MODELLING
GERMAN WORLD WAR I AIRCRAFT

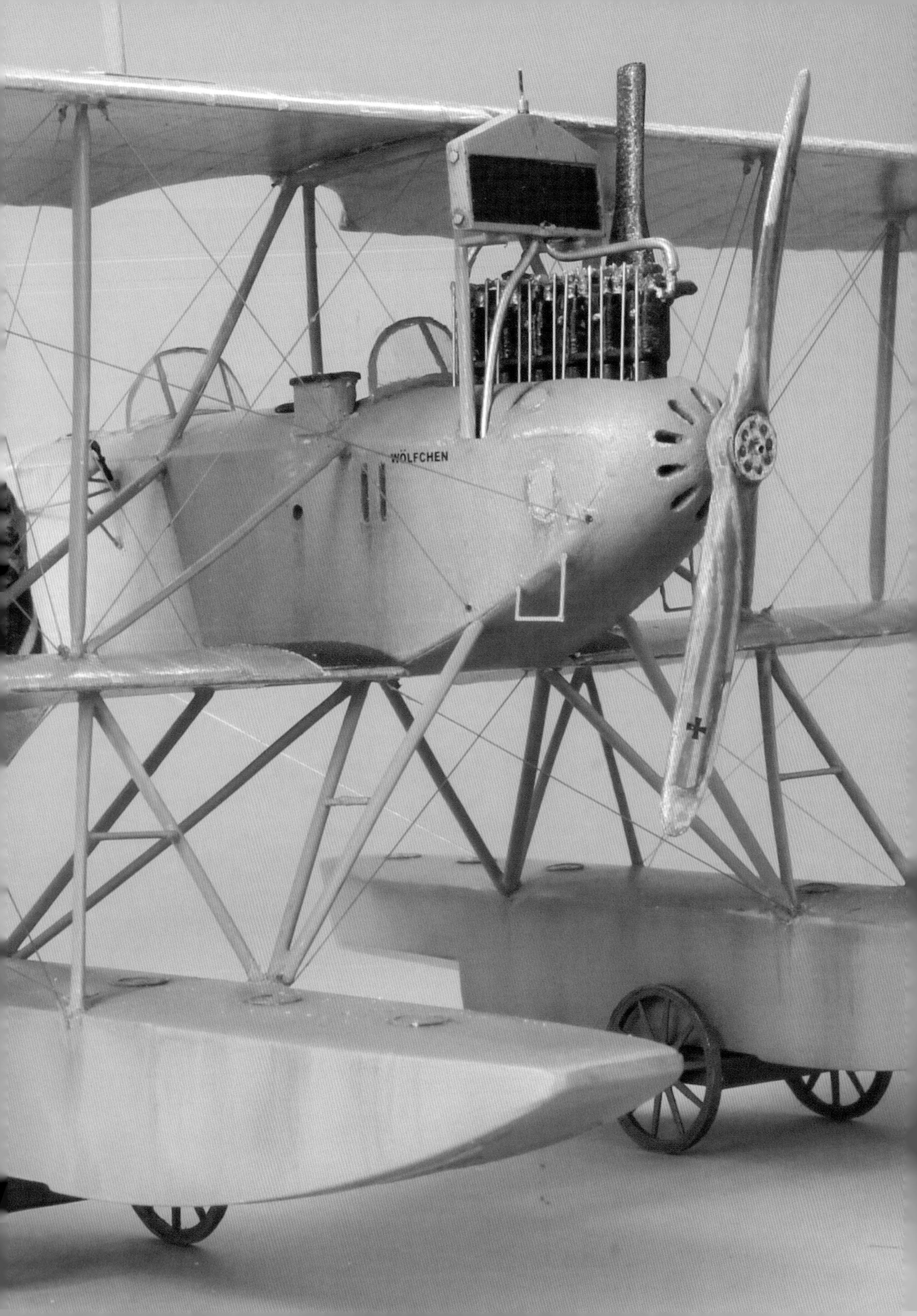
WÖLFCHEN

MODELLING GERMAN WORLD WAR I AIRCRAFT

Dave Hooper

THE CROWOOD PRESS

First published in 2021 by
The Crowood Press Ltd
Ramsbury, Marlborough
Wiltshire SN8 2HR

enquiries@crowood.com

www.crowood.com

British Library Cataloguing-in-Publication Data
A catalogue record for this book is available from the British Library.

ISBN 978 1 78500 884 9

Acknowledgements
Thanks to Richard Andrews for help and encouragement in writing this book. Thanks also to Jack Herris and Alf Small for allowing me to use photos. Many thanks to my wife and family for putting up with long periods of absence while writing this book and to the IPMS Great War SIG without whom this book would never have been written.

Typeset by Simon and Sons
Cover design by Blue Sunflower Creative
Printed and bound in India by Replika Press Pvt Ltd

Contents

Chapter One

The Basics

INTRODUCTION

When I was a young boy my father built a collection of aircraft models for me, which was displayed on a shelf in my bedroom. Along with the obligatory Spitfire, there were at least two World War I aircraft that I can remember: a Roland C.II and Fokker triplane. These aircraft caught my imagination and sparked a lifetime interest in early aircraft.

Thirty years later, I began to show an interest in modelling again after a break that had begun in my teenage years. Unsure of what subject I should choose, I decided to begin with the earliest aircraft I could find and work my way through in order of time period. What I didn't realize when I purchased my first few Airfix models, was where they would ultimately take me.

The Fokker triplane has always been one of the most popular World War I subjects.

The Roland C.II was one of the subjects that influenced a lifelong interest in World War I modelling.

I have now built over 150 models and have not moved very much beyond 1919 with my choice of subjects. There is something very compelling about these early machines made from wood, wire and fabric, and judging by the amount of interest that World War I displays generate at shows, I am not in a minority. However, World War I has always been considered to be a niche modelling genre, which I believe is mainly because of a reluctance to tackle these subjects with their fragile struts and intricate rigging patterns.

When displaying at shows, my colleagues and I are always kept busy answering queries around how certain aspects of the models are achieved. One comment I often hear goes something like, 'I'd like to be able to build these but…'.

And there is always a reason!

The truth is that modelling World War I aircraft is no more challenging than any other subject. Almost every genre of modelling has aspects that newcomers find daunting. It is just a simple case of learning new skills.

And that is what this book is essentially about. Starting from basics, by selecting and building an inexpensive kit, the intention is to provide a solid basis from which the modeller can confidently build almost any World War I subject. This book will concentrate on the construction of German aircraft and, as such, will contain techniques and historical information aimed at helping the reader build such subjects. However, much of the book's content will be equally suitable for building aircraft from any belligerent nation during the World War I period.

While this book is aimed at modellers with some experience, early chapters will concentrate on the raw basics, making the assumption that the reader is completely new to the hobby. It is my sincerest hope that this publication will encourage modellers of all ages and levels of experience to have a go and, most importantly, have fun building World War I subjects.

A Brief History of World War I Modelling

Some of the earliest commercial World War I model kits were produced and sold in the 1930s when a British firm called Skybirds produced a range of 1/72-scale kits that were predominantly made from wood.

The first plastic-injection moulded kits were produced during the post-war boom of the fifties. In America, a company called Aurora produced 1/48-scale kits of a number of World War I subjects. Many of these kits were copied by other manufacturers, most notably by a British company called Merit.

Airfix began producing plastic models in the early fifties and released its first World War I subject in 1956. Between 1956 and 1974, Airfix produced a total of eleven World War I kits in 1/72-scale, many of which are still systematically reissued.

In 1957, an American company called Revell produced a large-scale Fokker Dr.1 kit in 1/28-scale. In the following decade, the company began to release a steady stream of World War I subjects in 1/72-scale, which for many years would be considered to be some of the best small-scale World War I model aircraft kits available. Some of these subjects were copied by a Japanese company called Eldon. Eventually, these moulds were acquired by ESCI and are still in circulation, most recently used as part of Italeri's World War I centenary range.

By the early seventies, plastic modelling had evolved into an enthusiasts' hobby. As the modelling community demanded more esoteric subjects, small cottage industries sprang up to fill the void. By the mid-1970s, vacuum-formed kits began to surface. These were essentially sheets of plastic that were heated and formed around masters. The vacuum-forming process was perfect for the production of World War I subjects and provided

A selection of Revell and Airfix boxes from various eras.

The Xtravac 1/72-scale Albatros C.IX was one of a large number of vacuum-formed kits produced by the cottage industry.

the serious modeller with access to a huge choice of subjects.

In 1985, the first issue of a magazine dedicated to World War I modelling was published. *Windsock* was crude to begin with, but the magazine and *Datafiles* that followed would provide information and inspiration that helped to fuel a boom in kits.

The eighties would also see the arrival of some of the first short-run, plastic-moulded kits. These were typically very basic but provided the modeller with traditionally plastic-moulded kits of subjects that the large commercial companies would not touch. In the United Kingdom, a company called Merlin produced a series of World War I subjects of varying quality. By the late-1980s, Merlin had evolved into a company called Pegasus, who began releasing an extensive programme of good-quality, limited-run, World War I plastic kits in 1/72-scale. The company also began to scale up some of their products to 1/48-scale under the brand name Blue Max.

The fall of the Iron Curtain in 1991 sparked the beginning of a new golden era of World War I aircraft kits, as products from Eastern Europe began to make an impact. One such company was Eduard, who began exporting short-run, quality kits with photo-etch details in 1993. In the late-nineties, the company invested in new moulding equipment enabling them to compete with the mainstream model companies, after which Eduard continued to release a steady programme of World War I subjects.

Another company that benefited from the breakup of the Soviet Union was a Ukrainian manufacturer called Toko. From the mid- to late-1990s, Toko released a large number of

Toko and Roden produced high-quality World War I kits from the mid-1990s onwards.

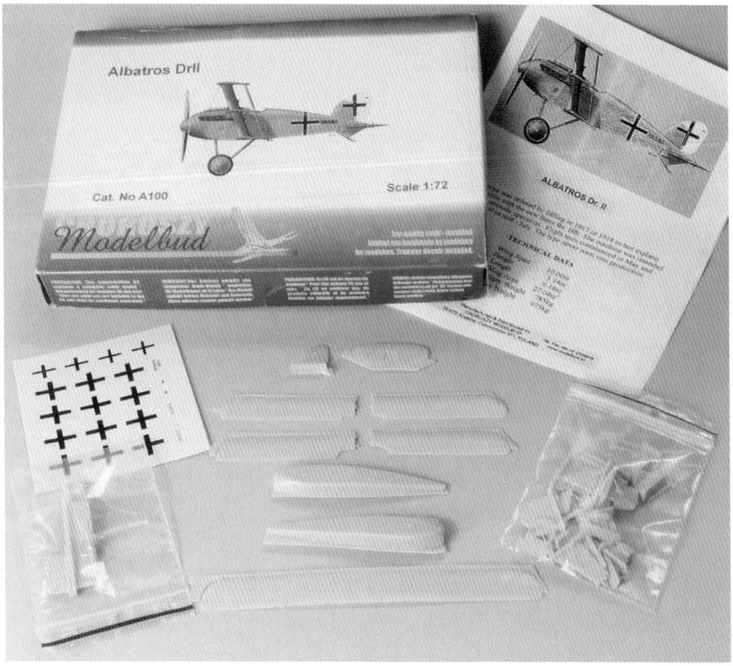

An example of a high-quality resin kit from the early millennium period. Companies such as Choroszy Modelbud were extremely prolific at this time.

high-quality 1/72-scale World War I plastic kits. In 1999, the company suddenly stopped producing models; reportedly to concentrate on manufacturing toiletry products. Those responsible for the modelling side of the business set up a new company called Roden that continued to produce new World War I kits, initially in 1/72-scale, but later in larger scales. Roden was one of the first companies to release a large number of subjects in 1/32-scale.

The Eastern Europeans were also instrumental in bringing resin products to mainstream modelling. Resin is a two-part polyurethane that, when mixed and poured into a silicone rubber mould, cures to produce a kit part. The process of making these kits is expensive because the moulds have a short lifespan and require replacing regularly. While Western companies had dabbled with resin for a number of years, the Eastern Europeans turned the medium into an art-form. The explosion of these kits on to the market signalled an end to the era of the vacuum-formed kit.

In 2009, the modelling world had something new to talk about. A company from New Zealand called Wingnut Wings, bankrolled by the film director Sir Peter Jackson, released their first four kits to almost universal critical acclaim. Not only were these kits well researched and finely moulded, but the presentation of the product itself was of a quality that had not been seen before in any modelling genre. Wingnut Wings' kits almost instantly changed the way that World War I modelling was viewed and many modellers who had never built biplanes before were enticed to buy these beautiful products.

Today, the modeller has a vast choice of scales, subjects, products and media to choose from. Enough new products are released and reissued each year to satisfy the market in all scales, while smaller cottage industries have benefited from the popularity of Wingnut Wings. The accessibility of 3D-printing has made it easier for modelling companies to create high-quality masters, and this has had a positive effect on all aspects of the hobby.

The Fokker D.VII was one of Wingnut Wings' most popular releases.

German Aircraft Designations

When Germany entered the war at the beginning of August 1914, its Air Service consisted of around 200 aircraft. The purpose of these aircraft was to provide reconnaissance information to the army. The military worth of the aeroplane was yet to be proved and was not taken seriously by traditionalists, who still viewed the cavalry as being the eyes of the army. As the war developed into stalemate, the aircraft became increasingly important on both sides of the conflict. The Germans initially designated their inventory into two distinct types of aircraft. Class A or A-type aircraft related to monoplanes, which during this period were mainly Taubes produced under licence by a number of manufacturers. Class B or B-type aircraft related to biplanes. During this period all aircraft were essentially unarmed and, as such, B-class aircraft came to be defined as unarmed two-seaters.

Having proved itself as a military asset, the aircraft itself became a serious threat to the opposition and the war in the air began. Aircraft on both sides of No Man's Land developed into fighting machines. In April 1915, the German Idflieg introduced a C-type designation, which was given to armed two-seat biplanes. These aircraft would essentially be the workhorses of the German Air Service during the war years.

As aircraft and roles developed, the Idflieg continued to add further designations throughout the war including:

E (*Eindecker*) – single-seat, monoplane fighters.
D (*Doppeldecker*) – single-seat, biplane fighters.
G (*Großflugzeug*) – twin-engined bombers.
R (*Riesenflugzeug*) – large, multi-engined bombers, with engines that could be accessed during flight.
Dr (*Dreidecker*) – single-seat, triplane fighters.
CL – lightweight, armed two-seaters.
J – armoured, ground-attack aircraft.
N – two-seat, night bombers.

In addition, naval aircraft were often designated as W-types.

WHERE TO BEGIN

Any new project begins with a spark of inspiration. This might be as simple as browsing the shelves of a model shop and finding a product that grabs your attention or seeing photographs of a built-up model. Inspiration may also be the result of a book that you are reading or even a movie that you have seen.

It is advisable to begin with a fairly basic subject that may have some aspects that are likely to provide a challenge. This may be a single-bay biplane or even a monoplane fighter. If the process of rigging is perceived to be daunting, then choose a model that has enough wires to provide a challenge without being too overbearing. The process of building a biplane itself might be a frightening idea, in which case a subject with upper wings that are fitted directly to the fuselage or a sesquiplane subject with V-shaped interplane struts may suit. Sesquiplane refers to a one-and-half wing configuration, such as used on Nieuports and a number of German aircraft of the period.

A selection of models for sale at a local model shop or show may provide the inspiration for your next project.

Aircraft featuring a sesquiplane design with V-shaped interplane struts are often good subjects to choose as a first biplane project.

A Question of Scale

The Fokker Eindecker *in the three most common aircraft-modelling scales, from left to right: 1/72, 1/32 and 1/48.*

World War I model kits have been produced in a variety of scales ranging from 1/144 up to 1/28 and beyond. Scale indicates the size of the model in relation to the full-sized original. For example, a 1/72-scale kit means that the completed model should be seventy-two times smaller than the full-sized subject.

1/144 is typically a wargaming scale, although some modellers do specialize in this size. The scale is probably more suitable for those who are interested in building a large number of models of the same subject in different markings. With a typical wingspan size of 5 to 6 centimetres for World War I fighter planes, there is very little scope for detail.

1/72 was championed by companies such as Airfix and Revell in the fifties and sixties and, as such, is the scale that most of us grew up with. This scale is especially suitable for those that have a small amount of display and storage space. 1/72 models have enough scope for a reasonable amount of detail, although much of this will be simplified. One of the beauties of this scale is the wealth of products that are available, although some of these are not currently in production. If you are intending to build an extensive collection based around one scale, then 1/72 is a perfect choice because some of the largest German R-type bombers will be close to the size of a medium twin-engine bomber in 1/32-scale.

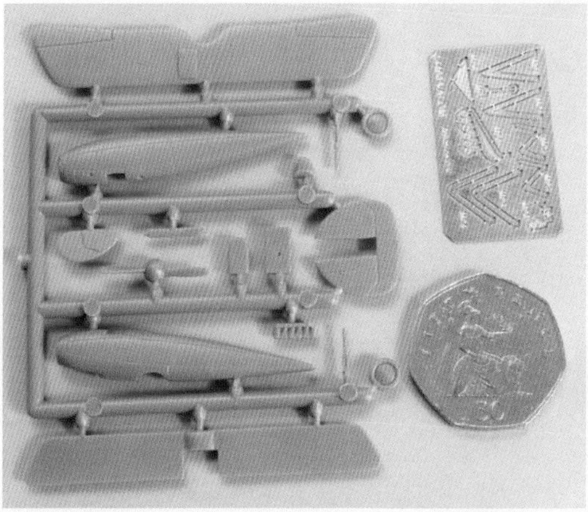

Valom has produced a number of reasonably priced World War I kits in 1/144 scale.

1/48-scale has been around since the mid-1950s, but became popular in the nineties when brands such as Eduard and Blue Max began to specialize in the scale. 1/48-scale is ideal for most World War I aircraft subjects, allowing for the inclusion of a good level of detail within a model of a manageable size. The 1/48-scale modeller has a reasonable choice of subjects to choose from, which are relatively easy to obtain.

1/32 became popular in the early millennium when Roden began releasing models in this scale. The scale's popularity had a major boost in the second decade of the millennium thanks to Wingnut Wings. The comparably large size of the model allows for a high level of detail, although this comes at a high price tag, with models in this scale typically selling between £60 and £130. One of the downsides of this scale is that subjects will be generally limited to production aircraft.

1/28-scale is limited to a few very old kits produced by Revell. The best German subject in this scale is the Fokker Dr.1, which is easily obtainable at a very good price, although the age of the kit means that a reasonable amount of work would be required to bring it up to acceptable modern-day standards.

Many of the huge R-type bombers would be impractical for most modellers in any scale larger than 1/72.

Choosing a First Kit

Once you have a subject and preferred scale, you should be ready to choose your first kit. It is always advisable to do some research before settling on a particular product. Magazine and internet articles can help you to refine your choice, although always remember that what you are reading is the personal opinion of the reviewer. I would avoid in-box reviews, as all these will ever hope to convey is the appearance of the kit in its unbuilt state. As a first-time builder, you are probably more likely to be interested in how the kit builds. There are also a number of dedicated World War I modelling forums and social media groups that can help steer you in the right direction. Another option is to talk to modellers at shows. There are dedicated World War I organizations, such as IPMS Great War SIG, that regularly display at events and often there will be built examples of the more popular subjects on club displays. Don't be afraid to talk to the modeller and ask his or her opinion on how easy the model was to build.

I would recommend starting with a cheap kit, even if it is not in the scale that you ultimately want to specialize in. It is wiser to practise new skills on inexpensive kits, so that if the unthinkable happens and you run into insurmountable difficulties, it won't matter so much financially.

Members of IPMS Great War SIG are always happy to answer questions about all aspects of World War I modelling.

References

Modellers will often spend as much time and effort acquiring and examining references as they will building the model itself. There are two main sources of reference material: printed publications and the internet. There can be pitfalls in both of these sources regarding accuracy of information; however, the internet is unregulated and there is, therefore, a greater chance of information being unreliable or misleading.

The most useful starting point when building a collection of reference material is a good set of drawings. It is not unusual to find anomalies between drawings and kit parts. This does not necessarily mean that the kit is inaccurate; it just means that the designers used a different set of drawings. For most of us, accuracy can be a minefield and the only solid advice I can offer is that if you are in any doubt concerning the accuracy of the drawings that you are working from, check them against photographs and period dimensions. Many World War I modellers use drawings from *Windsock* publications as a trusted source and more often than not kit designers base their products on the same drawings. However, do not fall into the trap of believing that these drawings are 100 per cent correct, as this is not always the case.

Try to collect as many period photographs as possible, including at least one photograph of the actual aircraft option that you are building. World War I production aircraft often varied between batches and were also often modified, overpainted or even fitted with replacement parts in the field, making them visually unique. *Windsock* publications are a good starting point for your collection but there are many other useful sources, including Osprey books, *Aeronaut* and *Cross and Cockade* publications, as well as social media and the internet.

Walk-around photographs of surviving examples and replicas are easy to obtain and can be very useful; however, it is important to remember that none of these aircraft will be in their original state. Most will have had any number of restorations, re-builds or modifications during their lifetime.

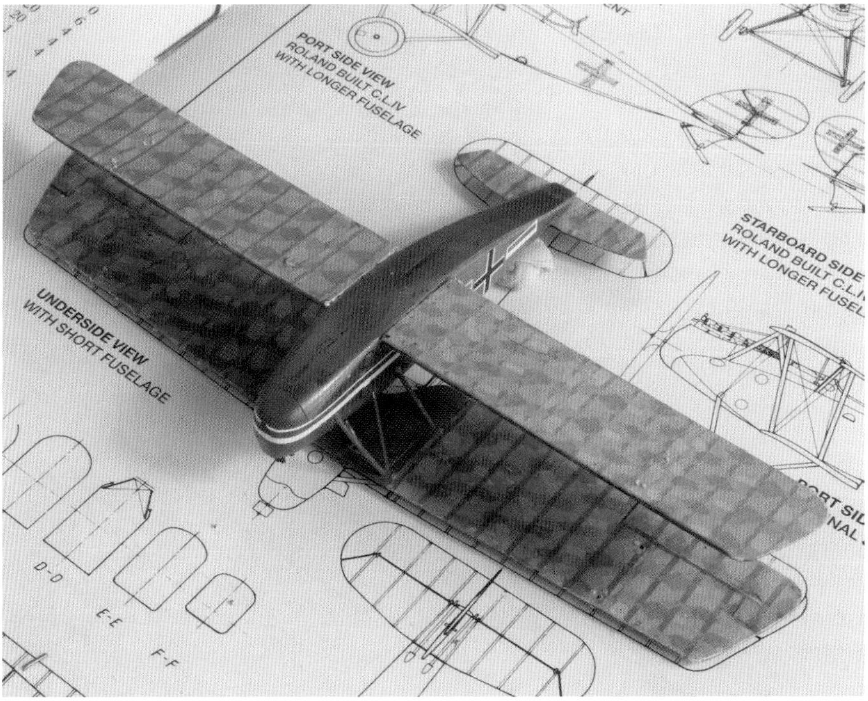

Scale drawings are an essential aid to constructing most World War I models.

A selection of useful reference publications, a number of which were used for projects built for this book.

The wood grain finish on this ex-Shuttleworth LVG is actually printed paper applied to the fuselage in a previous restoration.

BASIC TOOLS AND MATERIALS

Experienced modellers amass a large collection of tools and materials, some of which are used on a regular basis and some rarely touched. Many tools used by World War I modellers are identical to those used by builders of other modelling genres.

Cements and Fillers

Cements such as Liquid Poly and cyanoacrylate are widely used alongside the traditional tube of poly cement. It is not unusual to use different cements on different aspects of a build, using each product to its best advantage. For instance, cyanoacrylate cements are useful when a fast-curing cement is required that holds a part in position almost instantly, while poly cements are useful when cementing large areas together that require time to position.

White glue, such as PVA, is also very useful for cementing clear parts like windscreens, as other glues can fog or damage the plastic. Specific formulations can also be used to create transparent window panels by filling a frame, such as a photo-etch part, with glue and allowing it to dry.

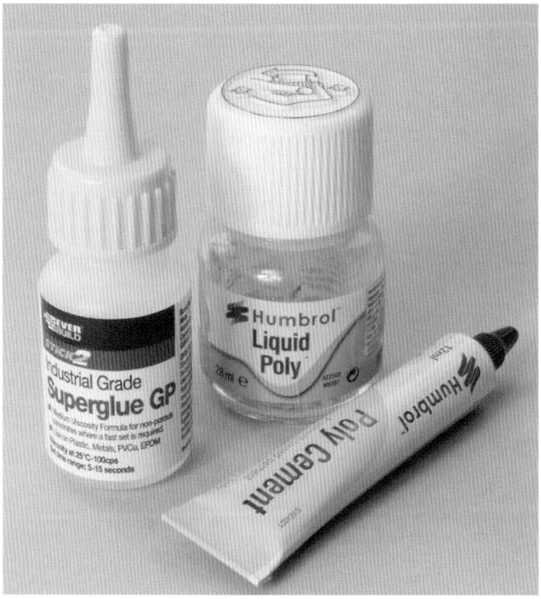

A selection of different cements.

Fillers are one of the most important materials on your workbench, correct use of which will mean the difference between a good model and a competition-winning model. There are plenty of products on the market designed for this purpose, but one-part, tube-based fillers are the most popular.

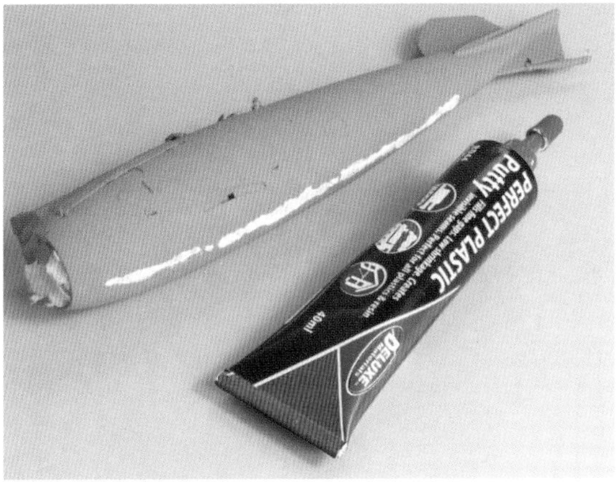

One-part tube-based fillers are a popular choice when filling gaps and surface defects on models.

When filling joints, I prefer to apply filler liberally and then sand it back to the plastic once dry, although some products will level when wiped with a reagent. Any detail lost during the filling process can be repaired once the part has been cleaned up. Most tube-based fillers work well with resin, although I sometimes prefer to use a two-part, car-body filler for this purpose.

Sanding Products

Once filler has been applied, the area can be levelled using a sanding product. There are a number of products currently on the market that are specifically tailored to modellers; however, a selection of grades of wet-and-dry abrasive paper should be considered a necessity.

Selections of sanding sticks are an essential part of most modeller's toolkits.

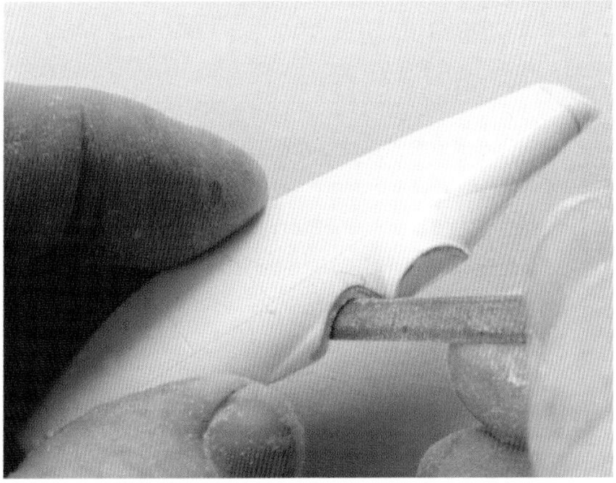

The cockpit opening of this vac-formed Albatros is being cleaned up with a crescent-shaped needle file.

Sanding sticks have become very popular in recent years and it is easy to see why, as these products often have advantages over abrasive paper, especially when dealing with larger seams.

For tight or small areas, I also have a few sets of needle files, with a selection of different shapes to choose from. Circular or crescent-shaped files are often useful when cleaning up curved edges, but care needs to be taken to avoid creating an unwanted trough or dip when using these tools.

Selection of a suitable grade of an abrasive product is essential. In general terms, when sanding an area that requires a lot of work, begin with a harsh grade of paper and then use finer grades to finish.

Delicate parts should always be cleaned up using a fine grade of abrasive paper. Harsher grades are more likely to catch and break the plastic.

One of the problems when tackling any sanding job is ascertaining when a surface or seam is completely smooth. One solution is to paint or prime the seam, which makes it easy to see whether it is smooth or not.

Sanding creates a large amount of airborne dust and it is advised that dust-masks are worn. This is especially important when dealing with resin, as the polyurethane dust is harmful.

Cutting Utensils

Selection of suitable cutting utensils is a matter of preference, as there are plenty of options available to the modeller. It is essential that blades are changed on a regular basis, as a blunt knife is more likely to damage delicate parts, and accidents to the model or the modeller are more likely to occur. A flat or curved blade can also be used to scrape away injection points or other unwanted details in areas that are hard to sand without damaging adjacent details.

Scribes are also very useful tools for cutting even grooves, such as panel lines, into plastic. Scribing lines on a model is virtually impossible to achieve without a selection of straight and curved line templates and I often use old photo-etch frets for this purpose.

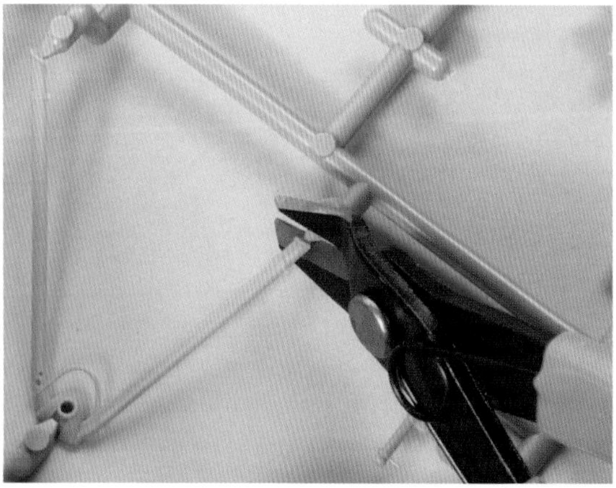

Snipping tools are useful for removing parts cleanly from their sprues.

Tweezers with square tips are a useful tool for manipulating struts.

Tweezers

Any modeller, regardless of what genre or subject they build, would be hard put to complete a model without a selection of good-quality tweezers. It is essential that the tips of the tweezers align with each other completely, otherwise wires and rigging materials will be almost impossible to manipulate. I also find wide, square-tipped tweezers essential when fitting struts or rods into position, as they reduce the risk of the part moving as you try to position it.

Drills and Drill Bits

Drills and drill bits are particularly relevant to World War I aircraft modelling. A good set of micro drills will usually contain a selection of bits ranging from 0.3 to 1.6mm in diameter. World War I modellers use a large number of 0.3, 0.4 and 0.5mm drills, and it is recommended that a reasonable stock of these sizes is maintained, as they are easily broken or bent.

A small, spring-activated pin vice is light and small enough to avoid over-stressing the drill bits. In some cases, I also drill holes by simply twisting the drill bit between my fingers. This technique can cause blisters but does reduce the risk of

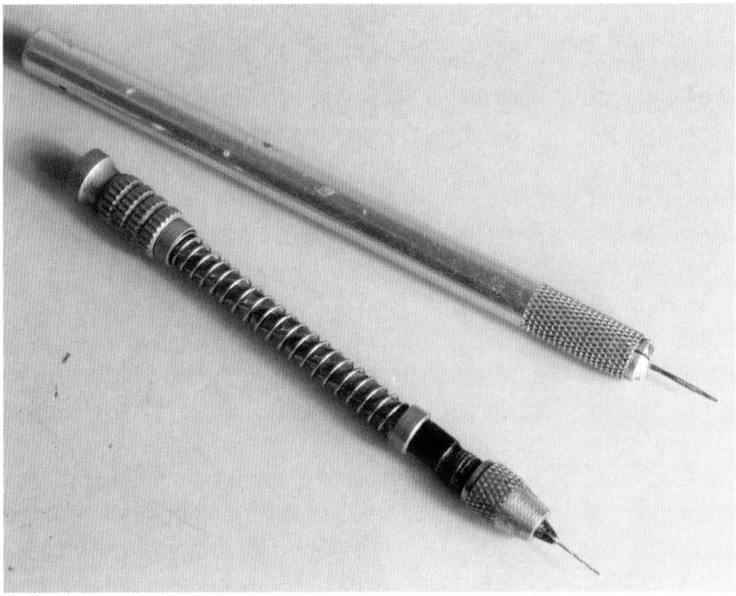

A pin vice and marking tool are useful aids to drilling, using small drill bits.

The undercarriage of this Halberstadt has been made from stock brass 'Strutz' and rod.

breaking very tiny drill bits. Pin vices can also be a useful tool for shaping small rods.

In conjunction with drills, I use a hand tool with a sharp needle fitted into the end in order to mark the precise position that I want to drill. Pre-marking with such a tool reduces the risk of the drill bit slipping.

Plasticard

Sheets of plastic are available in a large range of substances and are useful for a number of applications from filling gaps and repairing edges, to reskinning major parts, such as wings and fuselages. Plasticard can also be used as the basis of a scratch-build project.

Rods and Strips

A good stock of rods, strips and tubing is recommended, as they can be used in a wide variety of applications. Rods and tubes are available in plastic, brass and aluminium, and come in a variety of useful substances. The choice of plastic or metal products is a matter of preference, often based on application. Generally, if the rod needs to be bent to shape or is required to add strength to a vulnerable position, then brass is usually better than plastic.

Kits can also often be missing essential tubing or piping, especially between the engine and radiator, and these parts can be easily produced from stock items. It is also sometimes easier to replace a rod from a plastic kit than clean up the part.

Strips are generally available in plastic and have square or oblong cross-sections. Strips are often useful when creating internal or open structure detail.

Strut Stock

Strut stock is a little more difficult to discuss in contemporary terms as these products are no longer easily available. In the eighties and nineties, strut stock was fairly easy to obtain, either in plastic or brass ('Strutz'). Essentially, strut stock is a rod with an aerofoil-shaped cross-section. It is useful as a replacement for broken or poorly sized struts. In addition, modellers of resin kits would usually replace the kits' resin struts because they have a tendency to warp over time.

Occasionally, these products turn up at model shows and are well worth grabbing, as they can be extremely useful. Plastic strut stock can often be found packaged with vac-form kits.

Spares

Almost every kit that you ever build will generate a collection of spare parts. Probably 95 per cent of these will never be used, but the 5 per cent that you do use will often prove to be invaluable. You are likely to use spares as replacements for inferior kit parts, lost parts or even to add detail that the kit designer has omitted. While some spare parts, such as wheels, propellers, engines or machine guns, will be used as they are, sometimes you might be looking for a specific shape that can be cut or modified from an existing spare part.

ONWARDS

Once you have chosen a model and amassed a collection of basic materials and tools, you are ready to build your first World War I model, which will be covered in some depth in the next chapter.

This partially scratch-built Kondor III in fictional 1919 markings made use of a large number of spare parts from other kits including the propeller, a large proportion of the interior, the undercarriage, the elevators and the rudder.

Chapter Two

A First Build – The Fokker *Eindecker*

INTRODUCTION

The Fokker *Eindecker* could be described as the great-grandfather of the modern-day fighter. It was the first production aircraft to feature a forward-firing, fuselage-mounted machine gun, synchronized with the rotation of the propeller so that bullets would only fire when the propeller was not in the direct firing line. Anthony Fokker famously claimed that the idea for his invention was conceived, developed and tested within two days. In truth, a Swiss engineer called Franz Schneider had patented a synchronization device before the war and it is likely that Fokker and his engineering team, aware of Schneider's work, had been working on a system for some time.

The aircraft itself was a development of the French Morane–Saulnier Type G. Fokker replaced the Morane's wooden framework with steel tubing, while refining the flying and handling characteristics.

The introduction of the *Eindecker* made an almost immediate impact in the skies above the Western Front, heralding a period of dominance that became popularly known as the 'Fokker scourge'. A new type of hero – the Fighter Ace – was born, making household names of pilots such as Max Immelmann and Oswald Boelcke.

Why the Eduard *Eindecker*?

I have chosen this particular kit for a number of reasons, but mainly because the Eduard *Eindecker* provides a good introduction to modelling techniques specific to World War I, such as rigging, without having to worry about assembling two wings. The kit is also relatively inexpensive, especially if the stripped back, Weekend edition is selected.

The completed Eduard Fokker E.II.

An In-Box Assessment of the Eduard *Eindecker*

When you buy any kit, one of the first things that you will want to do is open up the box. For most of us this will purely be a visual assessment of the product itself, but a more experienced modeller will already be looking at the plastic with a view of what may require work. At this stage, you may be looking for flaws in the plastic, areas where you feel that detail could be added or even where there is too much detail that perhaps should be removed.

Other than a few injection marks in areas of the fuselage that won't be visible and some flash around the cowling, this kit looked pretty good on inspection. However, the kit designers have introduced detail into the model that shouldn't be there. The outside fabric sections of the fuselage are depicted as having raised lines to simulate fabric stretched over internal structure. Take a look at any period photograph and you will not see this. You may see some castor-oil staining around the structure positions, but the fabric surface itself should be smooth.

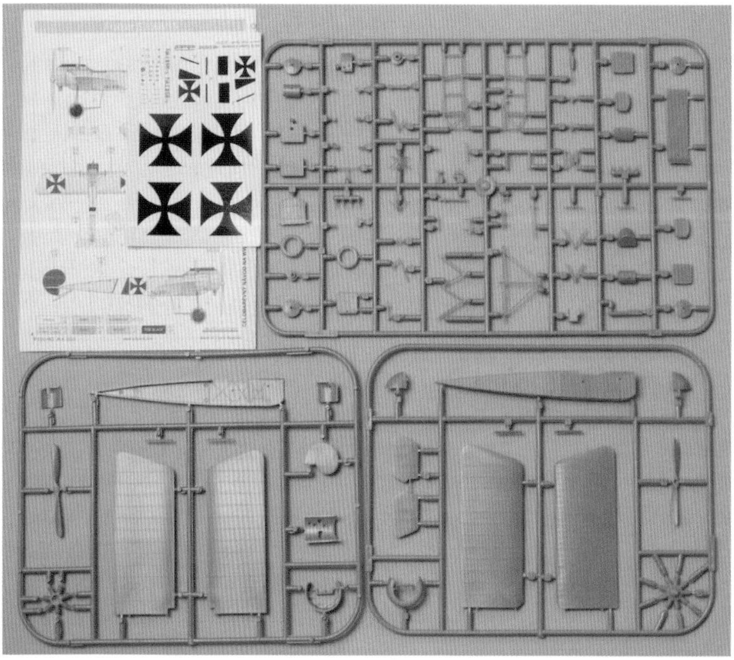

The contents of the Weekend Edition kit.

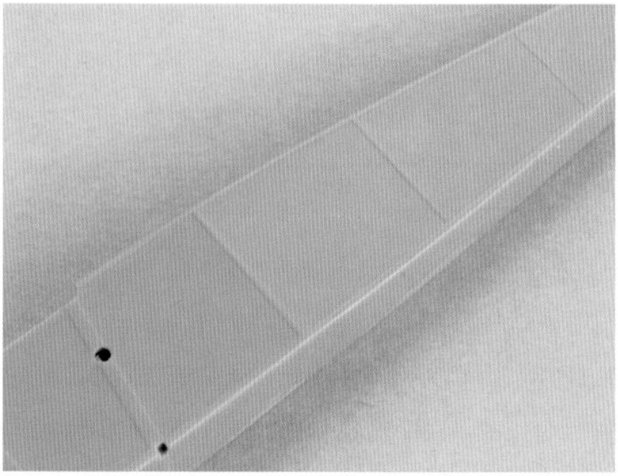

The fuselage rib detail is overstated and best removed completely. The optimum time to do this is once the two fuselage halves have been joined together.

References

At this stage, it is worth checking that the kit markings conform to period photographs of the subject as manufacturers often base their colour markings on published artwork that can be based on obsolete information. In the case of my *Eindecker* subject, there are three photographs in *Windsock Datafile no.91* showing 68/15 after a heavy crash. While the images are not ideal, there is enough information to confirm Eduard's interpretation of the markings.

In addition to the *Datafile*, I referred to two *Windsock Eindecker* specials and an Osprey book on early German World War I aces during this build. I also downloaded the instruction manual for the Wingnut Wings' kit, which I found to be extremely useful.

CONSTRUCTING THE *EINDECKER*

Basic Interior Assembly and Painting

The main interior sections were painted before assembly. I used the Wingnut Wings' instruction booklet alongside reference photographs as a basic guide to painting these parts. The fuselage sidewalls and floors were first sprayed in a basic fabric colour. Brown ink was then hand-painted around the frame and stitching positions

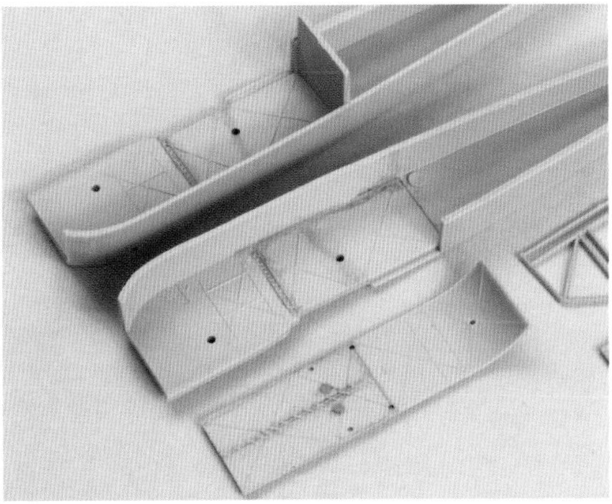

The interior fabric is weathered with a brown wash to simulate castor-oil staining.

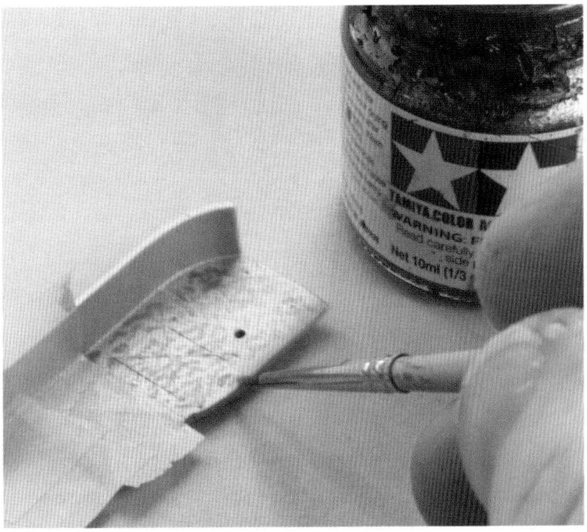

Metallic grey squiggles are painted on to an aluminium base to represent the milled finish.

to represent castor-oil staining. At this stage, the ink looked too overpowering and so these areas were sprayed with a second, light mist of the base colour to tone down the brown ink.

Masking tape was used to cover up all of the fabric areas and the exposed surfaces were then coated with a base coat of aluminium. *Eindecker* bare metal components were milled, which gave them a distinctive patterned appearance. To simulate this I used a small OO brush to paint squiggles of thinned metallic grey. All of the metal areas were then lightly over-sprayed with aluminium.

The sidewalls and floors now only needed finishing touches to complete the job. I used an HB pencil to highlight the moulded bracing wires, while a pale beige colour was used to carefully highlight stitching detail. Framework parts were painted with a pale grey-green colour to simulate German primer before gluing these parts and the floor section to the sidewall.

The kit includes a rear bulkhead and a pair of cross-frames that sit behind the main fuel tank. From an accuracy point of view, it would make more sense to fit the cross-frames directly to one of the fuselage halves, as the *Eindecker* did not appear to have a solid bulkhead in this position. However, these parts will not be seen once the fuselage halves are closed and so you may wish

The floor, side frames and rear bulkhead have been glued to half of the fuselage. The rear bulkhead will not be visible and has been included to aid alignment of the two fuselage halves.

to ignore them completely. I decided that the rear bulkhead would help to align the two fuselage halves, but the cross-frame parts were omitted.

Eduard has depicted the bulkhead that sits behind the pilot's seat as a fabric-covered frame. While this was true of many later Fokker types, the *Eindecker* typically had a wooden panel fitted in this position. For this reason, I sanded away frame and stitching detail. I then drilled a series of small holes that would later be used to thread control wires through. Holes were also drilled into each corner ready for the seatbelt attachments.

Holes ready for the control wires are drilled into the bulkhead that sits immediately behind the pilot's seat.

Interior Details

An *Eindecker* seat was essentially a tubular-framed structure, upholstered with fabric or leather. The seat can, therefore, be painted beige to simulate fabric, or black or brown to simulate leather. I chose to paint mine with a brown leather covering.

Weekend kits do not contain seatbelts, which are usually supplied as photo-etch details in the more premium versions of the model. For this particular build, I chose to use an aftermarket set of pre-painted photo-etch seatbelts produced by Eduard. Like most single-seat fighters of the period, *Eindeckers* were supplied with four-point harnesses. The lap straps fixed to the lower corners of the rear bulkhead can be difficult to attach with the seat fixed in position and so these straps were fitted before adding the seat. At this stage, the control column was assembled and painted. A hole was drilled into the base of the column to

Leather upholstery is simulated by building up brown washes over a lighter base colour.

A length of mending thread has been fitted into the base of the control column.

accept monofilament thread to simulate control wires. The completed column was then glued to the cockpit floor.

Once the column was firmly in place, each loose thread end was passed through the predrilled holes in the rear bulkhead. These were locked off with cyanoacrylate, ensuring that both thread ends were pulled tight enough to appear taut without putting stress on the control column.

With the control column in position, the control wires have been threaded through the bulkhead.

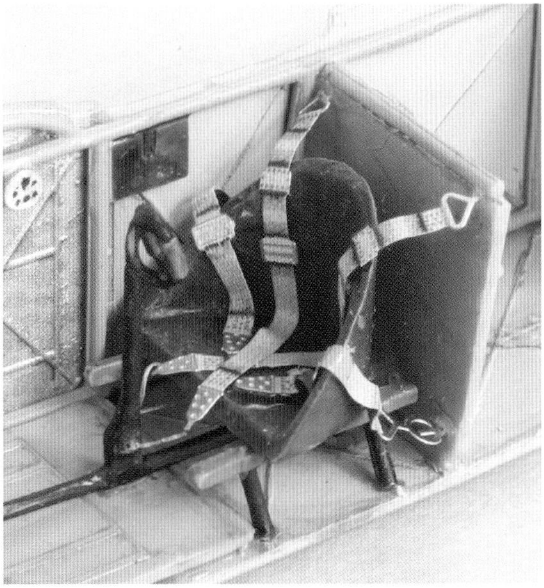

Photo-etch seatbelts located in the bulkhead are folded over the pilot's seat.

Once the seat was in place, the photo-etch lap straps were folded and glued into the seat. The ends of each shoulder harness were then glued into the top corners of the bulkhead before folding and cementing the opposite ends over the seat.

A significant length of plastic was cut away from the base of the vertical section of the rudder control bar, as its original length would ultimately result in the rudder bar being positioned too high above the floor. After gluing the revised rudder bar part to the cockpit floor, lengths of monofilament were extended between the bar and the remaining predrilled holes in the rear bulkhead to simulate rudder control wires. In hindsight, it would have been easier to do this before fitting the seat.

The two fuselage halves were then glued together. I used a combination of masking tape and clamps to hold the parts in place while the cement dried. A separate decking panel designed to fit behind the pilot seat is supplied with a centrally located hole for the fuel tank filler-cap to fit through. This hole is incorrectly positioned for the E.II variant, which should be slightly offset to the starboard side. The kit includes an alternative

More control wires are fitted between the rudder bar and bulkhead.

panel with no hole and so I used this part to create a replacement with the filler hole correctly positioned. I cut the filler cap from the fuel tank and glued this directly into the hole. The fuel tank will not be visible in the completed model and was consigned to the spares' box.

The completed forward coaming assembly.

Once the decking panel was fitted, the entire fuselage was cleaned up and the unwanted rib detail that was noted earlier was carefully sanded away.

The remaining interior detail is fitted to a forward coaming assembly. This was constructed as the instructions suggested, the only variation being that the tachometer that fits on to the port side of the empty ammunition belt box was pinned into position with a brass rod. This was achieved by carefully drilling a small hole into both parts and inserting a small brass pin.

The forward coaming assembly and firewall were then glued to the fuselage and all seams were filled.

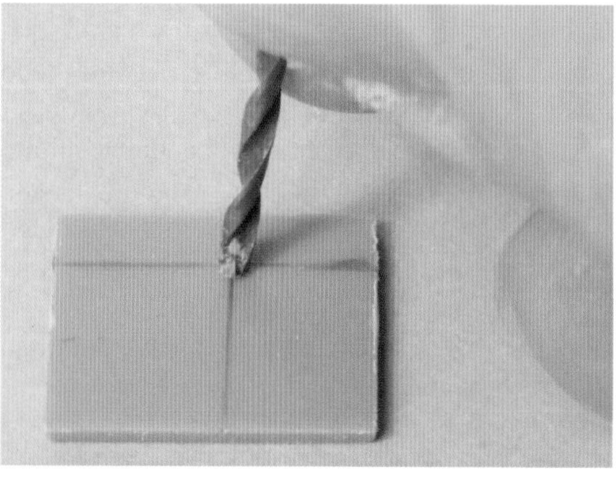

A hole for the fuel filler cap is drilled in its corrected offset position on a replacement decking part.

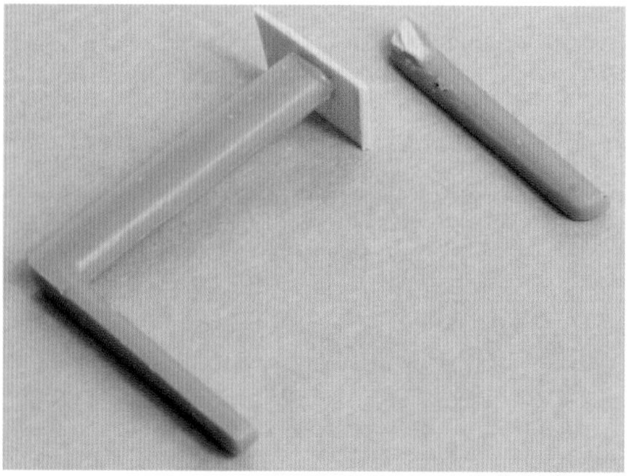

Plasticard is used to extend the width of the part depicting the padding around the cockpit opening.

A separate part, depicting the padding around the fuselage opening, appeared to be a little undersized. To rectify this, I cut the part into two sections and glued a piece of plasticard to the cut edge. Once dry, the plasticard was shaped and sanded flush to the shape of the original part. Both halves were then reassembled and fitted to the fuselage.

Elevators

The elevators come as a single piece of plastic. The central rod of this part is thin and brittle, which is likely to be damaged during handling. I, therefore, decided to replace this section with brass rod and tubing. Tubing was cut to the same length as the section of central rod that I was removing. A longer piece of rod was inserted into the tube, so that each end of this rod protruded from the tubing. Once the original plastic central section was removed from the part, a hole was drilled into each elevator in the same position that the central rod was cut from. The brass replacement was then glued in position between the two elevators, so that the protruding rod ends fitted into the holes drilled in each elevator.

Detailing the Engine

The provided engine is typical of a universal 9-cylinder rotary powerplant. While there are a number of details that can be added to make the engine appear more like an Oberursel U.I, I chose simply to add nine pushrods cut from a top E guitar string.

A sharp-pointed tool was used to mark where each pushrod would fit into the central crankcase and small holes were then drilled into these positions. Nine pieces of guitar string were cut to length and then glued in-between each hole and the corresponding cylinder tip, so that each rod was positioned centrally and parallel to the edges of the cylinder.

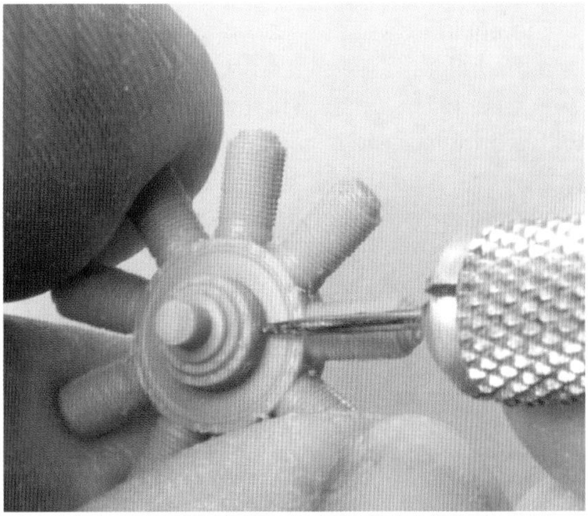

A marking tool is used to pinpoint the drilling position for each pushrod.

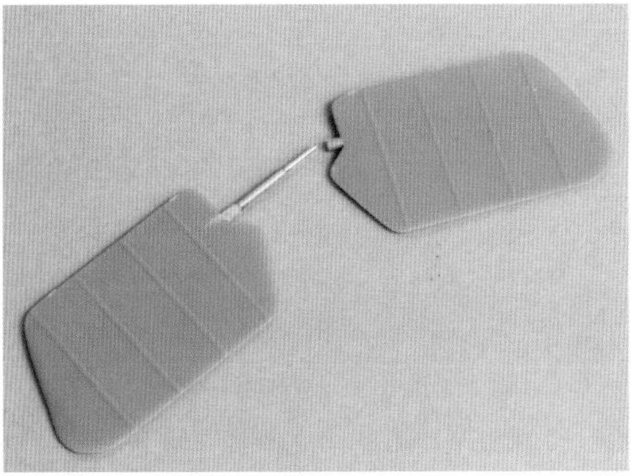

The weak central rod of the elevator section is replaced with brass rod and tubing.

The completed Oberursel U.I ready to be fitted to the firewall.

The engine was sprayed with aluminium paint and the cylinders were hand-painted in a metallic grey colour. The whole engine was then flooded with a brown wash to simulate castor-oil staining. Finally, aluminium was lightly dry-brushed over the entire engine and pushrods were highlighted by hand-painting them with aluminium.

Painting

As with all major paint jobs, the first step is to mask off any area that does not require painting. Masking is often thought of as being tape, but it can actually be any material that ensures that only the areas that you want to be painted are accessible. In this build, I used small pieces of kitchen roll to fill up the open cockpit area. I also used slithers of balsa to fill the ammunition holes in the forward coaming.

I always prime my models using a grey plastic primer. This is done for two main reasons. First, because it provides a strong base on which modelling paints will settle and adhere. Without a primer, acrylic-based paint can wear away in areas that are exposed to a lot of handling during the building process. A coat of primer will also show any flaws in the surface of the model where filling or further sanding is required. Some primers can result in a lumpy finish and, as such, it is worth experimenting with different brands before settling on a particular product.

Bare metal areas, including the cowling parts, were sprayed first. These areas were subjected to the same 'squiggle' treatment as the interior. The painted areas were then masked and the remainder of the fuselage and wings were sprayed with a clear doped linen colour. Dope is a treatment applied to fabric to tighten the weave after the wing has been covered. If the dope is clear then the colour finish is transparent, hence clear doped linen has become a common term to describe an early linen finish.

Eindeckers in the field suffered badly from castor-oil staining, which was often most prominent where fabric was in contact with interior structure. If the model depicts an aircraft in any condition other than factory fresh, then some kind of simulation of castor oil is recommended. I used a spray gun to add brown wash to areas where castor oil was likely to congregate, using photographs as references. This was sprayed freehand but could, alternatively, be hand-painted. A light overspray of the clear doped linen was then used, which produces a translucent effect. Other fuselage details, including the cockpit padding, were hand-painted. Once painting was complete, the engine, cowling and side panels were glued in place, ensuring that the starboard side panel

Bare metal areas are the first section of the fuselage to be painted.

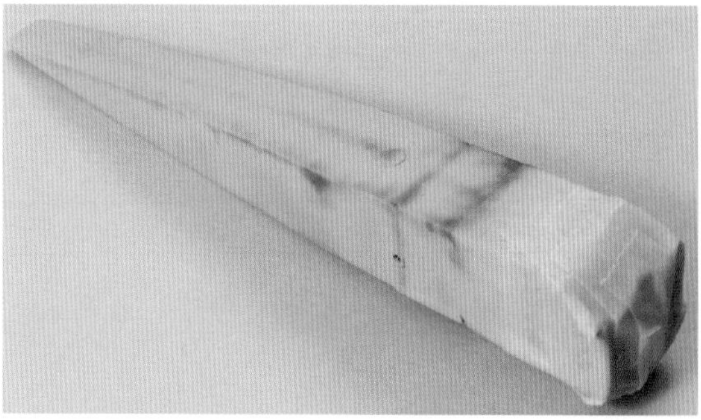

Brown wash is applied to the fuselage to simulate castor-oil staining. This will be lightly over-sprayed with the base fabric colour.

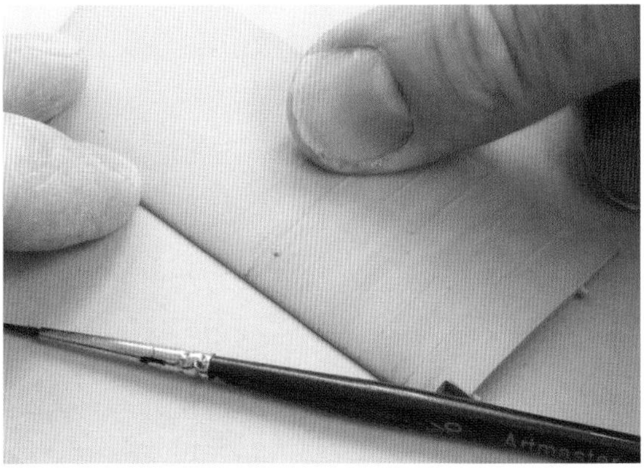

Wash is randomly streaked across the wing using a finger to spread the paint.

Poorly fitting decals left gaps that required touching up with paint.

was positioned so that the wing would fit into the panel once assembled.

A brown wash was wiped chord-wise across the wing in random positions to simulate general soiling before over-spraying with the base colour.

Decal Application

At this stage, I applied the decals to the fuselage and wings. The black and white striping behind the *Eisernes Kreuz* on the fuselage did not fit the shape of the fuselage perfectly. The side sections overhung the edges and were carefully trimmed back. The upper and lower sections were too narrow and, once settled, were touched up with paint.

Wings

The wings are fitted to the fuselage via a pair of lugs moulded on to the inside edge for positioning and reinforcement. I would, ideally, like to extend the shallow lugs with brass rod for greater reinforcement, but in this case any attempt to do so would be visible through the cockpit opening. For this reason, the wings on almost every *Eindecker* kit ever produced are difficult to maintain at a zero degree dihedral, once glued in position. However, use of a

As part of the wing preparation, holes are drilled ready to accept the rigging.

A simple jig made from packing foam is used to help maintain alignment of the wings during construction.

functional rigging material, such as monofilament, should help to support the wings and hold them in position.

Small holes were drilled completely through the substance of the wings in all of the rigging positions. Holes were also drilled into the fuselage ready for bracing and control wires.

I produced a simple jig from packing foam to help initially align the wings, which were then glued into place ensuring that alignment was correct when viewed from all angles.

Undercarriage

The kit supplies separate front and rear aerofoil sections that are designed to fit to the W-shaped forward section of the undercarriage. While the kit instructions suggest that the front and rear aerofoil parts are required, only the rear parts should be fitted to the E.II variant.

When preparing the main undercarriage parts, I am already thinking about the best way to rig it. Where possible, I like to drill rigging holes into the structure, but this was only possible in the front edge of the central horizontal post that is part of the triangular-shaped base section. I also drilled holes just inside of the four undercarriage location positions on the fuselage.

Most kit instructions recommend separate assembly of the undercarriage before fitting to the fuselage. While this is a good method on many subjects, complex designs such as can be seen on

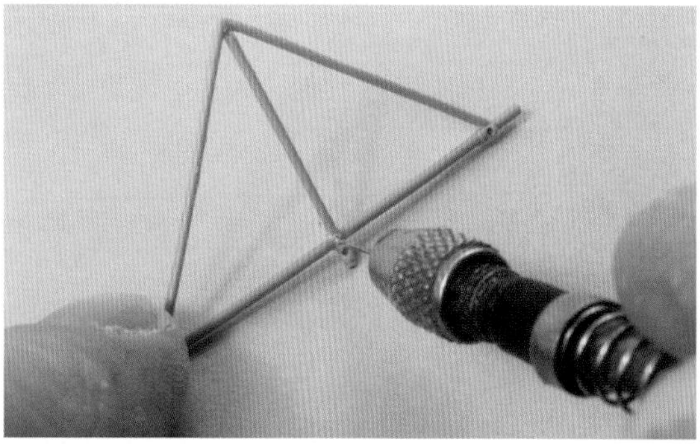

A hole for bracing wires is drilled into the central post of the triangular base section of the undercarriage.

Vertical sections of the undercarriage are initially fitted to the fuselage.

the *Eindecker* are sometimes better assembled directly to the underside of the fuselage in stages. I began by fitting the forward and rear vertical sections, referring to drawings to ensure that they were fitted at the correct angle. Once these parts were fixed firmly in position, the triangular-shaped base and axle section was glued in place.

Bracing wires were then added by gluing four lengths of monofilament into the holes that I had drilled in the fuselage. Each free end of the two

Undercarriage bracing wires are positioned so that they can be pulled tight while the cement cures.

rear threads was threaded through the predrilled hole in the front edge of the central horizontal bar. These thread ends were then pulled tight and cyanoacrylate applied to this position, keeping the threads taut until the glue had cured. The forward two threads were then positioned so that when pulled tight they rested on the triangular intersection each side of the horizontal bar at the rear of the central triangular base piece. Again, cyanoacrylate was applied to these positions and the threads held firmly until locked. Excess thread was then removed with a sharp scalpel.

Assembling the Machine-Gun

While the plastic gun included with the kit is perfectly acceptable, a huge improvement can be made with the inclusion of a photo-etch cooling jacket. I found a suitable replacement in my spares' box, but you can usually find them as part of detailing sets for almost any German World War I aircraft. Early- and later-style Spandau cooling jackets differed slightly, but, arguably, even the use of an incorrect style jacket would be a major improvement on the plastic moulded part.

The moulded cooling jacket was separated from each machine gun. I then drilled a hole near the base of the cut edge of the butt and inserted a length of brass tubing to represent the barrel. The photo-etch replacement cooling jacket was shaped around a cocktail stick.

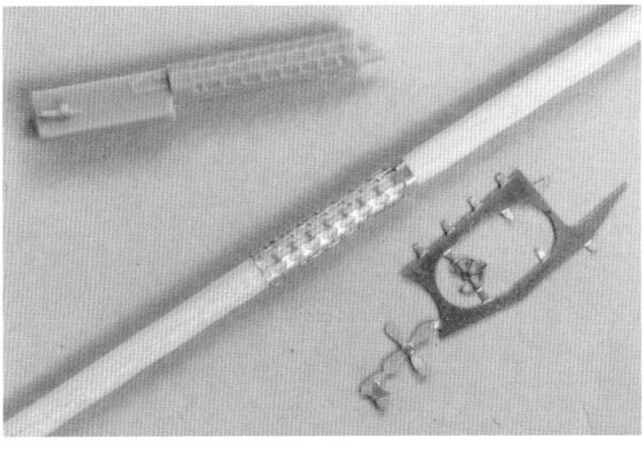

This photo-etch cooling-jacket replacement came from my spares' box.

The machine-gun, with magazine belt feeder, is fitted to the fuselage.

The cooling jacket was partially slipped off one end of the cocktail stick and cyanoacrylate applied to the exposed edge. The jacket was then carefully slid off the cocktail stick and attached to the edge of the gun butt. Once the assembly was solid, a small photo-etch front plate was glued on to the tip of the cooling jacket.

I sprayed the completed gun black and then brushed graphite, shaved from an HB pencil, over the surface to highlight the detail and give the part a realistic gunmetal appearance. The gun was then glued on to the fuselage.

A series of grooves was scribed across a piece of plasticard, which was then cut into a thin strip and fitted inside the magazine feeder to represent a magazine belt. The feeder was then glued on to the fuselage forward coaming.

Rigging

Most of the rigging and wing-warping wires connect to a central inverted V-shaped support pylon, which is fitted to the forward coaming on the fuselage. Before fitting this part, two holes were drilled into the tip of the pylon, one forward of the other. The pylon was then glued to the fuselage. Two small holes were also drilled into the forward coaming, forward of the base of each pylon strut

With the pylon and forward wires in position, the wings are ready to rig.

The first thread end is passed through the wing on the inside forward rigging position and locked in place.

position, and long strands of monofilament were glued into each of these holes. The free ends of monofilament were then threaded through the front hole in the tip of the pylon from opposite sides. A further long length of monofilament was threaded through the same hole, so that it was positioned centrally. A spot of cyanoacrylate was applied to this position and the two ends that

The initial thread was then pulled over the tip of the undercarriage and glued in place.

were initially glued to the coaming were pulled and held tight until locked.

I now had all of the forward rigging threads in position. Beginning on one side, I threaded one of the monofilament ends through the inside forward rigging position on the wing. Ensuring that the dihedral of the wing retained an angle of 90 degrees, the thread was pulled tight and locked with cyanoacrylate.

The loose end of this thread was then pulled tightly over the tip of the central undercarriage post and glued permanently in position. The process was then repeated on the other side of the aircraft.

I now had two options. I could cut both loose ends of thread from the undercarriage and repeat the process for the forward outer-wing rigging points, eventually ending up with four cut thread ends in the same position. Alternatively, I could

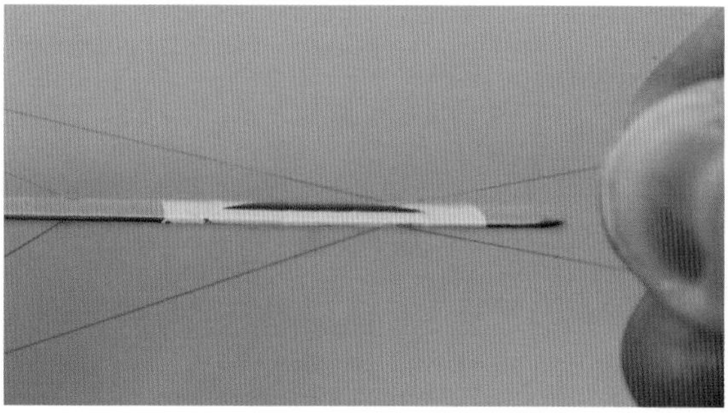

Thread ends from the pylon and undercarriage are threaded through the wing from opposite directions.

continue by threading each loose end through the underside of the forward outer-wing rigging position on the opposite side.

I chose the second option and once the original thread was in position, I took the remaining corresponding loose thread from the pylon and threaded this through the same rigging hole as the thread running from the undercarriage, so effectively I had two loose threads protruding from opposite sides of the outer rigging position in the wing. Both threads were then pulled tight and glued permanently into place. The loose ends were then cut flush with the rigging location hole and the process repeated on the opposite wing.

I repeated the same process for the rear rigging lines, but this time two long lengths of thread were initially threaded through the rear hole in the tip of the pylon. On the underside, the threads were located at the rear tip of the undercarriage central post.

Finally, there are two bracing wires that run from a point just behind the cowling on the fuselage to the forward inside rigging position on the wing. I drilled location holes into the fuselage and wings, and glued a piece of thread into each of the fuselage holes. Each loose end was then threaded through the corresponding hole in the wing, locked and tidied.

Finishing Touches

With most of the model now complete, the rudder and elevators were finalized by adding control horns. Plastic control horns are included in the kit but, in the case of the rudder, I replaced them with a part cut and shaped from a piece of photo-etch fret. This was done because individual control horns can be very vulnerable to damage and are also difficult to align accurately, so that they are in exactly the same position on both sides of the control surface. In order to fit my replacement, I needed to cut a slot into the rudder in the position that the control horns sits. I used a razor saw to create the slot, which, with a little cleaning up, was wide enough to accept the substance of the photo-etch control horn.

For the elevator control horns I used the kit parts. These were glued directly to the protruding plastic rim of the original elevator part, rather than the replacement brass rod and tubing. The elevators and rudder were then glued to the airframe.

For control lines I used an elastic thread, which is easier to glue to exposed tips than monofilament. Once each elastic thread was glued into the exit holes in the fuselage, I placed a small drop of cyanoacrylate on to the tip of each control horn and pulled the corresponding elastic thread in contact with the wet glue. This process was repeated

A replacement rudder control horn was cut from photo-etch fret.

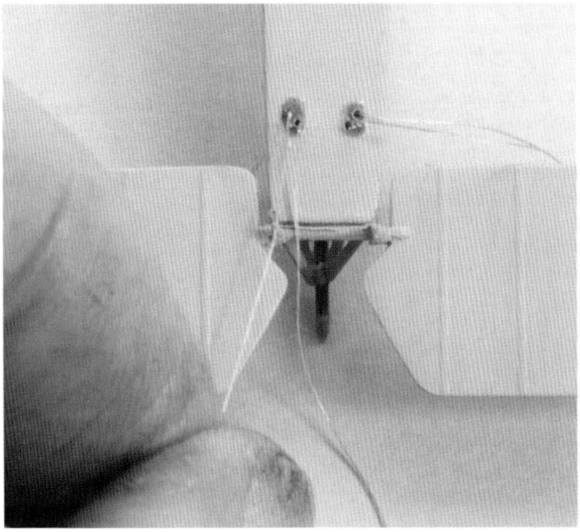

Elastic thread is used to replicate control wires.

Cocktail sticks are used as handling tools while painting the propeller and wheels.

for each control wire, beginning with the rudder lines. Excess elastic was then cut away.

A circular cutter was used to create masks for the black wheel covers. Tyres were sprayed with a pale-grey base colour, and a little light staining was added using an earth weathering wash. A dark-brown wash was also added to recesses.

Without any clear photographic evidence, the type of propeller used on E.II 68/15 is a matter of guesswork. I examined photographs of *Eindeckers* with serial numbers close to my subject, which suggested that either an Integral or Garuda propeller would be suitable. In the end I chose the Integral propeller, which appears to have been made from laminations of three different woods. Thin strips of masking tape were used to mark off and mask the laminations, which were hand-painted. The entire propeller was then subjected to a brown wash. Finally, the propeller boss was carefully picked out with aluminium paint. The model was declared finished once the propeller and wheels had been glued into position.

FINALLY

The Eduard Fokker *Eindecker* is unlikely to provide too many difficulties for a modeller with minimal experience of building World War I era aircraft. Eduard produces a number of very good German World War I biplanes that would make excellent follow-ups to the *Eindecker.* For example, the Fokker D.VII has very little rigging and, therefore, provides a good basis for practising the assembly of multiple wings. Alternatively, aircraft with a sesquiplane configuration are usually easy to assemble, which I hope to demonstrate with my next project.

A rear view of the completed Eduard Fokker E.III.

Chapter Three

Interiors and Engines

INTRODUCTION

Almost all World War I aircraft had open cockpits and exposed engines, which has the scope to provide modellers with plenty of opportunities to make improvements, no matter how good or poor the initial kit is. On average, most modellers will spend longer detailing the interior than on almost any other aspect of the build. The purpose of this chapter is to provide some hints, suggestions and, hopefully, inspiration on upgrading and detailing interiors.

INTERNAL COLOURS

The majority of World War I aircraft were predominantly constructed from wood and covered in fabric. Many German designs incorporated fuselages that were completely or partially covered in plywood and a few later designs, such as J-types, employed metal either as armour around the cockpit area or as the aircraft's primary construction material. All metal fittings would normally be coated.

Wood

The Germans typically used spruce and sometimes kiefer pine in the construction of their aircraft. Wooden panels were often made from plywood, which was likely to be manufactured from birch or alder. In addition, ash was often used in load-bearing areas of the structure. Internally, wood would typically be varnished or stained and, as such, the colour would vary greatly between

The interior and engine assembly of the Wingnut Wings' Rumpler C.IV.

manufacturers, even if the same base wood type was used.

Simulating Wood Interiors

Wood is difficult to replicate to a satisfactory level with a single coat of paint. For this reason most artists use a minimum combination of a pale base coat and darker translucent second coat. Examples of processes used to replicate the appearance of wood are discussed in greater detail in Chapter 7; however, a number of different types of wood may be visible from inside the cockpit and, as such, the practice of varying the colour can be used to create the illusion of an interior made from organic materials. I usually stick to two or three different wood shades, typically using a darker base colour shade for rib detail, which helps to accentuate the interior framework. Plywood panels are given a pale base coat, while large, wooden interior components, such as flooring and instrument panels, may either employ a different base coat or a different translucent coat to other areas.

It is important to remember that in most instances we are not trying to simulate wood itself, but the various treatments that were applied to the wood, such as varnish and staining. It is also possible that that wood was treated differently internally than externally and this may or may not have a bearing on colour selection.

Fabric

Until the introduction of printed lozenge fabrics in the summer of 1917, the interior side of the fabric would almost always appear in its original state, no matter what finish was applied externally. This is because the fabric would typically be doped before any further finish was applied. The coats of dope would effectively seal the fabric so that any pigments on top of the dope would not penetrate the fabric. Some manufacturers are known to have added pigment into dope, however British PC10 and PC12 finishes, which were essentially pigmented dopes, did not affect the appearance of the linen as viewed from inside the aircraft. Considering that British linens were not calendared and, therefore, more open than German linens, this suggests that penetration of pigmented dope to the interior was unlikely to occur.

Lozenge fabrics were printed using dyes that were known to have partially penetrated the linen giving the interior side a pale representation of the outer surface. Once attached to the airframe, the lozenge fabric would still be subjected to a doping process that would seal the surface. Any overpainting, such as personal or unit colours, would be unlikely to affect the interior appearance of the fabric.

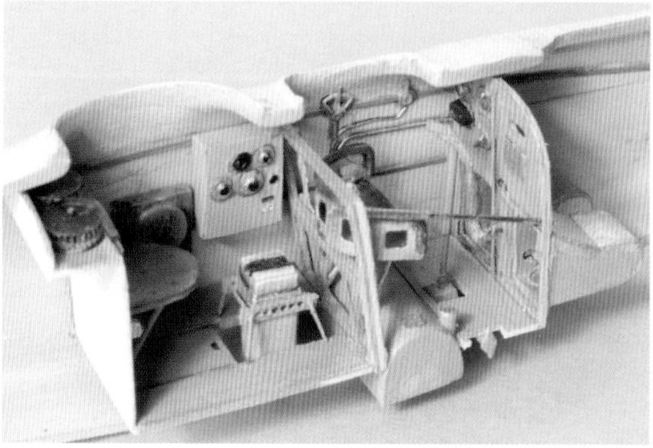

The interior of the Eduard Hannover provides a good example of how different wood shades can be used on different components.

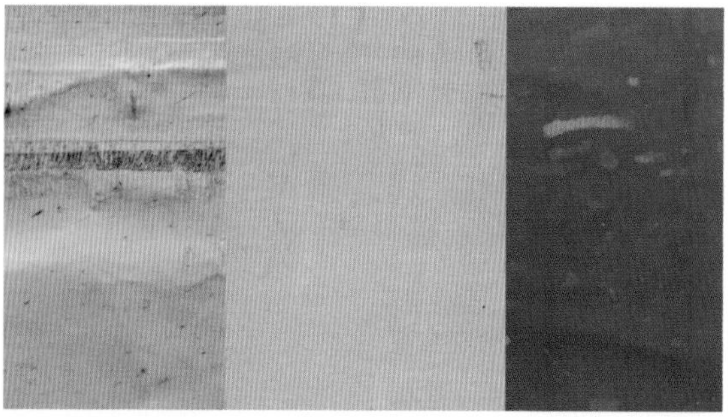

Three examples of fabric taken from the Shuttleworth SE5a. The clear doped and varnished fabric on the left and PC10 finished upper fabric on the right are both clearly different from the unfinished side of the fabric illustrated in the centre of the photograph.

Creating Fabric Interiors

The most important stage in replicating fabric interiors is selection of your linen base colour. In theory this colour should replicate untreated fabric and, therefore, could be different to the external linen finish, which is treated with dope and varnish, and subject to different ageing factors. However, in practice, most modellers will choose the same colour for both interior and external linen surfaces.

Replicating Interior Lozenge Fabric

The lozenge printed fabrics were introduced primarily to save weight. The covered aircraft only required a few coats of clear dope and varnish, negating the requirement for heavy pigmented finishes. While dyes used for the various colours did not fully penetrate the textile, dyes with larger colour particles, such as blue and black, would tend to break though the fabric less and, as such, appear paler on the inside than some of the lighter colours. The modeller has very few options with regard to replicating this interior appearance. As far as the author is aware at the time of writing, only Aviattic produce a decal lozenge to replicate the reverse side of a printed lozenge sheet accurately. It should be noted that the reverse side of the lozenge would normally only be applicable to the interior of the fuselage sides and floors. Any additional interior use of fabric, such as the panel behind the pilot's position, would be fitted with the exterior side of the fabric exposed.

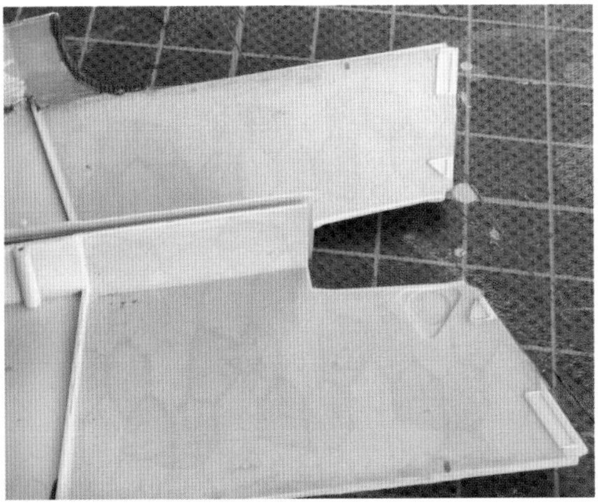

At the time of writing, Aviattic is one of the only companies to produce a decal to simulate the interior appearance of lozenge-printed fabric.

Weathering Interior Fabric

Unless the aircraft is fresh from the factory, some weathering is likely to have occurred to interior fabric. Rotary-powered aircraft suffered from castor-oil staining of the fabric, which typically followed the longerons along the aircraft, staining the fabric in areas where fabric contacted with structure and fittings. Interiors of aircraft powered by in-line engines are likely to have remained cleaner for longer, but would still be subject to a build-up of soiling and staining over time.

Oil staining can be simulated by applying a brown ink or brown wash to affected areas. This can be done with a normal brush but is sometimes more effective with an airbrush. Staining effects can be toned down by over-spraying with a light coat of the base fabric colour.

Interior Metal and Fittings

Metal fixtures and fittings were almost always coated to protect the metal. Typically, the Germans would either use a grey-green or medium-grey primer on metal structural components, while

The Wingnut Wings' AEG G.IV provides a good example of an interior predominantly finished with a grey-green primer.

performance fittings, such as the control column, could be finished in black gloss. The primer probably varied in colour shade depending on period and manufacturer. Plywood and wood interiors were also occasionally finished in primer. Pfalz, Halberstadt and AEG are known to have finished wooden interiors in this manner.

INSIDE THE COCKPIT

Internal Framework

While most modern kits include internal framework detail, many older kits do not. This kind of detail can be easily added using a combination of suitably sized plastic strip to represent wood framework and plastic rod for metal-tubed structures. The easiest method of adding framework detail is by gluing it directly to the inside of the sidewall using Liquid Poly cement. Often the blank sidewalls will require some preparation, especially if moulding flaws or injection marks are present. There may already be some poorly moulded or inaccurate detail that would be easier to remove and replace than try to correct.

Structural drawings in publications such as *Windsock* and *WWI Aero* can help with the positioning of framework detail, but sometimes guesswork may be necessary. It is usually easy to work out where the horizontal longerons should be positioned, as these will follow the edges of the main airframe. There will almost always be a vertical-positioned bulkhead behind the pilot's seat and there is likely to be another bulkhead close to the position of the instrument panel

Bracing Wires

Internal bracing wires can be added using either monofilament, elastic or stretched sprue. Elastic or stretched sprue is easier to apply to rib detail moulded to the sidewall because these materials can be applied without creating holes or slots.

I find monofilament perfect when simulating bracing wires on framework that is part of a separate cockpit assembly. Care needs to be taken to avoid adding substance to the outside edge of the framework, as this may affect fit. This can be done by cutting a series of slots and grooves for the thread to fit into. Alternatively, small holes can be drilled into corners of framework to accept thread or turnbuckle-style fittings.

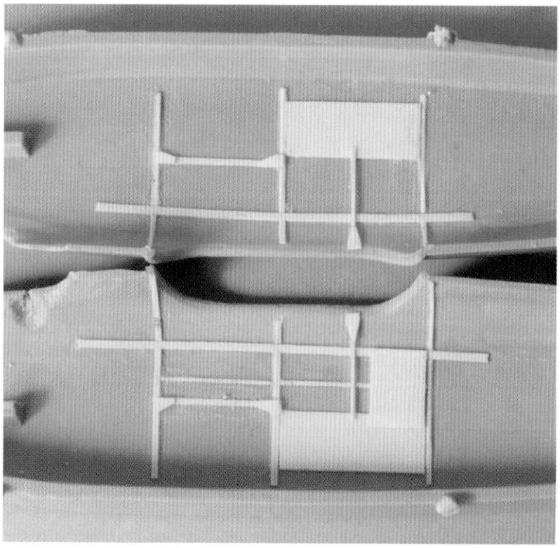

Interior framework detail is added to the sidewalls of the Blue Max Halberstadt CL.II.

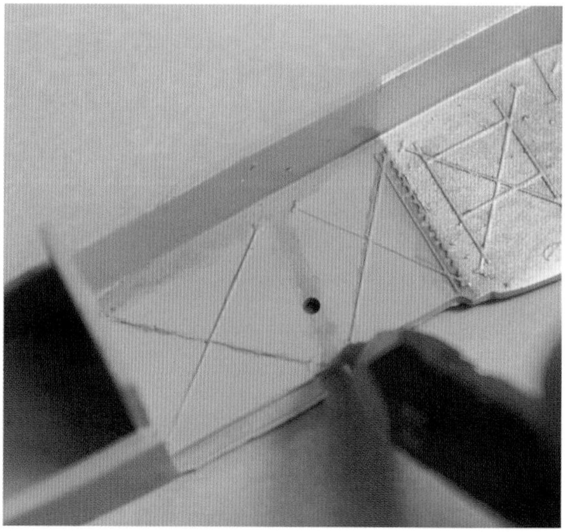

Moulded bracing lines can be highlighted with a pencil.

Some kits include bracing wire detail that is pre-moulded into the sidewall. This can either be removed and replaced with rigging material, or used in its original state. A pencil can be useful for highlighting moulded bracing detail.

Seats

Seating varied greatly between machines and manufacturers during World War I, ranging from wicker baskets to the duralumin-constructed seats fitted in Junkers' all-metal aircraft. While it's fair to say that the modelling industry has cleaned up its act, the majority of older kits will contain a piece of plastic or resin that bears very little relation to the genuine article. Typically, older kits will supply what is commonly known as a bucket seat. While a bucket seat may be acceptable in many cases, the shape of the seatback is often incorrect. Considering that the pilot's seat is probably the most visible part of any open cockpit, any improvement that can be made is worthwhile.

Improving Basic Kit Seats

Seats are not always the easiest part of an aircraft to research. This is because photographs of aircraft cockpits are often taken from the rear of the cockpit, looking forward and the seat is out of shot. A good source of research is period reports on captured aircraft, many of which include drawings and photographs of interior components. World War I aircraft restorer and replica-builder websites, such as the Memorial Flight in France and Vintage Aviator in New Zealand, can also be useful.

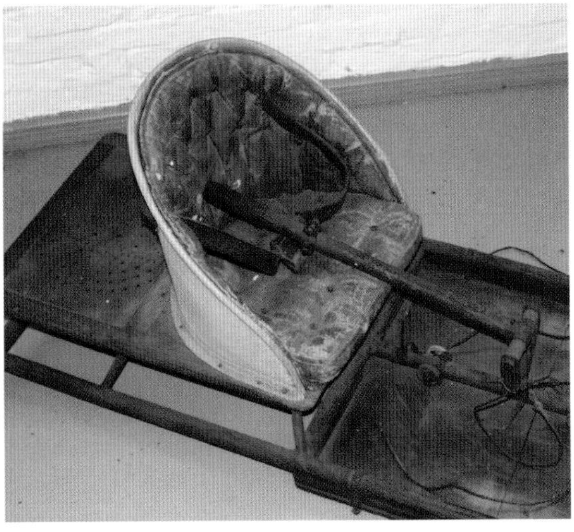

An example of a bucket seat displayed at Brussels Air Museum. ALF SMALL

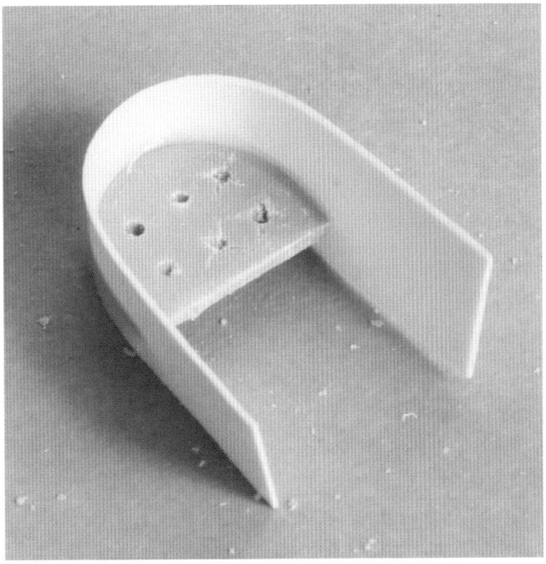

A replacement seatback for the Blue Max Halberstadt CL.II has been glued to the original base but still requires shaping.

Seatbacks often require the most work. The shape may be inaccurate or the substance too thick. Sometimes it is easier to replace the seatback completely with plasticard. Begin by removing the original seatback using a razor saw and clean up the base. Cut a strip of thin plasticard to a width that is approximately the same height as the required seatback and wrap the strip around the outside edge of the base, so that one of the edges of the strip is reasonably flush with the bottom edge of the base. Glue the strip in place using cyanoacrylate. Once the glue is completely dry, trim off any excess length of the strip and then use a sanding stick to shape the seatback.

Seat bases can also be made from thick plasticard. Suitably sized kit seats can be used to make a pattern for the base, but it's important to note

Masking tape has been applied to the seatback of a suitably shaped part so that the shape can be traced.

that the size of the pattern should be reduced slightly to compensate for the substance of the seatback.

Seatback patterns can also be made by wrapping masking tape around the seatback of a suitable kit part. The edge of the back is then traced with a pencil. Once removed, the masking tape can be placed directly on to the replacement material or used to create a more permanent pattern template.

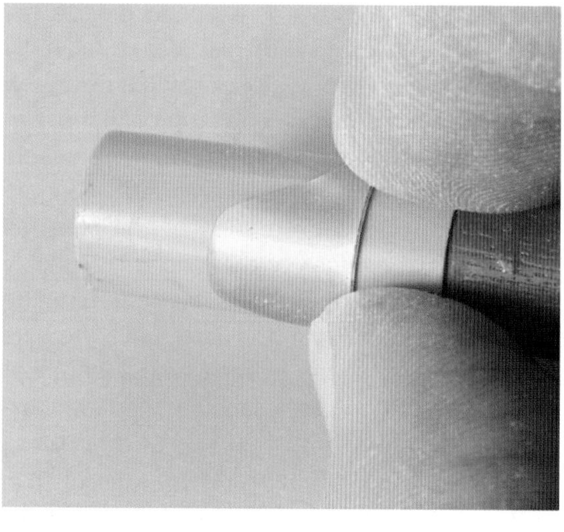

A photo-etch seat seatback is shaped around a pen.

Photo-Etch Seats

Photo-etch seats are sometimes included within a kit as an alternative to the plastic part or sold as an aftermarket improvement. These are constructed using a similar method to the plasticard replacements detailed above. The main difference with photo-etch is that the central part of the seatback requires preforming around a suitable-sized cylindrical item such as a drill bit. If the photo-etch replacement includes the seat base, it is advisable to mount this part on to plasticard, providing a wider area on which to cement the seatback.

Further Seat Improvements

Three-dimensional details, such as cushioned edges, can be added using thin plasticard or plastic strip, which, once glued firmly in place, can also be rounded using abrasive paper. Cushioning can easily be produced using putty products, such as Milliput.

Painting Seats and Simulating Leather

The colour of seats will be dictated by the materials from which they are made. Seats could be upholstered or made from plywood, aluminium or a combination of materials.

Many seats had areas that were upholstered in leather or fabric. The Germans used both leather and a synthetic material known as pleather to upholster seats. While there are many different types of leather finishes, modellers are often trying to simulate aniline leather, which has essentially had its natural features enhanced by creams and dyes. Simulating aniline-finished leather is a little like simulating wood, in that a fairly pale colour is used as a base and then washes are used to build up the final colour. I often dry-brush a light-beige colour in-between washing coats to accentuate the detail.

Pleather was a synthetic material akin in appearance to some modern synthetics. Aircraft manufacturers, including Fokker, are known to have used pleather as a seat covering. From a standpoint of simulating pleather, a simple semi-gloss base colour should be enough, perhaps with

This Albatros seat illustrates the difference in colour between the base coat (left) *and the finished part* (right).

a little dry-brushing or highlighting with a slightly paler colour. The finish of a synthetic material is likely to have remained in a pristine condition for longer; however, once wear or breakdown of the finish did occur, the result would appear to be more severe than on normal leather finishes and may include peeling of the synthetic coating.

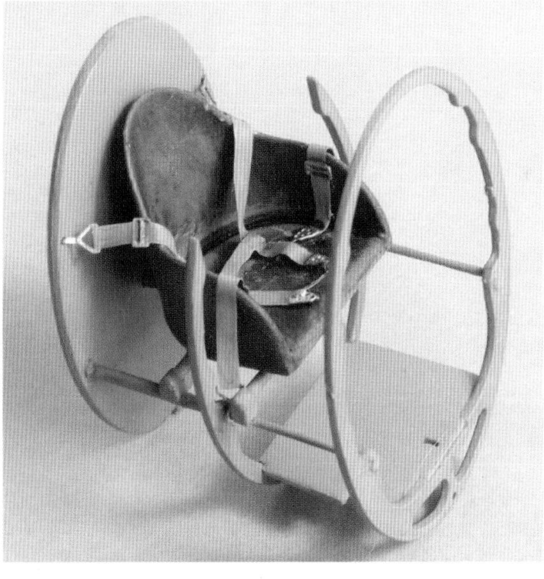

This assembly includes a four-piece harness, typically fitted in single-seat fighters.

Seatbelts

Typically, German aircraft were fitted with lap belts, while the addition of shoulder harnesses was standard on single-seat fighters. Seatbelts were usually fitted to the airframe, although often kits make a compromise by fitting the ends of the belts behind the seatback or to the sidewall of the seat.

Photo-Etch Seatbelts

Most modellers' first experience of seatbelts will be photo-etch parts included within a kit or as part of an aftermarket set. Kit photo-etch seatbelts are not always accurate, as many manufacturers use one seatbelt design for all of their kits. However, aftermarket photo-etch sets of seatbelts are easy to obtain in most popular scales.

Some photo-etch sheets are very soft and pliable, while others can be very rigid. If the latter is true, then the parts should be annealed. Annealing is a process by which the photo-etch is exposed to a cold flame, which has the effect of softening the metal. Seatbelt parts can then be removed from the fret, randomly folded over at various points along their length and then flattened to simulate natural creasing. Note that extra care needs to be taken with pre-painted seatbelts, as the paint will peel if the parts are folded too severely.

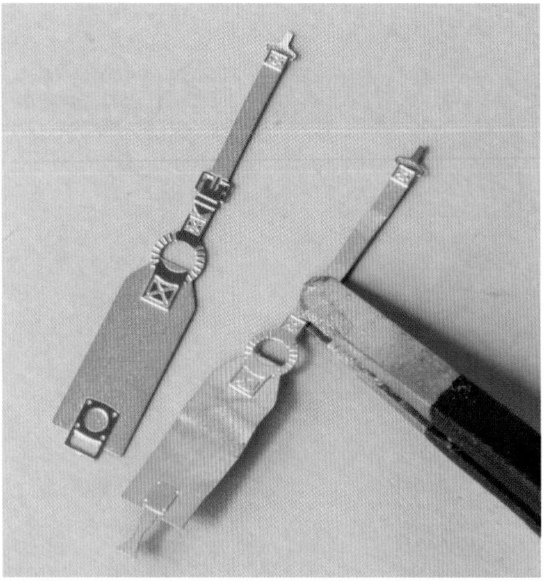

Photo-etch seatbelts can be folded in random positions to simulate creasing.

When fitting seatbelt sets into a cockpit, I usually begin with shoulder straps (if applicable), gluing the rear attachment points into position. Once the glue is dry, the shoulder straps are carefully bent down on to the seat, so that in its unglued state, the shape of belt reflects its final shape. Cyanoacrylate is then applied to the underside of the strap and the part is held in its resting position until dry. Once the shoulder straps have been fitted, I repeat the process for the lap straps.

Fabric Seatbelts

Some aftermarket product manufacturers offer fabric seatbelts. These sets usually consist of a dye-cut fabric material and a small photo-etch fret containing buckles and other seatbelt fittings. The seatbelt material usually needs to be carefully peeled from its backing and assembled in a similar manner to the way that a real seatbelt would be manufactured. Be careful to read the instructions fully, as often only certain types of cement, such as PVA, can be safely used on these products. Once the seatbelts have been assembled, they are fitted to the seat assembly using a similar process to the photo-etch belts. Typically, pastels can be used to weather and add depth to the flat colour of the seatbelt fabric.

Waste fabric can easily be cut into strips and used to make extra belts. The seatbelt sets usually come with extra photo-etch fittings, which are useful when making extra belts from the waste fabric. Further fittings can be sourced and shaped from unused parts on spare photo-etch frets.

Scratch-Building Seatbelts

Alternatively, seatbelts are relatively easy to make from a variety of materials, such as masking tape and baking foil. In 1/72-scale, a scratch-built seatbelt could be little more than a strip of your chosen material, with scrap photo-etch glued to one end to simulate the attachment fitting. In larger scales, seams can be folded around buckles and further fittings added to create something a little more detailed and accurate.

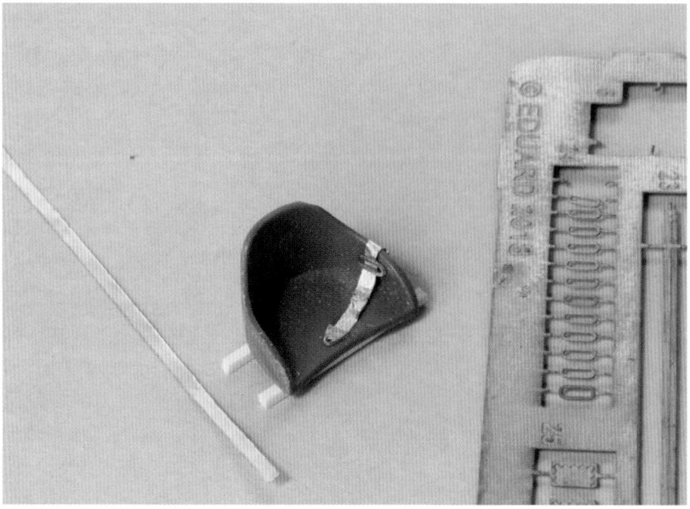

This 1/72-scale seatbelt has been made from baking foil and spare photo-etch.

Seatbelt Colours

Seatbelts were often made from strong textile webbing and, as such, should normally be painted in a pale, off-white colour. However, the Germans did sometimes make belts from alternative materials, including leather. Research can be difficult, as very little first-hand information, other than the occasional photograph, exists and, therefore, guesswork will often be necessary when selecting suitable style and colour seatbelts.

Control Columns and Rudder Bars

Control columns and rudder bars varied a great deal between manufacturers and aircraft. Control columns and rudder bars are fiddly, but fairly simple to modify or scratch-build from materials, such as brass rod and plastic stock.

Even the best and most accurate control columns can be improved. For example, there are usually wires that run from the trigger mechanism on the column to machine guns, which can be easily added to larger scale control columns. Additional details like brackets can also be simple to add.

Rudder bars also differed in design between aircraft but were typically single-piece bars that could be pushed one way or the other by the pilot. Rudder bars often included foot straps, which can be simulated by shaping spare photo-etch strip around a suitably sized rod.

Control Wires

Control wires running from the rudder and control column were often visible within the cockpit and can be simulated using a monofilament or elastic thread. Careful thought should be given as to when is the best time to fit control wires. Fit them too soon and you will end up with wires hindering assembly. Fit them too late and you may struggle to complete the process easily. It is often easier to drill holes into controllers while the part is still attached to its plastic sprue. Usually, a series of holes will also need to be drilled into a rear panel section behind the pilot's seat or observer's position.

Some modellers prefer to run the control wires all the way through the fuselage and through the actual positions where the control wires exit to the

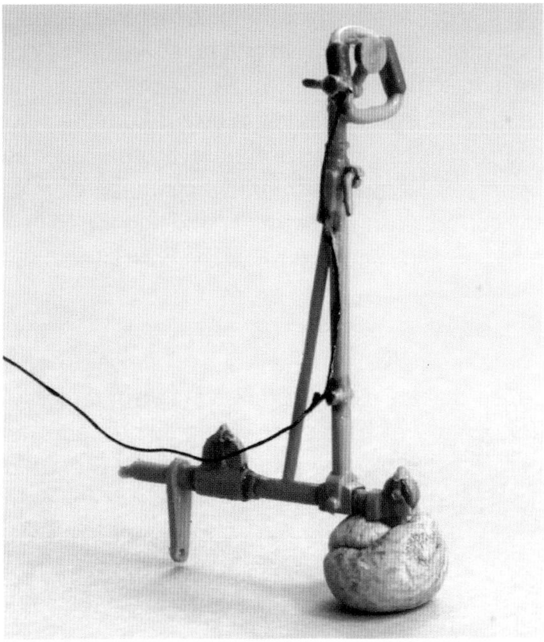

A 1/32-scale control column is large enough to include extra details, such as wiring.

This interior shot of the Techmod FF33e shows a simple control-wire arrangement running from the rudder to the rear of the cockpit.

outside. The problem with this method is that control wires get in the way of external painting and assembly and, as such, I prefer to extend my control wires only as far back as they will be visible.

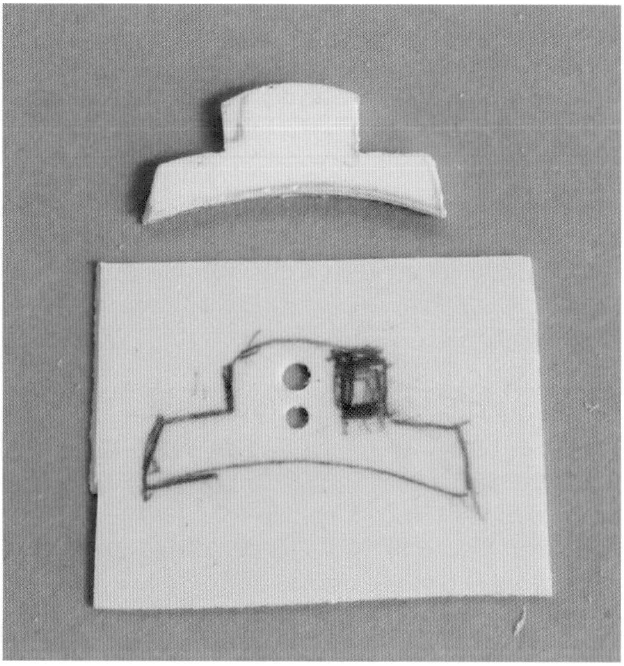

The two layers of a panel being constructed for the Blue Max Halberstadt CL.II.

Instrument Panels

Instrumentation on World War I aircraft was pretty basic and some cockpits did not have a panel, as such, just a few basic instruments that were fitted to the airframe. Most German aircraft were fitted with a tachometer, fuel selectors and starting magneto. Other instruments varied, dependent on manufacturer, machine or even batch. Most information that we have on instrumentation derives from the study of photographs, which, in themselves, are fairly rare.

Like many other interior aspects of models, instrument panels supplied within kits are not always accurate. This is not necessarily down to a desire by the manufacturer to deliberately produce inaccuracies, as information that we now take for granted wasn't always commonly available. As such, if you are building an older kit, there is a very good chance that some modifications will be required, if interior accuracy is considered important.

The first thing you may need to do is to revise the shape of the panel itself. Often instrument panels are assumed to be semi-circular to fit up inside the fuselage coaming. If the original panel is worth saving, then adjustment of the shape using sanding sticks and needle files may be all that is required. Alternatively, a new panel can be made from scratch.

Scratch-Building a Basic Panel

There are many methods of scratch-building panels, but I prefer to construct a panel from two layers of plasticard. The bottom layer has a substantial substance, while the top layer, which will contain any inlaid detail such as instrument faces, is cut from very thin plasticard. I usually begin by cutting the bottom layer shape first, using sanding sticks and needle files to tidy up the shape. This part is then used to draw the outline of the panel on to the thin plasticard. The position of any instruments or switches is also drawn and holes are drilled out to represent instrument faces. At this stage, the shape of the panel has yet to be cut from the plasticard. In this state, the bottom layer is glued to the upper layer ensuring that any instruments are in the correct position. Once dry, the thin top layer is trimmed and sanded flush to the base layer.

Photo-Etch Panels

Some kits and aftermarket sets include photo-etch panels that are usually supplied in two or three layers, one of which is a piece of printed clear acetate. Before assembly, the underside of the acetate is normally painted white or cream, so that the print on the dials shows up clearly. As an alternative to painting, the acetate can be mounted on to white plasticard. This method is especially useful if the panel itself is to be glued to fuselage sidewalls, as the extra thickness of the assembled part will improve the quality of the bond.

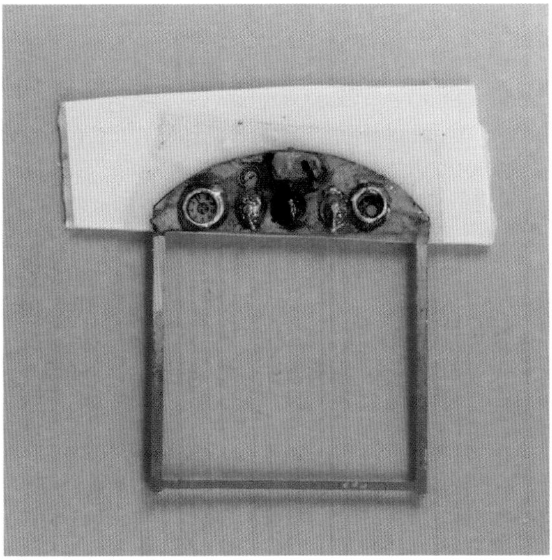

The PART photo-etch panel for the FF33e is glued to a piece of white plasticard.

Revising or Adding Instruments and Fittings

At its worst, a kit instrument panel can be completely blank or filled with a random selection of instruments and fittings that bear no relation to the genuine article. Alternatively, one or two instruments or fittings may need to be omitted or re-positioned. How these issues are dealt with will depend upon many factors, including scale, the level of detail of the existing instruments or even whether there is a desire to make the panel as accurate as possible. In some cases, instruments and fittings can be carefully shaved from the panel, using a sharp scalpel or razor blade, and then simply repositioned. This is not easy and care needs to be taken to keep the blade as parallel as possible to the panel face, while avoiding damaging parts of the panel that are considered satisfactory. If the process works, then the thin instrument is likely to have curled during the process and will need to be carefully flattened before repositioning. This method can also be used to add instruments and fittings removed from spare panels.

Alternatively, the offending item can be removed and a replacement scratch-built and fitted; however, something as simple as a bezel is difficult to produce in small scales. One possible method would be to cut slithers from suitably sized brass or aluminium tubing, but the substance of the tube wall would need to be very thin to produce a suitable-looking bezel. Photo-etch bezel sets are available in larger scales and can be extremely useful when revising instrument panels.

In smaller scales, it is sometimes easier to cut a cross-sectional slither of a suitably sized plastic rod to act as an instrument.

Other fittings, such as starting magnetos and wiring, can be added using basic scratch-building skills. For instance, a suitable starting magneto

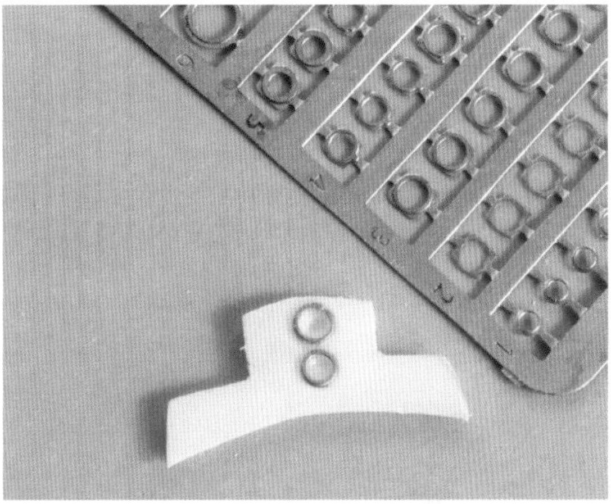

Commercially produced 1/48-scale bezels have been used to detail my scratch-built panel.

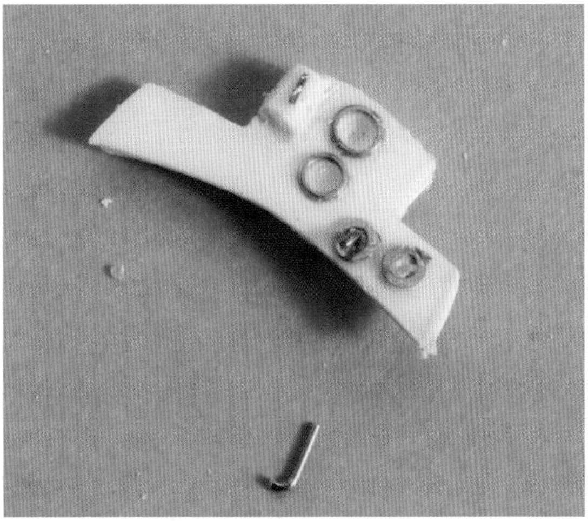

A magneto and a pair of selector switches have been added to the Halberstadt panel.

can be shaped from plastic strip. Most of the magneto can be shaped on one end of the plastic strip, so that it can be easily handled. Once a suitable shape has been fashioned, the part can then be cut away from the strip.

Even an accurate and detailed panel, such as you would find within a Wingnut Wings' kit, can benefit from some detailing. For example, fuel-selector switches are very rarely included as part of the mouldings. Rudimentary switches can be made from a thin brass rod, which is bent to a straight 90-degree angle at one end and then cut to a suitable length either side of the bend. A hole is drilled in the middle of each of the moulded selector dials to accept the switches.

Replicating Instrument Dials

Instrument dials are particularly difficult to paint to a satisfactory level and benefit from being replicated in decal form. Most modern large- and medium-scale kits include dial decals as part of the package, often including spares. Some modern sets also provide the option of dials as decals or pre-printed photo-etch instruments. Larger scale dial decals are also available in aftermarket sets.

Dial decals can also be relatively easy to produce on an ink-jet printer. The first stage of the process is to design or source your dial artwork. This can be as simple as finding a drawing of the desired dial and scanning it. Alternatively, the dial artwork could be hand-drawn and scanned or designed directly within a computer art program. If you are creating dials for a small-scale model, you will want to keep your dials fairly simple, otherwise once the artwork is scaled down, it will look a mess. In larger scales your design can be more realistic, dependent on the quality of your printer. Once you have your artwork, it can be scaled down using a number of different computer programs.

Dial decals can be printed on clear or white decal paper. The problem with using white decal paper is that you then need a satisfactory method of cutting out your dial as a perfectly sized and shaped circle. For this reason, I generally find it easier to print on clear paper, paint the base of the instrument white, applying the decal on top.

Images of authentic instruments have been cleaned up in an art program and are ready to scale.

Alternatively, effective dial decals can be produced by scratching details into the dial. Using this process, the base material needs to be the same colour that the dial details will be. This will usually be black or white. The base material is then painted in the background colour. Once the paint is dry, a needle point or similar implement is used to scratch details revealing the contrasting colour underneath. This process can work very well for small scales and is less time-consuming than producing homemade decals.

Further Cockpit Fittings

Cockpit fittings that are common to most aircraft include hand air-pump and throttle systems. On some aircraft types, magazine cases and empty cartridge boxes, or even fuel tanks, may be visible from inside the cockpit. In addition, forward-firing machine guns were buried on some aircraft and the butts of these guns are likely to be visible. On larger scale models, you may also want to represent brackets and other forms of attachment fittings.

Air pumps, if missing or inadequate, can be manufactured from suitably sized tubing or plastic rod. The handle at one end can be made from thin rod or spare material cut from photo-etch frets. Fitting detail can be added using a thin sheet material, such as aluminium foil or plasticard.

The throttle on the Halberstadt has been shaped from pieces of spare photo-etch.

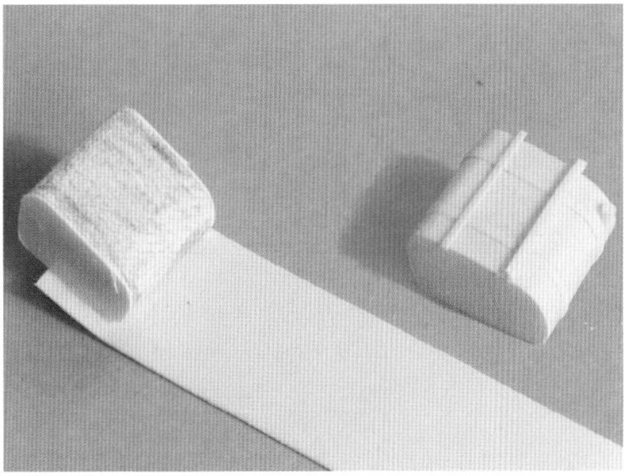

This fuel tank for the Halberstadt has been shaped from balsa and skinned in plasticard.

Throttles are much harder to produce from scratch, especially in smaller scales, although the structure is fairly basic. Waste or unused photo-etch material can be very useful when fashioning a suitable throttle.

Magazine cartridge boxes and fuel tanks can all be made from plasticard. Basic box-shaped parts can be assembled or cut from plasticard, while more complex shapes, such as fuel tanks, can be shaped from balsa wood, which is then skinned with thin plasticard.

The Observer's Station

The observer's position can contain a wealth of equipment, which is often not included within a kit. In particular, camera and radio equipment are often omitted. Storage for spare machine-gun magazines and photographic plates, or even small bombs, can also be missing. 1/32-scale builders have access to a number of sprues full of useful accessories that Wingnut Wings include in many of their two-seater kits.

In other scales, if a part is missing, begin by looking at your spares' collection. If you are lucky, you may find something that is suitable without too much remedial work. If not, you may find a

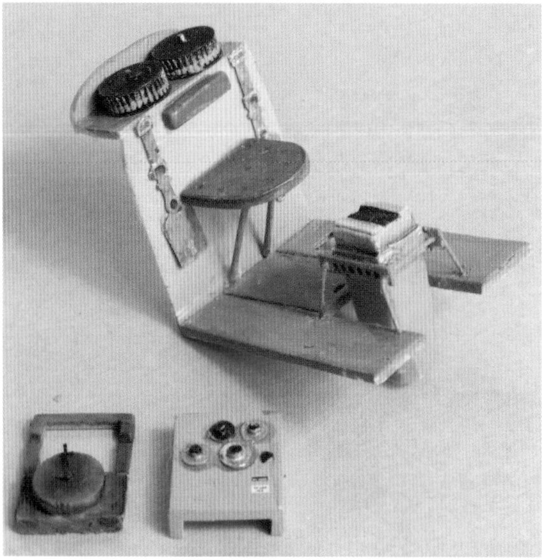

The observer's station for this Eduard Hannover includes a number of parts sourced from the spares' box, as well as scratch-built items.

shape or part of something that can be modified to your needs. If the spares' box proves to be barren, look to see what is commercially available or begin to think about ways that the part you need can be scratch-built. Items such as machine-gun magazine reels and internal bombs are likely to be quite easy to source, as there are often spares left over once a kit is completed. Cameras are more difficult to find, especially when building in smaller scales.

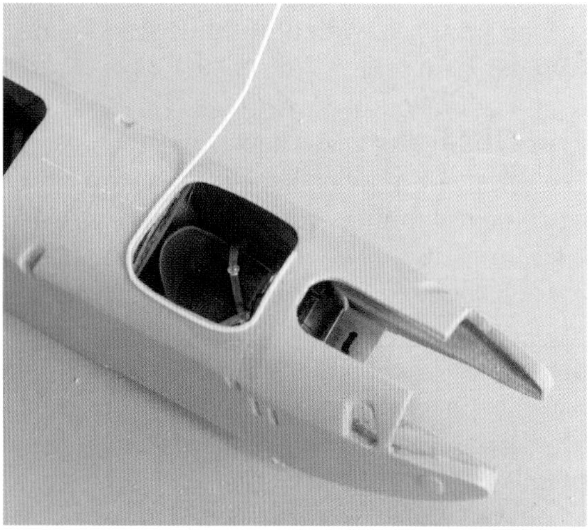

The Techmod FF33e fuselage had no cushioning detail. This was added by gluing plastic strip around the edge of the opening.

Cockpit Cushioning

The cushioning around cockpit openings can be simulated by gluing plasticard strip around the edge of the opening with Liquid Poly or cyanoacrylate. Once dry, the shape can be rounded to simulate cushioning. Alternatively, putty products such as Milliput can be used, although I personally find this option messy.

ENGINES

Engines of the World War I period can be broken down into two basic types: rotary and in-line. Rotary engines typically had nine or ten cylinders that were arranged around a central crankcase. In flight, the entire engine spun on a central axis, which helped to maintain a steady temperature.

In-line engines typically had six to eight cylinders mounted in a single or pair of straight lines on top of the crankcase. Unlike rotary engines, in-line engines required a separate radiator for cooling. The radiator could be mounted in front of the engine, on the leading edge of the upper wing or even in the wing.

Model engines can be represented by a number of forms from a lump of plastic moulded to look like cylinders, to very accurate-looking replicas. However, even the best kit engine can benefit from some simple modifications, such as the addition of pushrods or wiring.

Scale

In most cases, kit engines are designed to be under-scale. This is necessary because the engine needs to sit inside a cowling, which has a scale thickness much greater than the genuine article. Scale reduction is not usually noticeable but, occasionally, can be severe enough to be apparent. In this situation, the best course of action may be to

A selection of in-line engines of varying quality.

replace the kit part with a more suitable item. This can either be sourced from spares, replaced with an aftermarket item or scratch-built. The cowling may also require thinning from the inside to accept the replacement engine.

References

Photographs are perhaps the best source of reference for German engines. Period photographs are preferable, but walk-around images of surviving power units are also very useful. A good source of information, which is fairly cheap and easy to obtain second-hand, is *Jane's Fighting Aircraft of WWI*, which contains a large and extensive section on World War I engine references in the rear of the book.

Updating a Basic Kit Engine

Almost all kit engines can benefit from simple upgrades; however, areas most appropriate for upgrading will depend on such factors as scale, the initial quality of the kit part and how much of the engine will be on show when the model is complete.

Crankcase

Typically, in-line engine crankcases will not be seen once a model is complete; however, in extreme cases, the crankcase shape may be missing or be so poor that remedial action may be required. Normally this can be done by revising the original kit part (if present) but, occasionally, part or all of the crankcase may need replacing. I would typically carve upper and lower sections from thick plasticard, using scale drawings as an aid to defining the correct shape. Thin plastic sheet can be the basis of the central wider rim. Larger scale crankcases could be shaped from balsa and then skinned with plastic.

The basic shape of a rotary crankcase can be cut and shaped from wood dowelling, which can then be completely covered with thin plasticard and detailed. The dowelling should be of a smaller diameter than required to compensate for the additional covering of plasticard. Plastic sprue of a suitable radius may also make a suitable basis for a rotary crankcase.

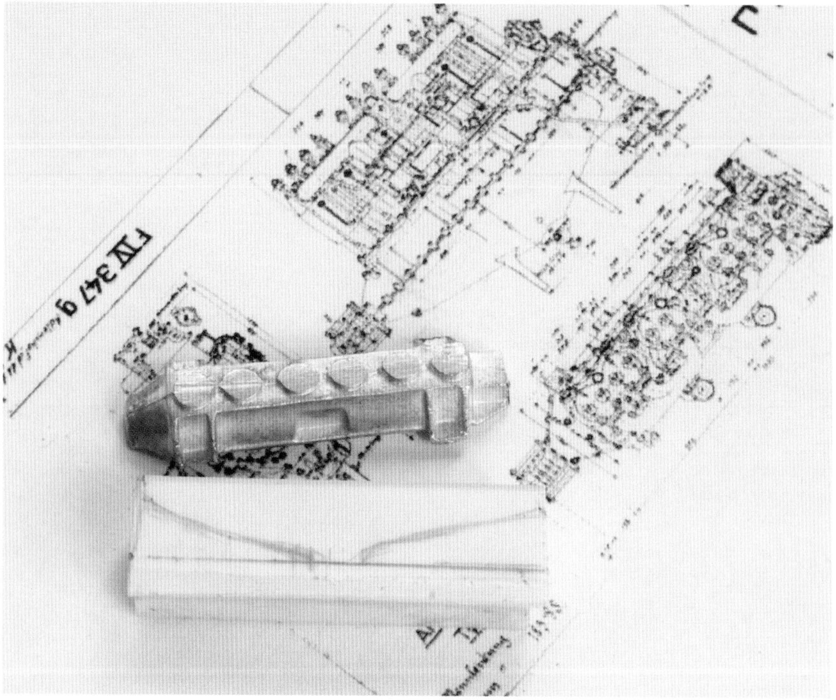

In the case of the Eduard Hannover, the Opel Argus engine was so poorly depicted that the lower half of the crankcase was replaced from an item shaped from plasticard.

Cylinders

Cylinders can be cut from plastic rod. In-line engine cylinders were often smooth with shaped heads. Rotary engine cylinders typically had a grooved surface. This can be replicated by winding thin gauge wire or thread around plastic rod. Alternatively, suitably sized screw threads can be cut down and used as cylinders. In very small scales, wound guitar strings may be suitable.

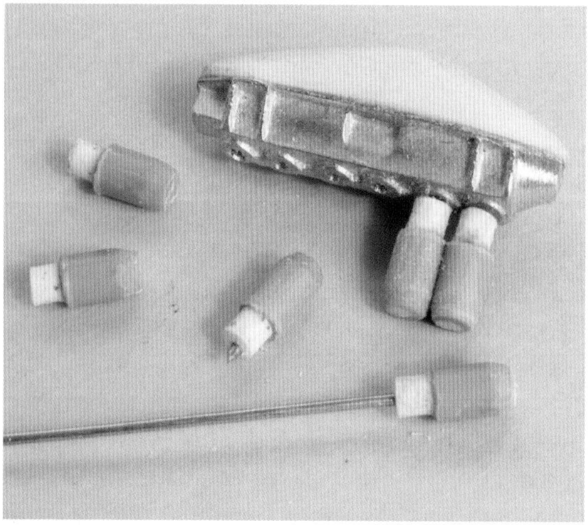

Cylinders for the Opel Argus were made from a combination of plastic rod and sprue, reinforced with brass rod.

Pushrods

Perhaps the simplest upgrade that can be made to almost any engine is to add pushrods. Pushrods are

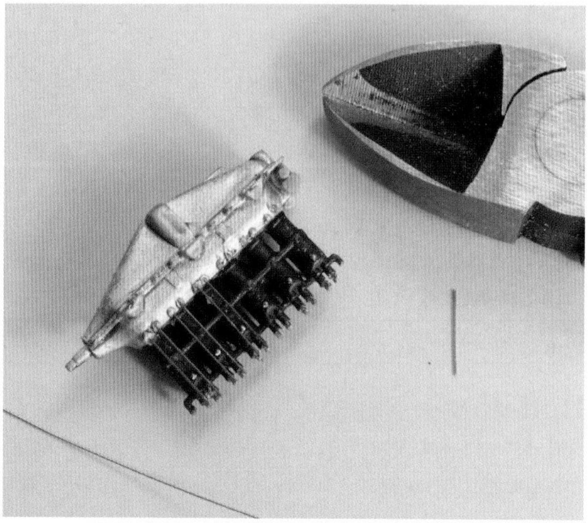

Guitar strings are being used to simulate pushrods on this Benz Bz.III engine.

often either missing from a kit engine or moulded into the cylinder. When pushrods are included as part of the kit engine, they often look over-scale or are supplied as a flat, photo-etch part. Suitably sized brass rods or guitar strings are perfect replacements for pushrods. How they are fitted depends on the original kit part but, typically, a small hole is drilled into the crankcase to accept the rod. If rods are initially part of the moulded cylinder detail, it is advisable to remove the detail before fitting replacements.

Rocker Springs

On larger scale engines, rocker springs can be added or improved. Springs can be made from thin plastic rod, which is glued into predrilled holes in the cylinder head. Once dry, cut a length of thin gauge wire and cement one end to the base of the rod. Apply glue to the rest of the rod and then carefully wind the wire around the rod until you reach the top. Ensure the end is glued down before trimming away the excess. Rocker springs can also be made from wound guitar strings.

Wiring and Spark Plugs

Wiring and spark plug detail can be added to larger scale engines. Spark plugs can be made from any rod of a suitable diameter, but I find it easier to cut plugs from brass or aluminium tubing. This allows

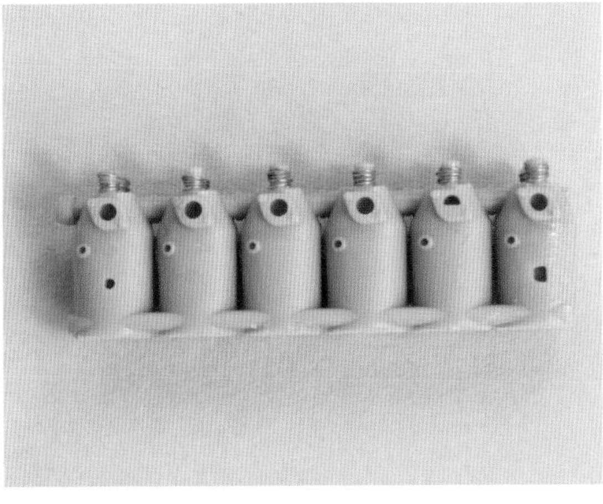

In this example, wire has been wrapped around existing moulded rocker spring detail.

Spark plugs made from aluminium tubing and wires have been fitted to this Mercedes' engine.

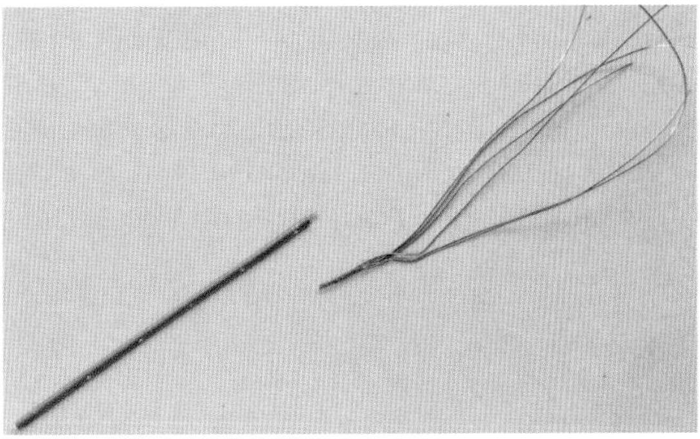

In this example, three wires have been folded and twisted to simulate the six spark wires that exit the wiring tube.

the spark plug wire to be fitted into the tubing resulting in an easier bond.

In-line engines have wiring tubes that are, essentially, cable tidies. Even if the kit includes these parts, it can often be advantageous to replace them with tubing. This allows simulation of wires exiting the end of the tube that fit to the magneto. The required number of thin-gauge wires are twisted together at one end and locked with superglue before trimming. This end is then glued inside the tip of the wiring tube.

Holes can either be drilled into the magneto to accept the wiring, or wire can be looped around each fixing nut and glued in place.

Pipes and Hoses

In-line engines usually have a number of pipes and hoses connected to them. Even the best kits do not include all of these parts, but they are easy to add using suitably sized brass rod. Curves can be shaped by bending the rod around a suitable sized drill bit. In this way, a realistically shaped pipe can be manufactured and then fitted into position.

Engine Colours

When I began building World War I aircraft, I assumed, incorrectly, that all engines were metal in colour. In reality, crankcases were typically unfinished metal, but cylinders and other engine parts were often painted black. Exhausts are often depicted in kits as a rust-brown colour but a rust wash would be more applicable. I usually paint exhausts with a black base that is dry-brushed with a steel colour. I then apply a number of coats of a rust wash until I am happy with the results.

Brown washes or inks can be very useful when weathering an engine. Dry-brushing can also be a useful technique to master. Grey can be dry-brushed on to a base of black to subtly add some depth to cylinders, while a light dry-brush of the base colour to the crankcase after an ink wash will help to highlight details.

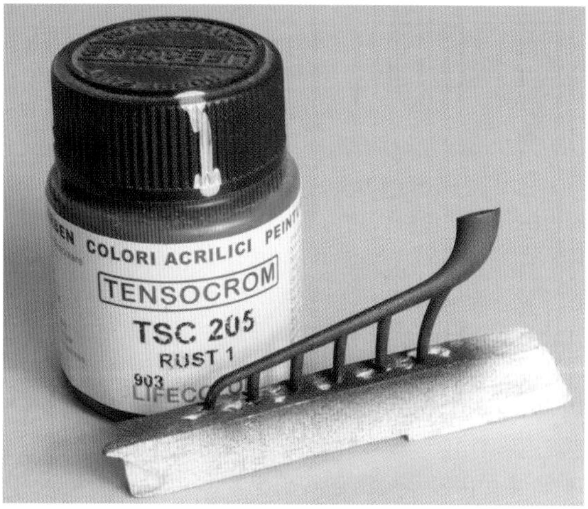

I often use Lifecolor Tensocrom washes to simulate the burnt brown appearance of exhausts.

Radiator pipes are often missing from kits, requiring the modeller to manufacture suitable parts from brass rod.

Black cylinders can be dry-brushed grey to highlight details and add depth.

Chapter Four

Building an Albatros – a Simple Biplane Configuration

INTRODUCTION

When I thought about the subject that I would like to feature as a second build, it was an easy decision. Besides being one of my favourite subjects, the Albatros features a sesquiplane configuration that makes it reasonably easy to assemble and rig.

There are many Albatros kits on the market in almost every scale you can think of but I have chosen the Wingnut Wings' 1/32-scale D.Va kit. It is not the simplest Albatros kit to construct, but it is the most accurate and can be built without any modifications.

This chapter will focus on three aspects of the build. First, some of the interior and engine-detailing methods that were discussed in the previous chapter will be put into practice. Second, I will begin to look at colour; in particular, wood simulation and lozenge application. Finally, and most importantly, will be the assembly of the biplane configuration, including an alternative method of rigging to the one described in the *Eindecker* build.

The completed Wingnut Wings' Albatros D.Va.

Many other aspects of the build follow the processes detailed in Wingnut Wings' excellent instruction manual and I see no profit in describing these areas of construction in too much detail.

Historical Background

The Albatros was designed at a time when the *Eindecker* was beginning to find itself outclassed against a new generation of allied fighters. The Albatros had an all-wooden semi-monocoque fuselage and was powered by a Mercedes' 6-cylinder in-line engine that had previously only been fitted into larger two-seat aircraft. The extra power from the engine meant that two Spandau guns could be mounted forward of the cockpit.

The Albatros made an immediate impact on the air war above the Western Front when it began to filter to front-line Jastas in September 1916. By the spring of 1917, most Jagdstaffeln were equipped with the Albatros by which time the Germans had regained the upper-hand in the fight for air superiority.

The D.V began to arrive on the front in the late spring of 1917 but was viewed as a disappointment by many pilots, as it had very little performance advantage over its predecessors. Despite this, the Albatros continued to be produced in large numbers and remained in front-line units until the end of the war.

The Wingnut Wings' Albatros D.Va

Wingnut Wings' kits are of an extremely high standard, both in terms of product quality and accuracy, which has earned the company large numbers of faithful followers worldwide. The Albatros is one of the company's earlier kits, which has been re-issued in different guises on a number of occasions. The kit essentially consists of good-quality, injection-moulded plastic with a small number of essential photo-etch parts, such as seatbelts and cooling jackets.

References

It is not difficult to find reference material for the Albatros and I quickly assembled a large collection of publications that might be helpful. These included two *Datafiles* and an *Albatros Special* from the *Windsock* series. I also found the collection of photographs printed in *Albatros Aircraft of WWI: Vol. 4* by Jack Herris very useful. Another Aeronaut publication that became a significant reference was *Royal Bavarian* Jagdstaffel *23* by Bruno Schmäling, for reasons which will become apparent later.

An accurate replica of the Albatros D.V on display in the Royal Air Force Museum at Hendon.

CONSTRUCTION

Building the Interior

The interior of this kit consists of three major sub-assemblies. The cockpit assembly is made up of three interconnecting bulkheads on which the seat fits. The fuel tank and machine-gun magazine assembly is fitted to a single bulkhead designed to slot into the sidewalls. The engine-bearer assembly is a collection of four bulkheads that are connected to the bearers on which the engine sits. All other interior details either fit directly to the sidewall or slot in between assemblies.

Cockpit Assembly

I began by painting the insides of the fuselage halves. To simulate plywood I used a technique whereby a thin layer of yellow ochre oil paint was wiped over a pale base colour in the direction that I wanted the woodgrain to follow. An old, stiff-bristled brush was also used to induce a woodgrain appearance into the wet oils. Longeron and rib detail were then hand-painted in a darker acrylic wood colour.

I also assembled and painted the bulkhead parts for the cockpit section. During this process, one of two thin horizontal bars that the seat fits on to snapped. As the breakage would be difficult to repair, I decided that it would be easier to replace both bars with plastic rod. The original sections were cut away and holes drilled into the bulkheads where the original bars had fitted. Lengths of plastic rod were then threaded through the holes. Once glued in place, excess rod protruding from the end of each bulkhead was removed.

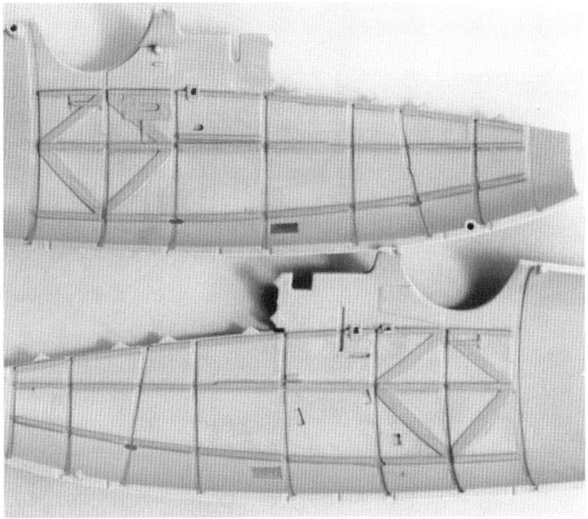

The painted interior sidewalls.

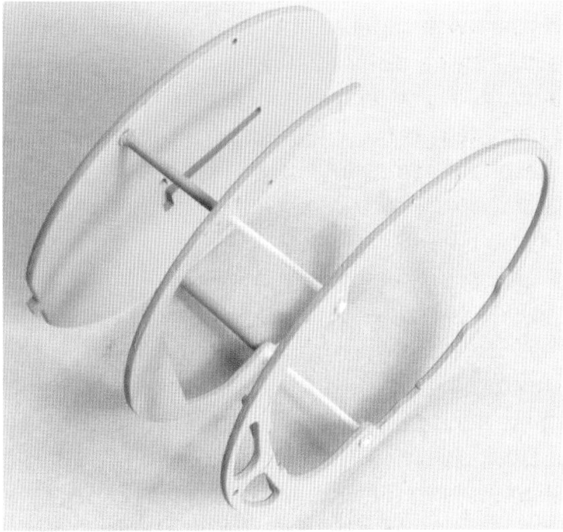

The basis of the cockpit assembly with replacement horizontal bars.

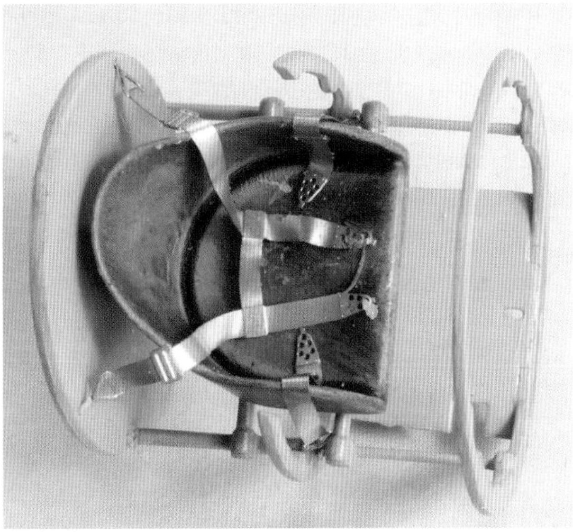

Annealed photo-etch seatbelts have been fitted on to the cockpit assembly.

The pilot's seat was given an ochre earth base coat over which a number of coats of brown washes were applied. I dry-brushed the surface with a beige colour between washes to simulate a worn, aniline leather appearance. The seat was then fitted to the internal cockpit assembly and the photo-etch seatbelts annealed and glued in position. The cockpit assembly was then ready to fit into the sidewall.

Cockpit Fittings

The largest of the cockpit components is the control column to which I made a few very basic improvements. On some period photographs, a small switch with wire running from it can be seen fitted to the left handle of the controller. To simulate this switch, a length of wire was glued into one end of aluminium tubing, which was then cut down to the approximate size required for the switch. I drilled a hole through one end of a piece of plastic rod and the aluminium tubing was slotted through the hole so that the end with wire extending from it protruded slightly from one side of the plastic. The other end protruded enough to simulate the actual switch. After gluing the tubing in position, the plastic rod was carefully cut flush with each side of the tubing, so that it resembled the base of a switch. The completed component was then glued to the handle and the protruding wire was glued in various positions along the vertical bar of the control column.

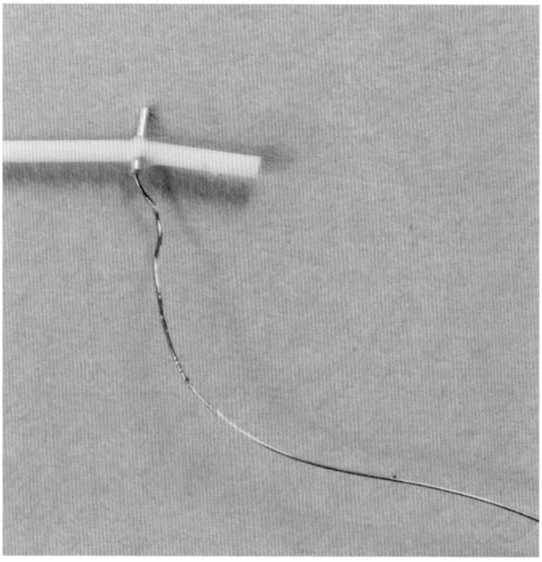

A small switch unit to be fitted to the control column handle is in the process of being made from tubing, wire and plastic rod.

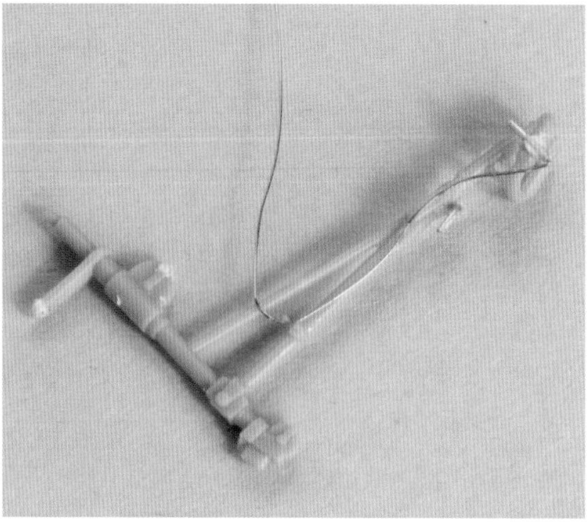

The control column with the addition of the switch unit and an adjustment handle.

In addition, a small handle, presumably intended for adjustment of the column height, was made from brass rod and glued into a predrilled hole on the vertical bar of the control column.

The fuel and air selector switchboard is supplied without any selector switches and so I drilled holes in the centre of each switch position and made some rudimentary switches from brass rod. The

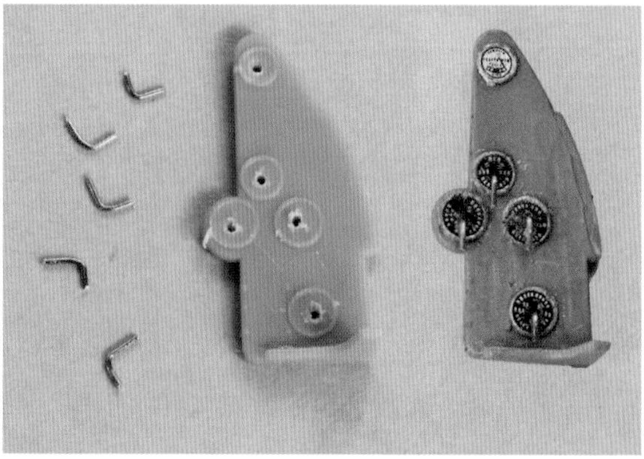

Before and after: the fuel and air selector switch board with switches made from brass rod.

switches were not actually glued in position until after the board had been painted and decaled. A needle was used to reopen the holes, covered by decals.

Pipes leading to the grease pump were manufactured from brass rod and fitted to the sidewall once the cockpit assembly, grease pumps and selector switchboard were in position. Reference photographs also show some partially visible pipework that fits behind the fuel and air selector switchboard. This part was simulated using a combination of brass and plastic rod and tubing.

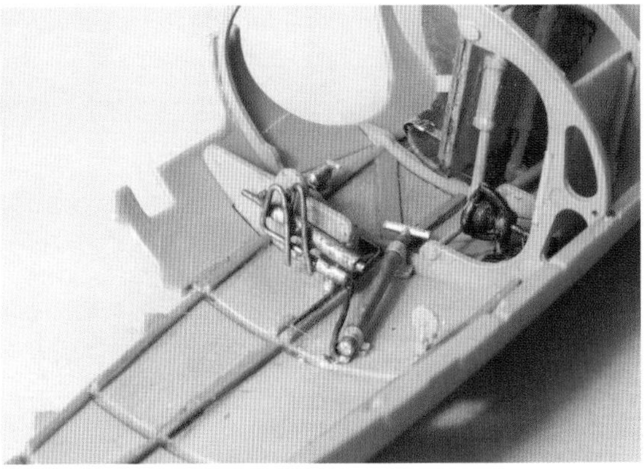

Additional pipework made from brass rod was fitted behind the fuel and air selector switchboard. Pipework for the hand air pump and grease pump were also fitted to the sidewall.

The control column is slotted between the cockpit and the fuel tank assemblies. Control wires are not easy to fit in such a confined space.

Once I was happy with the assembly, it was fitted in position at the rear of the panel.

The fuel tank and machine-gun magazine assembly was built, painted and fitted to the sidewall as detailed in the instruction booklet. The control column slots in-between the fuel tank and cockpit assemblies. Control wires were particularly difficult to fit, although some of these will not be visible. I used a combination of elastic line and monofilament for this purpose, but did omit a few of the more obscured wires.

The Engine and Bearer Assembly

Before assembling the engine, I modified the rocker springs on top of each cylinder by wrapping wire as evenly as possible around each of the plastic spring protrusions.

The basic parts of the engine were then assembled and painted. I replaced wiring tubes that fit to each side of the cylinder stack with brass tubing. To simulate wires that run from each wiring tube to the magneto, three pieces of thin-gauge wire were combined and folded. The folded end was then twisted tightly and spot glued, resulting in six wires connected at one end. The twisted end was cut to size and then inserted into one of the open edges of each wiring tube.

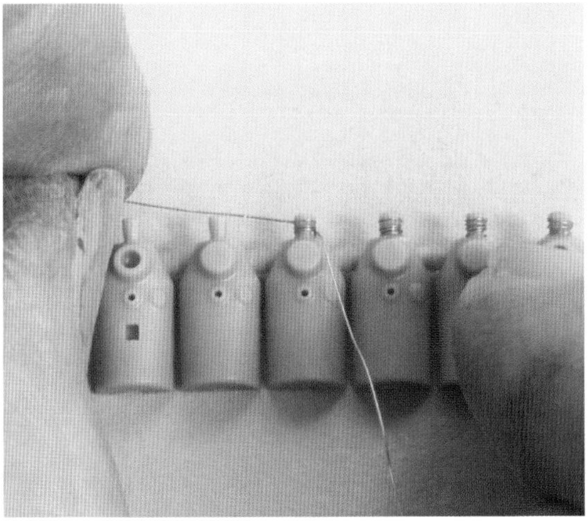

Thin-gauge wire is wrapped around each moulded rocker spring.

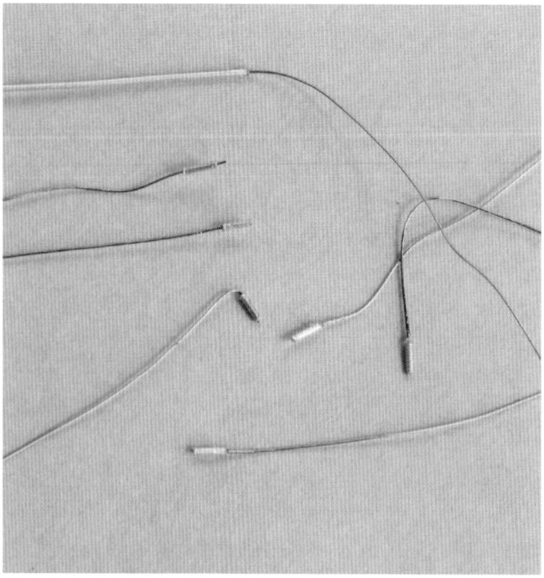

A collection of spark plugs made from tubing and wire.

Spark plugs were manufactured from wire and aluminium tubing. Holes were drilled into the cylinders ready to accept the plugs. Once the spark plugs and wiring tubes were glued to the engine, I gently teased each loose spark plug wire into a curved shape that was then attached to the underside of the tube. Excess wire was trimmed with a sharp scalpel.

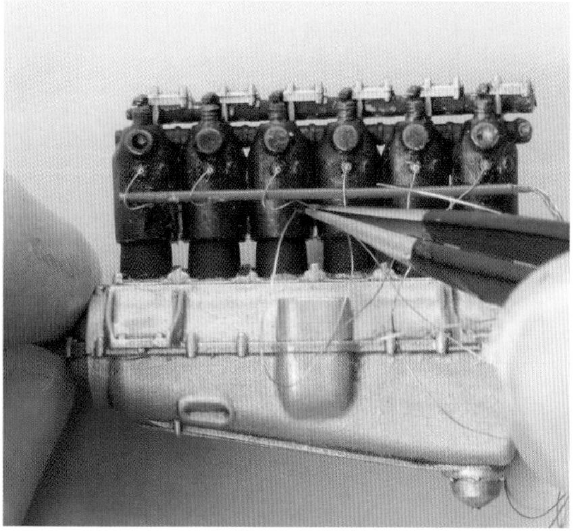

Each spark plug wire is teased into a curve and glued to the underside of the wiring tube.

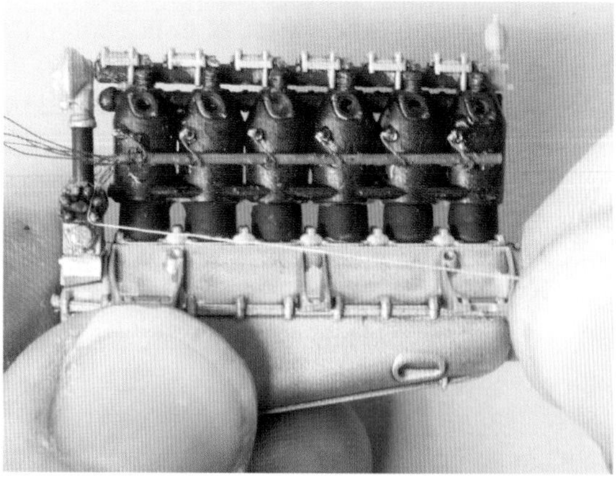

Wires running from the wiring tube to the magneto were fitted.

The completed Mercedes' D.IIIa engine.

Further kit details, including the magnetos, were added to the engine. The six loose wires extending from each wiring tube were separated and then individually glued to the connections on the magnetos. I found that the simplest method of achieving this was to apply glue to each connection nut and then pull the wire around each connecting nut until the wire fixed permanently in position.

The remainder of the engine was built according to the instructions, although the radiator

The completed engine-bearer assembly.

water-pipe that fits to the rear of the engine did not remain fixed in place for very long. I decided that it would be easier to deal with this part later in the build and so it was removed for the time being.

The engine-bearer assembly is a five-part jigsaw that has the potential of becoming misaligned during the construction process. To avoid this risk, the assembly was dry-fitted inside the two fuselage halves, while the glue holding the engine-bearer assembly together was still wet. This part was then painted before the engine, and a few further details from the kit were glued on to the bearers.

The two fuselage halves were now ready to close. Wingnut Wings' kits are developed on CAD systems. This should mean that fit is almost always guaranteed, but in reality it can sometimes result in problems because the tolerances are so tight that too much paint, slightly inaccurate positioning of a component or even a spot of cured glue in the wrong place can cause fit issues. Luckily I had no such problems when joining these two fuselage halves together.

Painting the Fuselage

The open cockpit and engine were masked using a combination of tissue and masking tape before priming the entire assembly.

Albatros fuselages are known to have been finished in a yellow varnish, which resulted in some allied pilots describing them as 'flying bananas'. I sprayed the plywood areas with a pale-beige colour and then used yellow ochre oil paint to simulate the varnish, using the same method as described earlier for the interior. However, this time each plywood panel was treated separately. This was a slow process, but the intention was

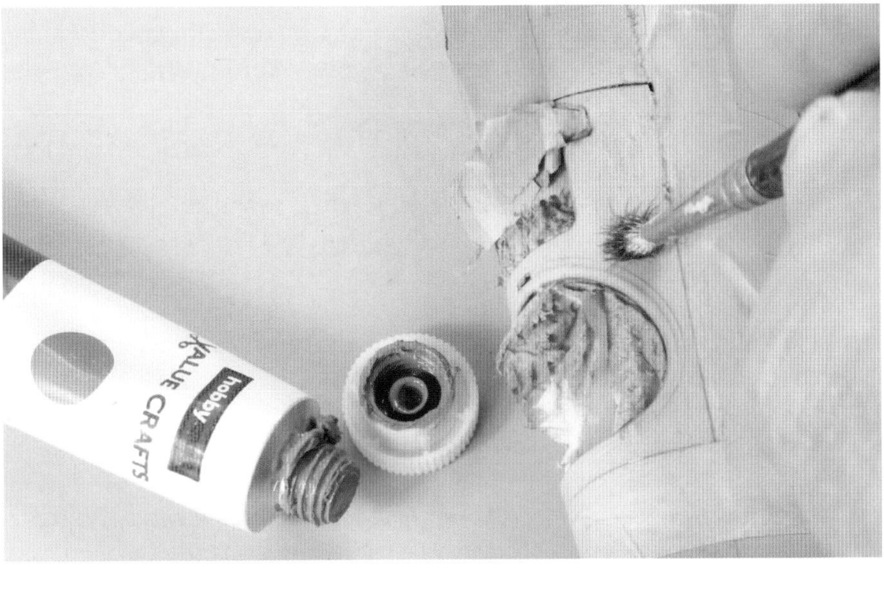

Treating one panel at a time, oil paint is applied and an old brush with splayed bristles is used to simulate grain.

The treatment of individual panels is deliberately varied.

that, once completed, each panel would appear slightly different to those around it. To help create this illusion, I deliberately treated each panel slightly differently with regards to the amount of excess oil paint that was wiped or brushed away.

Creating Markings

One of the most enjoyable parts of building a subject like the Albatros is choosing a colour scheme. The kit comes with five decal options, but there is plenty of scope for a little more individuality, as many companies produce separate aftermarket decals for this subject. For this project I wanted something really eye-catching but also a subject that was a little unusual. I finally found inspiration within the pages of a book on *Jasta 23* by Bruno Schmäling. This book contained photos of many colourful machines that I had not previously seen, but my eye particularly fell on an OAW D.Va with a *Münchner kindl* motif adorning the side of the cockpit.

There are no decals available for this particular subject and so I essentially had to create my own. I only needed the *Münchner kindl* motif as other markings could be sourced from a combination of the kit decal sheet and spares.

The first stage to producing my own decal was to create the artwork. I could have scanned artwork already present within the *Jasta 23* book, but chose instead to hand-paint my own version. This was painted in a much larger size than required, so that I could add a reasonable level of detail.

Once happy with my artwork, it was scanned at a very high resolution. The scan was then cleaned up in Adobe Photoshop. I also used Photoshop to scale the artwork using a scan of a 1/32 side-view plan to help me get the size exactly right. Once I had scaled my motif, it was copied and pasted on to a blank A4 page and printed on to paper.

This paper version was used to confirm that the artwork had been scaled correctly and was also

Painting the Münchner kindl *motif using an original photograph as my primary reference.*

The motif artwork after scanning and clean-up.

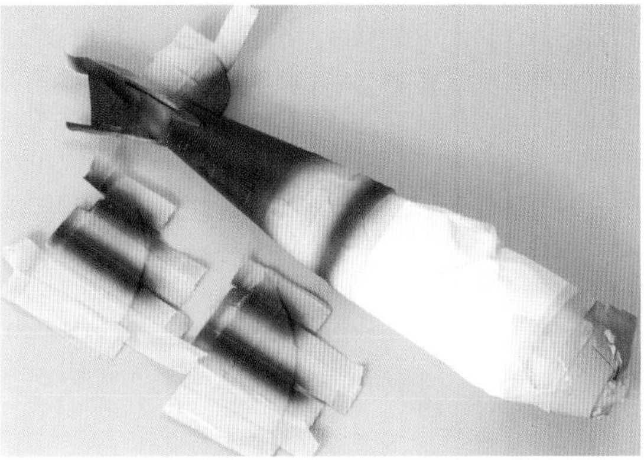

Black and white Jasta 23b unit markings were masked and sprayed.

used to help mark out the width of the white band around the fuselage, which on photographs is only very slightly wider than the motif. This area was masked and sprayed white. After further masking, the front edge of the white band and rear section of the fuselage were sprayed black. At this stage, the black and white striped tail section was also masked and sprayed. Before removing the masking, the black paint was over-sprayed with varnish to seal in the colour. Rich colours such as black and red can sometimes have a tendency to smudge adjacent white areas during handling if not fixed immediately.

Lozenge and Decal Application

Flying surface colours on Albatroses varied depending on batch and manufacturer. The OAW-built subject that I was building was covered in a five-colour lozenge fabric. For this model I chose to use a set of pre-shaped cookie decals designed by Aviattic to specifically fit the Wingnut Wings' kit. The advantage of using cookies is that you do not have the long and laborious job of applying rib tapes, as they are already printed in the correct positions. The lozenge cookies are available in a number of different variations, but I chose a set with salmon-pink rib tapes. These decals are printed on clear continuous decal paper and, therefore, should be applied to a white base colour in order to maintain their intended colour.

One advantage in using lozenge decals printed on clear paper is that you can add some weathering effects to the model surface prior to applying the decal. There are various methods of achieving these effects, but I chose to simply wipe a wash of brown paint chord-wise with my finger as I had done for the *Eindecker*.

When applying lozenge decals, I always begin with the paler underside. The front edge of the decal is positioned correctly along the leading edge of the wings and then a soft cloth is used

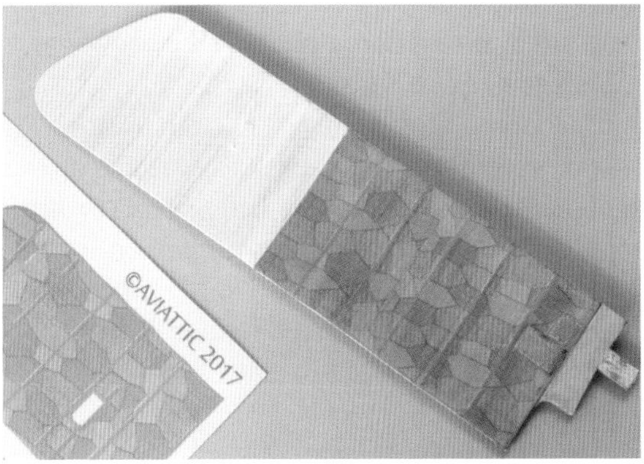

The Aviattic lozenge cookies are applied in easy to manage sections. Note the weathering effect, which is visible through the clear-backed decal.

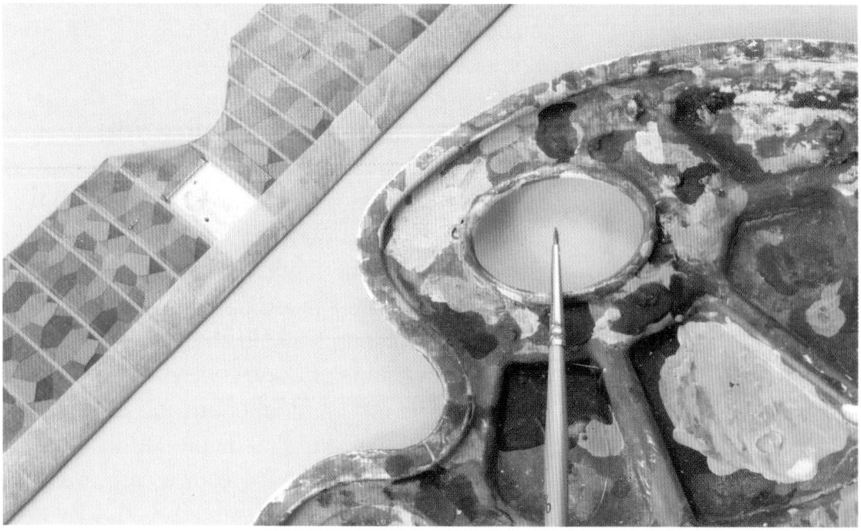

The leading edge tape on the upper wing was repaired using masking tape to ensure that the repair had a straight and clean edge.

to push pockets of air out from under the decal toward the trailing edge. Once I am happy with the result, the part is set aside overnight to allow the decal to settle properly. Any excess decal from the tips or trailing edge of the wing is then trimmed away. The process is then repeated for the upper side lozenge.

Once all of the flying surfaces were completely covered, the lozenge decals were sealed with a few coats of varnish. I had a few issues with the leading edge line on the top wing where I had overstretched the decal, so that I was missing the salmon-pink leading edge tape in a few places. To rectify this problem, I trimmed the offending areas and then painted a replacement line using masking tape to ensure that the line I painted was clean and straight.

Marking decals were sourced from a variety of spares when nothing suitable was available on the sheet supplied with the kit. The *Münchner kindl* motif that I created earlier was printed on to clear inkjet decal paper and sealed with varnish prior to application. National marking decals were also applied to the wings at this stage.

Back to the Fuselage

When building subjects with fuselage-mounted machine guns, I always delay fitting the guns in place until just before the upper wing is fitted. This reduces the risk of accidental damage to the guns while handling the model.

The two Spandau machine guns were assembled using the kit's photo-etch cooling jackets. These are made from very thick brass and required annealing before it could be rolled. Once painted, the guns were then fitted into position on to the fuselage of the model. Cowling panels were also painted and fitted.

At this stage of the build, the horizontal stabilizer was fitted to the fuselage. Control surface attachments on Wingnut Wings' kits are typically some of the weakest areas of the models. If it is

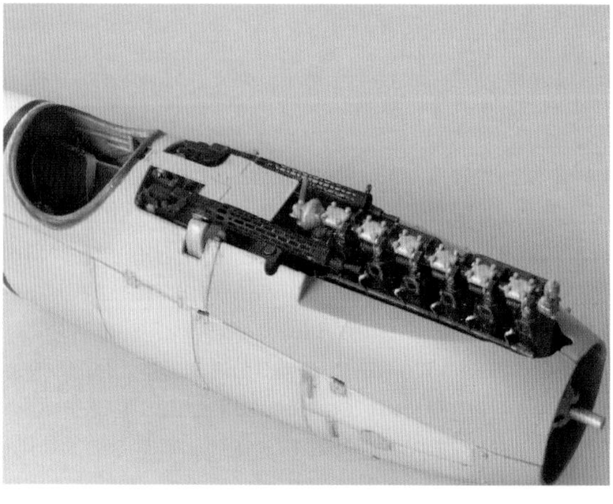

The cowling panels and Spandau machine-guns have been fitted to the fuselage.

The elevator was pinned to the stabilizer to strengthen the joint.

possible to do so, I always like to reinforce these attachments with brass rod. The substance of both the stabilizer and elevator was thick enough to reinforce the elevator attachment. Finally, the lower wings were permanently glued into place.

Wing Assembly

The cabane strut parts were pre-painted before gluing to the fuselage. It is important to check the fit of all the strut attachment lugs to the fuselage and upper wing before attempting final assembly. If the fit is too tight, then either the location lug on the strut end or the corresponding recess should be modified, otherwise the risk of breaking struts during assembly increases.

I intended to use Gaspatch turnbuckles as part of the rigging. These aftermarket parts are brittle and should be fitted into holes that are drilled at approximately the same angle as you want the turnbuckle to sit; otherwise they are likely to snap if too much stress is applied while adjusting their position.

I did not have specific Albatros turnbuckles at hand and so I modified my parts to simulate Albatros fittings. Turnbuckles tend to be fitted to the lower wing and fuselage and so small holes were drilled into these rigging locations with enough depth to hold the end of the turnbuckle in place. For the upper-wing attachment, I made my own looped pins by twisting wire around a

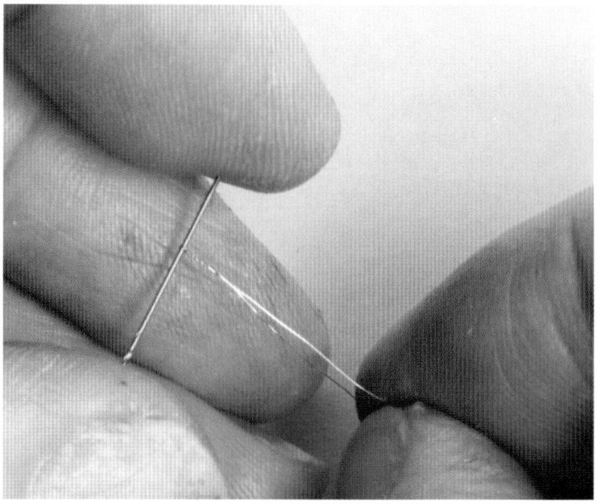

Rigging attachment loops are manufactured by twisting wire around a small drill bit.

0.3 mm drill and then cutting off the end to create a small pin.

After painting the turnbuckles, they were fitted into the rigging location holes on the lower wing, while the homemade loop pins were fitted into the upper-wing positions. For this build, I trialled Gaspatch's recently developed resin-based turnbuckles.

When attaching the upper wing to the lower wing, I always try to initially fit the wing in position by gluing the minimum number of attachments that I can get away with. In the case of the Albatros,

Turnbuckles are fitted to the lower wing at an approximate angle to the angle that the bracing wire will follow.

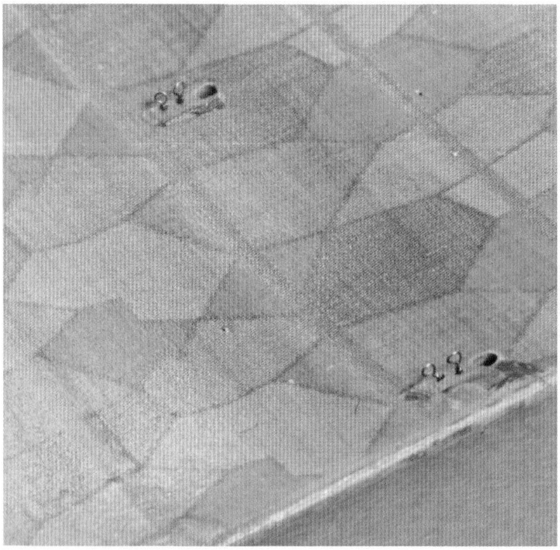

Rigging attachment loops were fitted to the underside of the upper wing.

it is easier to initially fit the V-shaped interplane struts to the upper wing, so that when the wings are assembled there will be only one interplane attachment on each side to worry about rather than two.

The water pipe that had broken away from the engine earlier was glued to the underside of the radiator encapsulated into the upper wing. The upper wing could then be fitted. This was performed in an upside-down position with the upper surface of the upper wing placed face down on a flat surface. I applied a small amount of glue on to each of the four upper-wing cabane strut ends and the fuselage/lower-wing assembly was

Interplane struts are initially glued to the upper wing.

The upper wing is initially glued to the cabane struts in an upside-down position.

then carefully lowered into position on to the upper wing without the aid of any kind of jig. At this stage, the interplane strut attachment points were slotted into position without cement.

Once the cement holding the cabane struts in place was completely dry, each interplane strut was carefully teased from its slot, glue applied to the recess in the wing and the strut replaced back in its original position.

Rigging

I used a monofilament mending thread as my rigging material, as this helps to provide strength to

The thread end from the upper-wing loop is carefully threaded through the turnbuckle eyelet and tacked in place using cyanoacrylate.

Once tacked, the thread is knotted once. Note that white paper placed under the area being rigged can help to make the process easier to see.

what is a fragile model in its unrigged state. I usually begin from the centre and work outwards. Typically, the thread would be fitted to the turnbuckles first, but I soon discovered that this did not work very well with the resin turnbuckles, as the action of attaching the thread to the turnbuckle was enough to snap the part. The process worked better if I started from the homemade loops in the upper wing. This way, when the thread was pulled down and through the opposite resin turnbuckle, the turnbuckle attachment was supported by the thread.

Each strand was first threaded through a loop in the top wing and knotted once. The knot was then fixed with cyanoacrylate and excess thread cut carefully away once the glue was dry. The remaining end of thread was then pulled through the eyelet of the corresponding turnbuckle and tacked into place using cyanoacrylate. The thread was then knotted, locked and cleaned up using the same process as had been employed on the opposite end of the thread.

Undercarriage

Unlike the *Eindecker* in the earlier build, the Albatros' undercarriage can be completely assembled as a separate entity before fitting to the fuselage. Wingnut Wings' instructions go even further by suggesting that the wheels can be fitted at this stage, but I prefer to wait until later.

Holes for the undercarriage bracing wire were carefully drilled out before fitting the undercarriage to the fuselage. These holes were drilled completely through the undercarriage struts, so that the thread could be pulled tightly through

Undercarriage bracing wires are initially fitted into holes in the fuselage.

the hole. The monofilament was initially glued into holes drilled into the fuselage. Each loose end was then threaded through the corresponding hole in the undercarriage, pulled tight and locked with glue. Care needs to be taken during this process to ensure that the undercarriage struts are not pulled out of alignment.

Finishing Touches

The wheels were assembled and painted using the OAW-style wheel covers included within the kit. The wheels were then glued in place along with the exhaust and radiator pipework. Ailerons were reinforced with brass rod, using the same method as the elevator, before fitting them to the wings and adding control wires.

I manufactured a replacement propeller from laminations of wood veneer. This is a process whereby the thin layers of veneer are glued together and then carved into the general shape of the propeller. This process is covered in more detail in Chapter 9. Finally, the windscreen was painted and fitted into place.

FINALLY

The Albatros is a good example of a simple biplane construction; however, beginners may prefer to practise on the smaller, cheaper Eduard Albatros or any similarly configured fighter, such as the SSW D-type. While significantly smaller than the Wingnut Wings' model, the Eduard kits are likely to provide many of the same challenges. In the next build, I'll be focusing on the construction of a multiple bay two-seat subject that requires a slightly different method of wing construction.

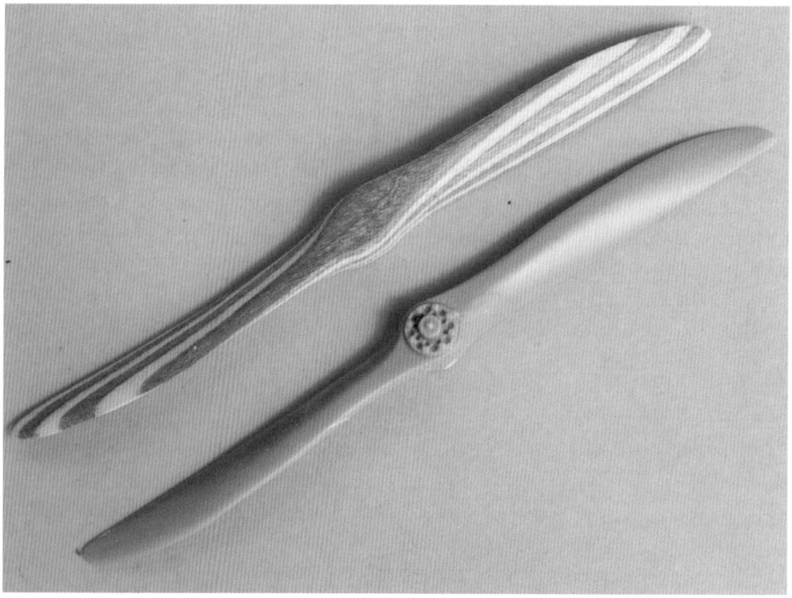

The kit's propeller was replaced with an item made from laminations of veneer.

Chapter Five

Wings and Rigging

INTRODUCTION

Perhaps the most challenging aspect of any biplane build is the assembly of the wing section. This is often cited as the main reason why modellers are discouraged from building World War I subjects, but, in reality, the processes employed are not difficult to master. This section takes an in-depth look at wings, struts and rigging, and the processes involved in successfully completing wing sections.

PREPARATION

Flying Surfaces

The majority of World War I period flying surfaces were made from a wooden structure covered in fabric. The fabric was pulled tightly over the structure and stitched to the ribs. Rib tapes, cut from strips of fabric, were glued over the stitching and the entire surface of the fabric was then doped, which effectively tightens and seals the fabric weave.

The three-bay Friedrichshafen FF.33e is a challenging subject to construct and rig in any scale.

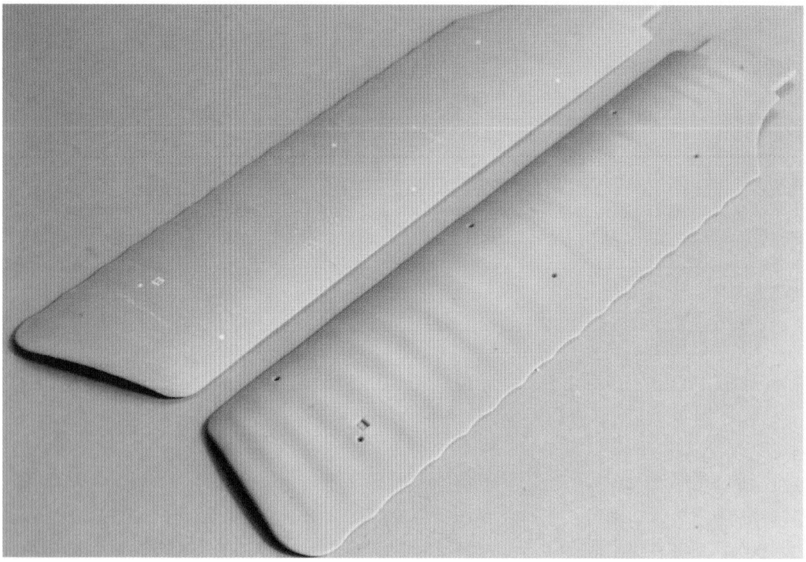

Out of the box, the Techmod FF.33e wings have an unrealistic 'starved cow' appearance, as illustrated by the wing at the bottom of this photograph. The surface of the wing (illustrated at the top of the photograph) has been heavily sanded in an attempt to improve the wing surface.

Kit manufacturers have traditionally depicted wing surfaces as a series of concave curves representing the space between each rib. In reality, the surface of fabric-covered wings should be almost flat in appearance, as any excessive sagging of the material would affect performance.

One method of rectifying such issues is to sand the wing surface almost completely flat and then apply strips of a thin material to simulate rib tape. The main problem with this method is finding a suitable material that is thin enough so that the rib tapes do not look over-scale. In smaller scales, decal strips are perhaps the best solution. Anything much thicker will appear out of place. In larger scales, 5-thou plasticard strips can be employed, but these will normally need to be thinned down once they have been glued to the wing. Heavy coats of primer applied at regular intervals during the sanding of plasticard ribs helps to clarify what the finished appearance will look like and will also create a very slight dip between rib tapes, which can look pleasing.

Heavy or oversized rib-tape detail can also sometimes be a problem. This is usually easy to rectify by reducing the substance or removing the detail with a sanding stick.

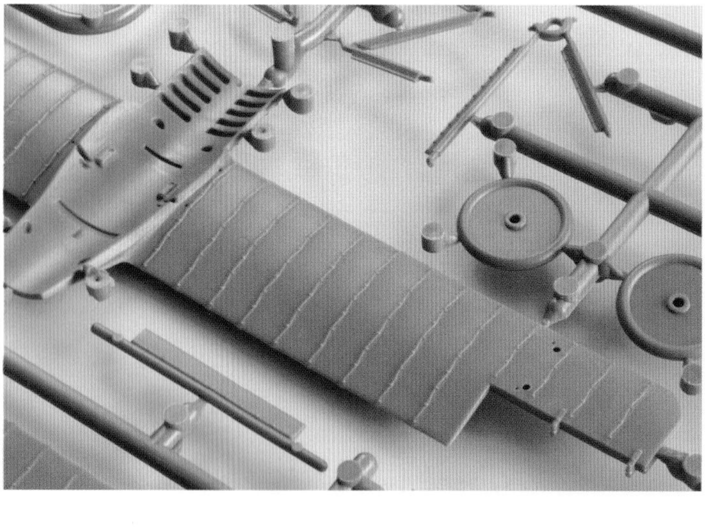

The wings of the Eduard SSW D.III are a good example of when rib tape detail can be considered to be overdone.

Rib tapes can also be simulated using a pair of scalpel blades spaced with a piece of plasticard of a suitable width. The blades are used to score pairs of lines simulating the rib-tape edges. This technique can sometimes work well on smaller scaled wings.

Skinning Wing Surfaces

Another method of updating wing surfaces is by skinning. This is a process whereby a new surface layer of plasticard is applied to the sanded and levelled surface of the kit part. Rib detail is scored into the plasticard using a blunt object such as a fine black biro. The surface of the wing is then attached to the scored side of the plasticard ensuring that the ribs are correctly positioned. Good-quality, double-sided tape can be used to attach large surface areas, initially. Edges can then be sealed with thin cyanoacrylate. Once the entire area of the skin is in place, excess plasticard is trimmed away and the edges tapered. I tend to use 5-thou plasticard for this purpose as I find that the thinner substance is less likely to stretch when the ribs are scored into its surface. Poly cements and Liquid Polys should not be used as they can melt the thin plasticard. I have also had problems where the wing has warped over time, because the poly cement had not entirely cured between the two materials.

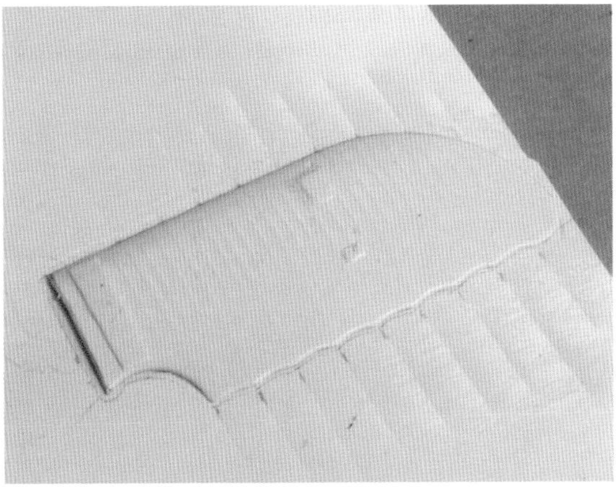

Rib positions are scored on to plasticard, which is then glued to the wing core. In this example, underside rib detail is being added to a vacuum-formed wing.

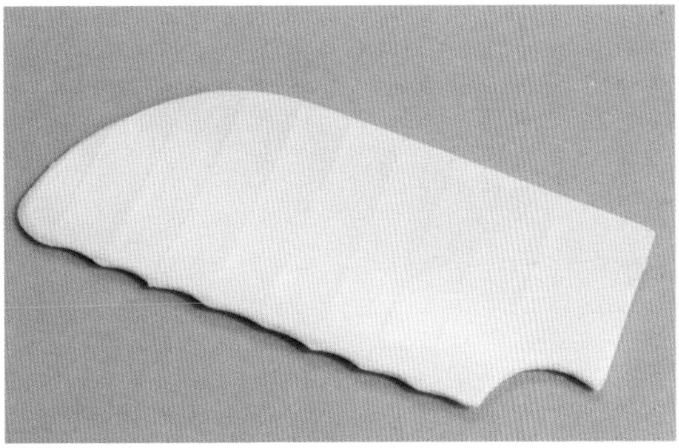

An example of the kind of effect that can be achieved by skinning a wing surface.

Trailing Edges

The trailing edge is the rear edge of a wing, as opposed to the leading edge, which is the front edge. A full-sized, fabric-covered biplane wing will often taper to a very thin edge, which, if scaled down to model size, could be depicted as a sharp edge. Kit wings can often suffer from thick trailing edges, which appear over-scale. This is particularly true of limited-run plastic kits, but the effect can also be seen on some injection-moulded kits.

Fixing an oversized trailing edge is a relatively simple process of reducing the substance of the plastic toward the rear of the wing with a sanding stick. It is preferable to thin a trailing edge from the underside, as any loss of detail will be less noticeable. However, because of its concave shape, the underside may be more difficult to blend, resulting in a noticeable dip toward the trailing edge. In these cases, it would be preferable to reshape the trailing edge from the upper side or from a combination of both surfaces. While you will almost certainly lose some rib detail, this may not look out of place. If loss of detail does become a problem, then it may be preferable to remove all rib-tape detail and then replace it.

Reducing scalloped edges can provide added issues as the substance of the scallop at the centre of its curve may be greater than at the edges. To rectify this issue the centre of the curve will need to be reduced and blended in.

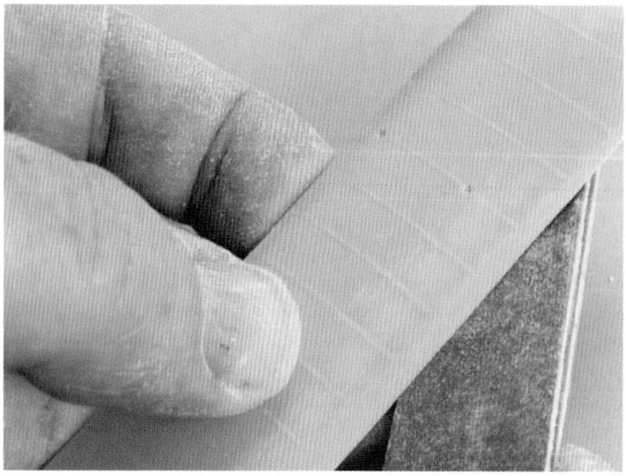

The trailing edge of the Blue Max Halberstadt CL.II is being reduced from the underside of the wing.

Reinforcement Pins

Often the attachment points on the wing root are absent, undersized or poorly defined. A poor attachment fitting may be strong enough for your needs, dependent on a number of variables, including scale and how your model is likely to be treated once it is completed. For example, a small 1/72-scale, limited-run kit, with the tiniest of dimples on the wing root and corresponding shallow recesses on the fuselage, may be good enough if your model is going to sit on a shelf gathering dust. However, if you are likely to be transporting your model between displays, then you will probably want to create a much stronger bond by reinforcing the attachment.

This is simple enough to achieve. Essentially, holes are drilled in the attachment positions on both the wing root and fuselage. A length of suitably sized brass rod is glued into each hole in the wing root and, assuming that the fuselage recess holes align correctly, the wing can then be slotted into the fuselage and cemented firmly into position.

The same procedure can be used to assemble upper wings that are provided in more than one piece or to reinforce the attachment between control and flying surfaces.

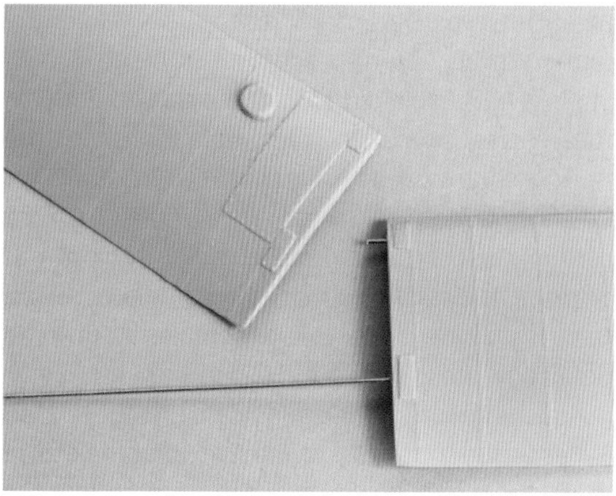

The original flat ring root of the wing, illustrated by the wing on the left, is pinned with brass rod.

Fixtures and Fittings

Often a wing surface will include fixtures and fittings, such as foot plates, inspection panels, aileron hinges or even strut-mounting fittings. Most of these can easily be simulated with plasticard, which I usually cut into strips of the required width, from which multiple fittings of the same size can be cut.

Control Surfaces

If control surfaces, such as the elevator, rudder or ailerons, are moulded to the wings, you may wish to alter their position. Typically, this is done by completely removing the control surface and then reattaching it at the required angle, but, occasionally, the surface can simply be scored and bent to

The moulded aileron of the Halberstadt has been completely removed, so that it can be repositioned.

the required angle. A line of thin cement will help to hold the repositioned control surface in its new position. Reinforcement pins can also be fitted to the separated parts for a stronger bond. Hinges can be cut from plasticard strip.

Determining Strut-Attachment Positions

You cannot always trust strut-attachment positions. Sometimes upper and lower strut positions do not align, which will result in struts that will look as if they are leaning sideways once the wings have been assembled. Occasionally, strut positions are not even visually apparent on the original part.

With the lower wings fitted to the fuselage, check that the upper and lower wing interplane strut attachments align by laying the upper wing beside the assembled airframe and parallel to the lower wings. Assuming that the interplane struts are intended to be angled at 90 degrees, the upper and lower wing strut-attachment positions should align. If the struts are not intended to be angled at 90 degrees, then compare the strut positions on your model to a reliable set of drawings.

Next, measure the distance between the forward strut positions and the leading edge on both wings. Compare this measurement against the side-views of your drawings.

Finally, measure the distance between the front and rear strut-attachment positions on both upper and lower wings. These should align reasonably well with your drawings and if the front and rear struts are parallel to each other, then the corresponding positions on both the upper and lower wings should be identical.

If any of the above measurements are incorrect, fill in the location that you believe is incorrect, drill a new hole at the corrected location and recheck the positions.

This may sound like an extreme process, but it will save a lot of bother later on in the build if there are inherent strut-alignment issues with the original kit.

Struts

Wing-support struts are usually divided into two distinct types. The inner struts, which are usually positioned between the fuselage and the upper-wing centre section, are typically defined

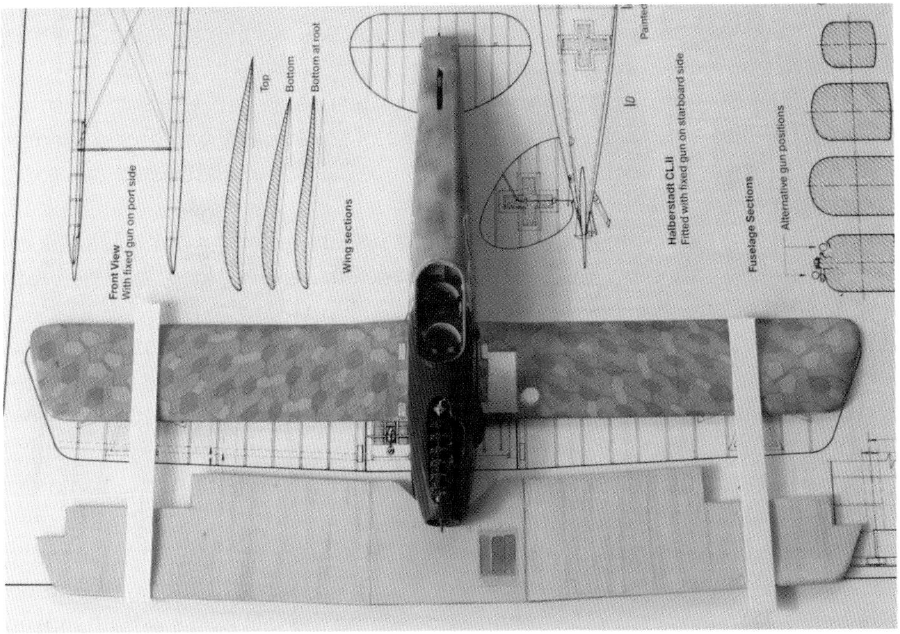

Strips of card have been used as a simple aid to checking that upper and lower strut positions line up with each other.

as cabane struts. Outer struts, which usually sit between the wings, are known as interplane struts. Each space between two sets of struts is known as a bay. For example, a fighter with one pair of interplane struts each side of the fuselage would be classed as a single-bay aircraft.

Perhaps one of the most common and annoying issues with biplane kits is strut length. While the major manufacturers do generally provide struts of the correct length, even the best can get it wrong. The more limited or esoteric the kit, the more the likelihood will be that the strut length will need to be adjusted. If struts are too long, then they can easily be reduced in length; however, if they are too short, then replacement is the only option.

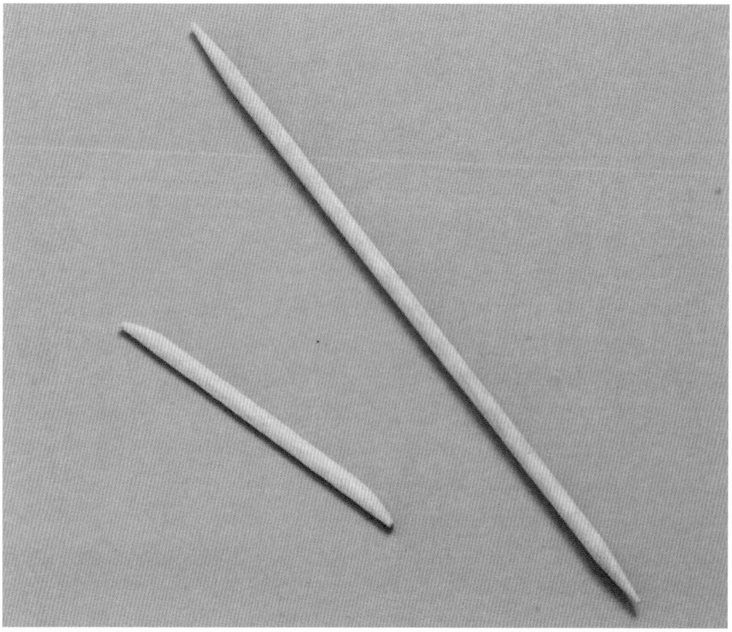

Two opposite sides of a cocktail stick have been shaped so that its cross-section represents that of a strut.

Short struts may not be the only reason why you may want to opt for replacement. If you are building a resin kit and the struts are unreinforced, then it is recommended that they are replaced as they have a tendency to warp, so that your completed model may develop unwanted curves in its struts over time.

The substance of kit struts may also be a problem that you may opt to rectify with replacements. Struts may even break, making it easier to replace than try to repair.

Unfortunately, replacing struts is more of a problem today than it was fifteen or twenty years ago when various sizes of plastic strut stock were easily available from Contrail or brass strut lengths were sold as a product called 'Strutz'.

The good news is that it is not too difficult to manufacture your own replacement struts from strip or rod-shaped materials, such as wood, bamboo or plastic. For smaller scale struts, items such as cocktail sticks can be quite easy to shape into realistic strut stock. For larger scales, strips can be cut to the correct width from ice-cream lolly sticks and then shaped. Wood can be strengthened by applying coats of thin cyanoacrylate to the surface. The glue will soak into the wood grain, which will ultimately result in stronger raw material that can be safely sanded to a thinner substance than non-treated wood.

Plasticard of a suitable substance can also be cut into strips of the desired width and shaped; however, a single length of plastic strip can easily become bent and damaged while shaping and, as such, it is better to begin with a lamination of two or three thin layers glued together with cyanoacrylate.

Another option open to modellers who regularly build biplane models is to keep a stock of spare unused struts from completed models, which can be reshaped and sized, as required.

It is possible to repair broken struts, but in order to do so successfully, it is recommended that reinforcement, such as 0.3mm brass rod or top E guitar string, is used to pin the repair. Drill corresponding holes into the split edges of both broken

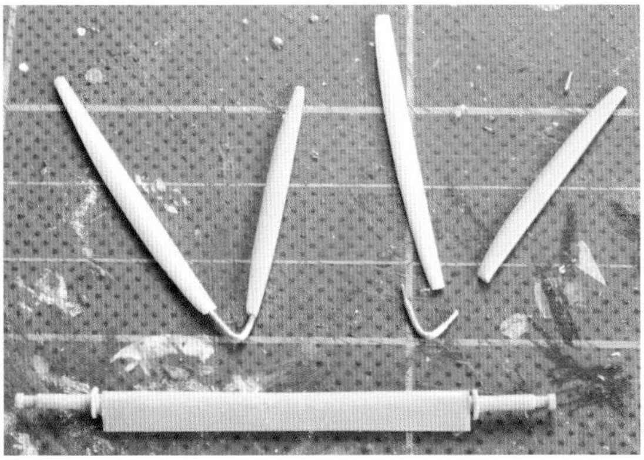

The undercarriage of this 1/32-scale Kondor has been made from reshaped spares.

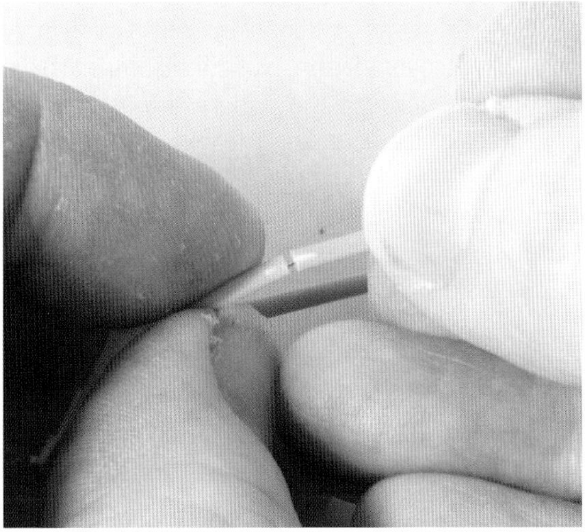

One of the cabane strut parts from the Wingnut Wings' Rumpler was broken on the sprue, requiring a repair.

pieces in which to insert your reinforcement. Once glued back together, the struts will require some sanding to hide the join.

Dihedral and Angle of Incidence

The position of the wing in relation to the fuselage of an aircraft is defined as the dihedral and angle of incidence. The dihedral is the angle of the wing when viewed directly from the front. The angle of incidence is the invisible line between the leading edge and trailing edge in relation to the longitudinal axis of the fuselage.

Unless both lower wings are supplied as one single part, the dihedral will need to be set by the modeller when gluing the lower wings in position. This is usually done by making a visual comparison with scale drawings, although jigs can be constructed for this purpose.

If the upper wings are provided in sections, then the correct dihedral will also need to be set. Some manufacturers have even been known to mould upper wings without dihedral when there should be an angle, in which case each wing would need to be cut from the centre section and repositioned to the correct dihedral.

The lower wing angle of incidence is unlikely to require adjusting in most instances; however, the upper-wing angle of incidence should, typically, be identical to that of the lower wing.

WING ASSEMBLY

There is no right or wrong method of tackling wing assembly. For most projects this will probably depend on personal preference and experience, although the process may vary depending on the type of aircraft, quality and scale of the kit.

Typically, the first step will be to glue the lower wings in position, although this may not always

The Eduard Hannover provides an example of a subject where it can be beneficial to attach the upper wing before the lower wings.

be the case, as it may sometimes be beneficial to attach the upper wing first.

Most kit instructions advocate fitting all struts in place before attaching the upper wing. The main problem with this method is that when you come to fix the upper wing into position there will be a large number of attachments that all need to be positioned and glued at the same time. For this reason, it is often easier initially to attach the upper wing to a small number of struts and then spring-fit the remaining struts in place individually. One of the advantages of assembling the wing in this manner is that if there are any anomalies in strut length, they can be adjusted, as long as the lengths of the initially fitted struts are correct.

In most instances, cabane struts will be fitted first, but, occasionally, it may be beneficial to begin with some or all of the interplane struts.

Jigs

The use of jigs can be useful during the wing-construction stage. A jig is almost anything that will help you to assemble and align wings correctly with a minimum of fuss. Jigs can be made from almost anything from cardboard to Meccano. I have even known modellers who use Lego bricks to aid alignment. There have been a few attempts at commercially made jigs, most notably an adjustable jig produced by Aeroclub. However, this jig was designed for use on smaller scale models, no bigger than 1/48. Pheon Models have included patterns for jigs with some of their decal sets, which are designed to be backed with card and assembled. The important thing to remember with any style of jig is that it will need to provide easy access to any work that needs to be carried out while the jig is in use, otherwise the jig will be more of a hindrance than a help.

Determining Strut Length and Spring-Fitting

Kit manufacturers can sometimes provide incorrectly sized struts within their kits, which may only be discovered once your initial struts have been positioned and the upper-wing assembly is dry-fitted. In these cases, it is important to have a good set of scale drawings to hand, as the first step will be to try to estimate how much larger or smaller the struts need to be by comparing the model to the drawings.

Once the original struts have been removed, clean up and re-drill the attachment positions on the airframe. Begin by adjusting one set of struts, which will usually be the forward cabane struts.

Packing foam has been used to hold the upper wing in the correct position on this 1/72-scale Albatros C.IX.

The cabane struts for this Albatros have been correctly sized and positioned with the aid of scale drawings.

Either modify your existing struts or use these struts as a pattern for making replacements to a slightly longer length than you have estimated.

Using a small amount of cyanoacrylate, tack the forward struts into position on to the model's airframe, ensuring that angles from all directions are correct to your drawings. Once the glue is dry, carefully position the upper wing on to the struts and compare the distance between the upper wings and fuselage decking and/or lower wings to your drawings. If the upper wing looks too high, remove the struts and make a slight adjustment, repeating the process until you are satisfied. Repeat the process for the rear struts, also checking that the angle of incidence of the upper wing matches the lower wing and that both wings align when viewed from above.

Sometimes, rather than removing the oversized struts, small adjustments can be made by adjusting the depth of the strut-attachment recesses in the top wing; however, this method is only suitable for very minor alterations.

Once the initial set of struts is correct, then the remaining struts are fairly easy to resize. This is done by gluing the upper wing permanently in position on to your initial group of struts. A simple jig may need to be constructed to help support the upper wing while in this state, but the wings must align correctly when viewed from all angles.

Carefully dry-fit one of the remaining struts in-between the upper and lower wings. Assuming that the strut is not so overly long that it will not fit between the two points without forcing the upper and lower wings apart, observe the alignment of the two wings when viewed from the front. If the alignment looks incorrect, remove the strut and make a very slight adjustment to the length and retry. By a process of trial and error you should arrive at the correct length, assuming that the length is not over-adjusted to a point where it is too short, in which case a replacement strut will need to be manufactured.

Once the correct length of the strut has been determined, test fit the same strut into the same position on the opposite wing. If the strut fits into this position without throwing the wing out of alignment, which should be the case, use it as a template to cut and shape a second strut. Test fit

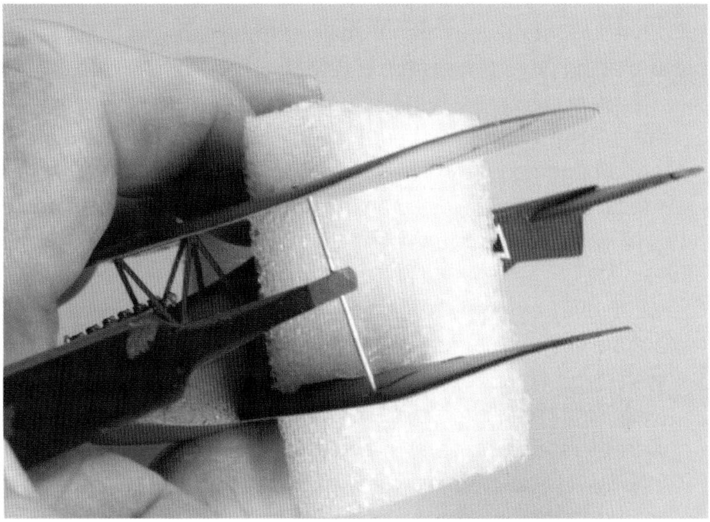

Each interplane is repeatedly dry-fitted and adjusted until the strut fits perfectly.

the second strut and if this is judged to be correct, then glue both struts permanently in position. Repeat the process for the remaining struts.

RIGGING

'Rigging' is a naval term describing a series of ropes or steel cables used to strengthen the structure of an area of a ship that is subject to stress, such as a mast. Rigging has also become a term that encompasses all wires on aircraft, whether they are performing a structural function or not.

The main types of wires on aircraft are:

1. **Landing wires** are wires that are intended to resist forces as an aircraft drops height. On single-bay aircraft, landing wires would usually run from the uppermost tip of the central cabane strut to the base of the outer interplane strut.
2. **Flying wires** are wires that are intended to resist the forces of lift as an aircraft gains height. On single-bay aircraft, these would normally run from the base of the fuselage to the uppermost tip of the outer interplane strut.
3. **Incidence wires** are bracing wires that run between corresponding forward and rear struts.

All other structural wires are normally termed simply as bracing wires (for example, undercarriage or internal bracing). Wires used to steer or control the aircraft are normally described as control wires.

German rigging wires were typically made from high-tensile steel. The Germans used two main types of wires during the World War I period:

1. Hard wires or single-strand round wires were almost like piano wires. These types of wires were typically used for internal bracing.
2. Multi-strand cables consisted of many wires that were themselves made up of a number of strands. Information on German wires of the period is limited, although some period drawings and technical assessments do provide limited information on sizes, which appear to have ranged from around 3.5 to 6mm. The British typically produced multi-strand cables in 7 × 14 or 7 × 19 formats, meaning that each length of cable contained seven wires made up of either 14 or 19 strands; the Germans would have almost certainly used a similar format. Multi-strand wires were typically used as external wires.

This model of the FF.33e includes examples of landing, flying and incidence wires, as well as float bracing wires.

Choosing Rigging Material

There are many different materials that are suitable for use as rigging; however, all of these products have pros and cons associated with using them. The selection of rigging material may be governed by personal preference. Alternatively, scale accuracy may be important, which is likely to limit choice.

Wingnut Wings are one of the only modelling companies that suggest rigging diameters within their instructions. Typically, a specification for the use of a 0.15mm thread would be intended to represent rigging with a diameter of 5mm.

Another important factor in choosing rigging material is whether you require the rigging to be functional.

A selection of rigging materials used by modellers.

Functional and Non-Functional Rigging Materials

A functional rigging material is a material that provides support and is an integral part of the structure of the model. Functional rigging is recommended if you tend to move your model around regularly, such as travelling to and from shows. It is also recommended on aircraft or models where the structure without rigging support is likely to be 'wobbly'. Functional materials can also sometimes be useful to correct slight misalignment of the wings. Good examples of functional materials are monofilament thread (for example, mending thread, fishing line) or wire.

A non-functional rigging material is simply a visual representation and provides no support to the structure of the model. Good examples of non-functional materials include elastic (such as EZ line) and stretched sprue.

Monofilament Thread

Monofilament thread is available in many guises, the most common of which are fishing wire and mending thread. The model requires a lot of preparation before using monofilament thread, which will certainly include drilling location holes. If scale accuracy is important, then fishing line is probably the best material as you can buy this product in multiple gauges. If scale accuracy is not so important, then I would recommend mending thread, which tends to look equally at home when used on a variety of scales from 1/72 up to 1/32. Try to buy a product that is smoke-coloured, as this will negate the need to colour your rigging material.

Monofilaments are very strong and durable but can respond slightly to changes in temperature, so it is important to get the tension right during the rigging process. Tension monofilaments too loosely and you may find that you have sagging lines on a cold day, while if tensioned too tightly, you may end up with curved struts.

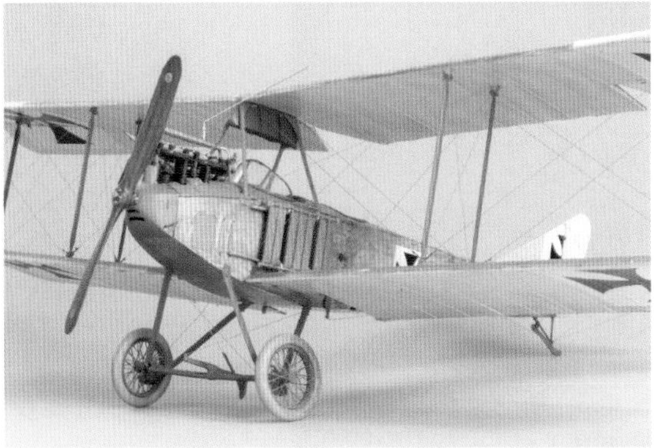

Large aircraft with a delicate structure, such as this Wingnut Wings' Albatros B.II, benefit from functional rigging.

Smoke-coloured mending thread has been used to rig this 1/72-scale LVG C.II.

Wire

Wire can be very problematic to use as a rigging material but can be used successfully. One of the biggest problems associated with using wire is that it is easy to produce kinks in the strand during application or handling. Another potential issue is temperature. I have seen examples where wire has responded badly to varying temperatures. I personally have not used this material but I have seen successful use of wire. Success or failure may be determined by choice of product, as I suspect that you can purchase wires of varying quality, some of which may be more suitable as a rigging material than others.

Elastic

Elastic has become very popular as a rigging material in recent years. It is a non-functional material and, as such, provides little or no support to the structure of the model. Most materials on the market have a flat edge, which can look out of place when simulating German multi-strand cables or single wires. These threads are made up of many small strands of elastic that, with practice, can be split into smaller sizes; the main problem with this being that it is very difficult to control the size of the strand that you split.

Unlike monofilaments and wires, elastic threads do not, necessarily, need to be threaded through holes, although some kind of locating preparation is recommended. Elastic threads are also easy to repair, as you can usually get an almost immediate grab when using cyanoacrylate. Not all elastic threads are made from the same raw materials and some threads have been known to perish over time. Another downside is that elastic is extremely difficult to thread through holes due to its non-rigid structure. It is, therefore, not necessarily a quick and easy material to use. It is also very likely that you will need to colour the thread as, typically, the colour of these products is white. Ushi van der Rosten produces a black elastic thread in various gauges, but in my opinion black rigging visually stands out too much.

Cementing elastic thread takes practice, as its ability to virtually instantly stick can be both a pro and a con. Always apply cement to that part of the model to which you are gluing the elastic, never to the thread. If you have located the thread into a hole, be very careful not to touch the thread with the applicator, otherwise it will probably stick to the applicator. If your first attempt does not work,

An example of why wire can be problematic as a rigging material.

Elastic thread is ideal for simulating control lines because of its ability to instantly stick to a surface.

cut the end off the thread and try again – don't attempt to reuse the edge that is already contaminated with glue.

Stretched Sprue

This is perhaps the most traditional method of rigging plastic models. Scrap plastic sprue is heated and stretched over a flame until a thin thread of plastic is created. Typically, a length of stretched sprue is glued in place between the two attachment points with cyanoacrylate. Do not use poly cements as the solvent will eat into the sprue. A tiny amount of heat, such as from an extinguished match, can be held close to the attached rigging to tighten loose or sagging threads. Longevity can also be a problem as, over time, the stretched sprue can split. The risk of breakdown is greater the thinner the sprue has been stretched or the poorer the quality of the plastic. Try to create all of the sprue strands from the same source, as this will make it easier to produce reasonably consistent batches of thread.

Given all of the alternatives out there, it is very rare that you will see a model rigged using this method any more, but the process may still be useful for certain aspects of rigging, such as control wires.

Turnbuckles and Rigging Attachments

Turnbuckles are devices that are used to tension rigging. Turnbuckles fit to one end of a bracing wire, which would normally be in the position that is easiest to maintain, so in most cases turnbuckles will appear as lower-wing fittings. The opposite end of the bracing wire is usually attached via a loop attachment.

The decision to simulate turnbuckles is a matter of personal preference, which, for me, is often dictated by scale and intended rigging method. Smaller scales are less likely to benefit from any kind of turnbuckle simulation.

Perhaps the best commercially available turnbuckles are the Gaspatch 3D-printed products, which are available in both 1/32- and 1/48-scales, although many modellers use Gaspatch's 1/48-scale turnbuckles on 1/32 projects. When using Gaspatch turnbuckles and loop attachments, it is important that the location hole is drilled to the approximate angle of the bracing wire, as overstressing the 3D-printed product by trying to bend it will cause it to break.

Many manufactures have tried producing photo-etch turnbuckles to varying degrees of success. My favourite product to date is made by RB Productions. These are folded in on themselves

Turnbuckles fitted to the replica Albatros D.Va on display at the RAF Museum in Hendon.

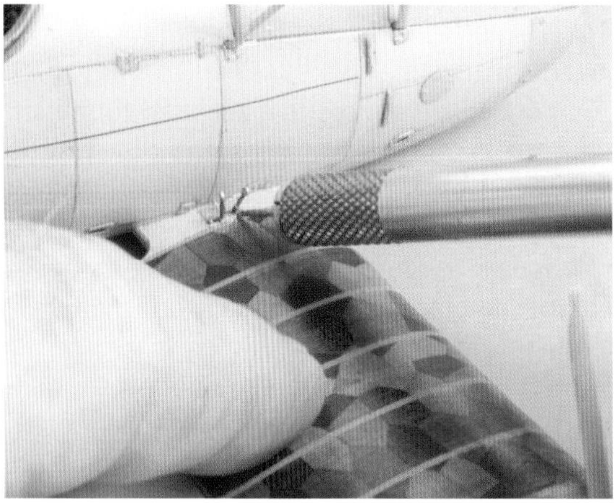

3D-printed turnbuckles should be fitted at the approximate angle that the bracing wire follows.

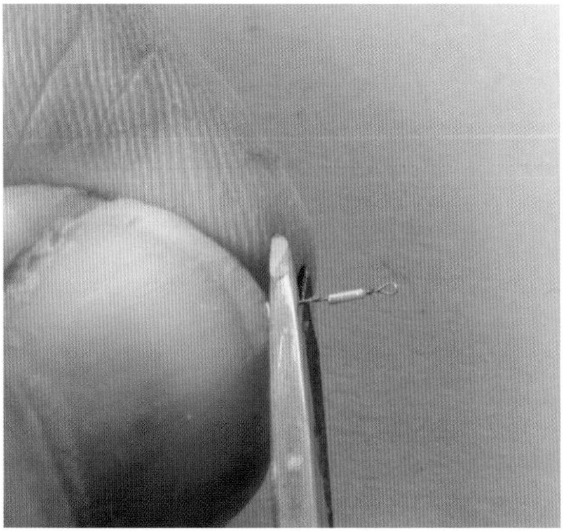

Excess wire is trimmed from the end of the turnbuckle leaving enough to act as an attachment.

to produce a three-dimensional shape, which is reasonably to scale. Most other photo-etch turnbuckles are flat simulations, sometimes with holes that are too small to thread rigging material through.

Another option is to manufacture your own turnbuckles from wire and tubing. A length of wire is twisted around a small drill bit of around 0.3 or 0.4mm, so that you end up with a length of twisted wire with a loop at one end. If you are making a turnbuckle with a single loop, simply thread the twisted wire through a small piece of tubing that has been cut to size, glue in place and trim the exposed twisted end of the wire, so that there is enough length remaining to anchor into a drilled hole on the airframe.

To manufacture turnbuckles with a loop at each end, make two loops and cut the twisted end of each loop to about half the length of the aluminium tube. Then insert and cement the loops into each end of the tubing.

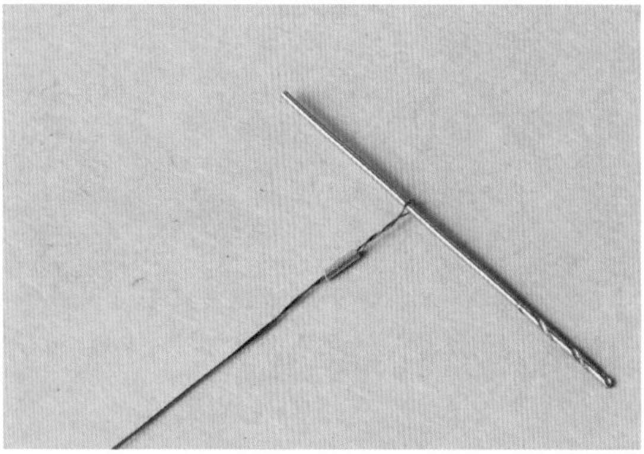

Wire twisted around a small drill bit is threaded through a length of tubing to simulate a single loop-style turnbuckle.

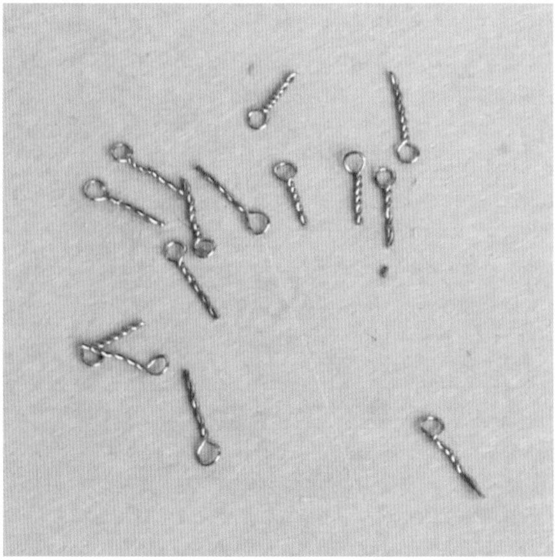

I usually create a reasonably sized batch of rigging loop attachments for a project, including a number of spares.

Rigging loop attachments for the upper wing are made simply by twisting wire around a drill bit and cutting the loose end short to create a pin.

The downside of making your own turnbuckles and attachments is that they will often look oversized. The smaller the tubing that you use, the closer to scale the turnbuckle will look, but the trade-off comes when the tubing is too small to insert the loops into.

Rigging Methods

If you strip everything back to basics, there are two methods of producing viable rigging. In the first method, an attachment point is produced, the rigging is threaded through the attachment point and secured. In the second method, the rigging is glued directly between one position and another. Most modellers will opt for the first option, although they may use the second option in some areas.

The first method is suitable for most flexible rigging materials, including elastics, while the second method, in its purest form, is more suitable for elastic or stretch sprue materials.

Method One

The first question you need to ask yourself is whether or not you want to use separate rigging attachments, such as eyelet loops or turnbuckles. If the answer is 'no', then you are going to need to drill completely through the parts that you are going to fit your rigging to on at least one end of the rigging. This is so that you are able to tension your rigging, which you can only do to a satisfactory level by pulling through the object that you are fixing to. For example, let's suggest that you need to fit a flying wire between the fuselage and the upper wing. In this case, you will drill a hole completely through in both locations, glue one end of the rigging material into the hole in the fuselage, thread the other end through the upper wing, pull tight and cement.

This method may sound like hard work, but actually it is one of the easiest and simplest ways to successfully rig a model. The downside is that

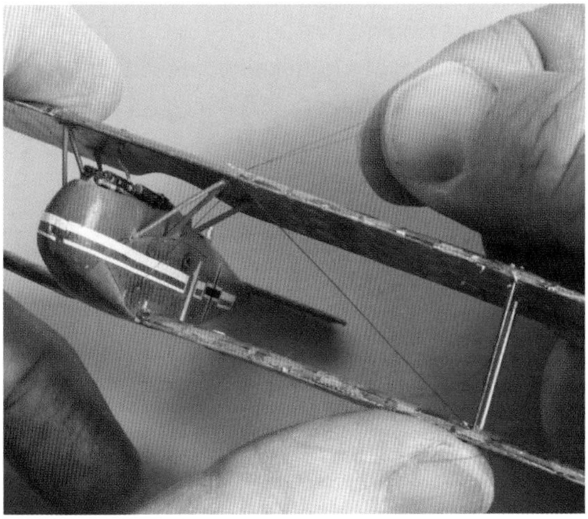

In this example featuring a 1/72-scale Halberstadt CL.IV, two rigging lines, one attached to the fuselage and one to the lower wing, are being tensioned through a hole in the upper wing.

you have to clean up and re-paint the upper side of the wing. The first rigging point in the fuselage does not need to be drilled all of the way through, as this rigging point only needs to be located, but if working in smaller scales, it may be safer and easier to drill completely through, thereby giving you a decent substance to cement your rigging into.

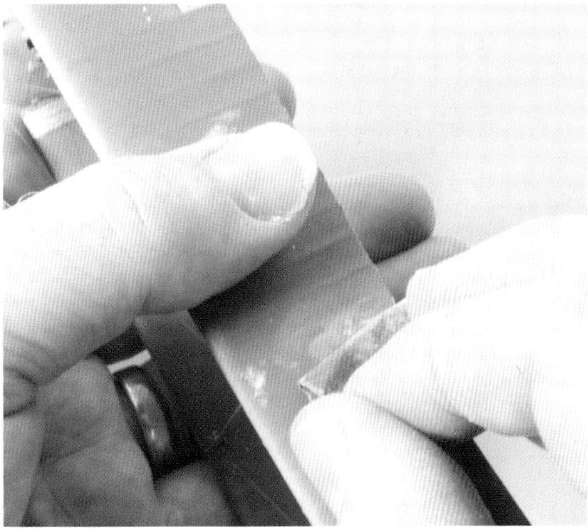

Rigging positions through the upper wing are cleaned up with abrasive paper prior to touching up the affected areas with paint.

I advocate rigging through the wing rather than struts. This more accurately simulates the way that rigging is attached on original aircraft. In addition, I have seen examples where elastic has pulled struts out of their sockets.

If you intend to use a separate rigging attachment, then all holes are partially drilled into each location that you are going to rig. The attachments are then cemented into these holes, usually before the upper wing is attached. The rigging material is attached and locked through the first attachment loop and allowed to dry. The loose end is then threaded through the second loop at the opposite end of the rigging arrangement and locked off. There are various methods of locking the thread to the attachment. I initially tack the rigging material in place with cement and then create a small knot. This is also locked off with cement before trimming the excess thread away. It is not ideal, as the cement can often accentuate the attachment, but the knot not only serves the purpose of creating a stronger attachment, but also prevents the rigging material from looking like it is sitting one-sided in the attachment loop.

Method Two

This method is more applicable to the use of non-functional materials, such as elastics and stretched sprue, but can also be applied to functional materials in areas such as booms and control horns. Glue one end of your rigging material into the start position of your rigging arrangement. Gently pull the loose end of the rigging material to the opposite rigging position and cement. You may need to use a pair of tweezers or pointed implement to hold the second attachment in place while the glue dries. Once fixed firmly in position, carefully trim away any excess.

You can also use one piece of thread to rig multiple sections using this method. A good example would be if rigging a tail boom on an Otto pusher. With careful planning you can literally rig the entire boom with two pieces of rigging material just by continuously cementing your thread from one rigging position to the next.

In some cases, you may opt to use a combination of methods 1 and 2. A good example may be when fitting control wires; you might cement one end of your material into a location hole and the other end directly to the tip of a control horn.

Once tacked in place, the thread end is knotted around the turnbuckle loop.

In this example, float bracing wires were glued directly to the float after initially being located into a hole drilled into the fuselage.

Colour

The colour of rigging often becomes a personal preference rather than a subject of accuracy, which seems a little strange given how much time we spend elsewhere to make an accurate model. The rigging materials that we use are usually naturally white, black, translucent, metallic or smoke-coloured, depending on what we use. The best advice I can provide is to consult references, although if in doubt, a dull matt steel colour is generally a good bet for most German aircraft.

If you have to colour your rigging material, then there are various ways to do so, but the most popular are with the use of permanent markers or a thin wash of paint. You would tend to colour rigging using markers before attachment, while painting is often better to do post-attachment. However, care should be taken to avoid flicking paint all over your model and, as such, it is better to use diluted paints, allowing them to flow along the rigging material.

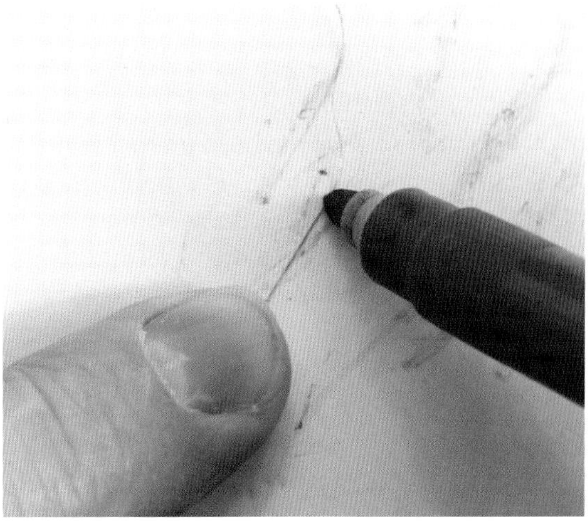

A permanent grey marker is being used to colour this white elastic thread.

Fine rigging on this scratch-built 1/144th scale P-class Zeppelin is made from elastic using method 2. The ends of the elastic are so flexible that they are almost impossible to thread into holes, so they are simply glued to the surface of the Zeppelin's envelope.

Chapter Six

Building a Rumpler Two-Seater

INTRODUCTION

In this chapter I am going to build a larger two-bay subject that employs a slightly different method of wing attachment than used in the previous builds in this book. In addition, the build will include the use of homemade turnbuckles and will also focus on producing a three-colour camouflage scheme with blended demarcation lines.

I have chosen the Rumpler C.IV as the subject of this build, which I have always considered to be the prettiest of the larger German two-seaters, especially in its later configuration with a rounded nose.

Historical Background

The C.IV was the most successful of the Rumpler family of two-seaters, which began with the design of the C.I. Much of the success of the C.IV was down to the ability of the aircraft to fly faster and higher than the enemy. It is thought that over a thousand C.IVs were produced between early 1917 and the end of the war.

The Kit

For this build I have chosen another Wingnut Wings' kit, mainly because alternatives at the time of writing were limited to either resin products or very small scales. The Wingnut Wings' kit was

The completed Wingnut Wings' Rumpler C.IV.

originally released in 2011 and contains eleven sprues of various sizes. It is an example of one of Wingnut Wings' finest designs. As with all kits from this company, the boxing provides five decal options, mostly sporting three-colour camouflage schemes. The decals themselves are from a period in the company's history when their quality was at its best. For whatever reason, many modellers, including myself, have found decals in later Wingnut Wings' kits and reissues to be more fragile and problematic to use.

I decided that I would build one of the examples with a three-colour camouflage scheme. While flicking through the collection of reference photographs on the Wingnut Wings' website, I came across a picture of C.8037/17 with its ornate scarab motif painted on the side of the fuselage. This subject is included as one of the schemes in the kit, but I had initially disregarded it because I had been unable to find photographic references.

References

There is a surprising amount of good reference material available on the Rumpler C.IV. Perhaps the most useful of these are a pair of *Windsock Datafiles* detailing the aircraft. In addition, the Air Ministry produced a technical report on the captured Rumpler C.IV 8500/16, which has surfaced in a variety of publications over the years. The report includes a detailed technical description of the aircraft and a large number of detailed drawings, which make useful modelling aids. Aeronaut has also published a reference book on *Rumpler Aircraft of World War I* with almost forty pages of C.IV coverage.

Finally, a surviving restored Rumpler C-type is displayed in the Deutsches Technical Museum in Munich. A search of the internet will result in many useful walk-around photographs of this aircraft.

CONSTRUCTION

Interior

The interior of this kit is almost entirely built as a separate entity, which, once assembled, fits inside the two fuselage halves. Injection marks are present in areas that will not be visible, such as the underside of the flooring.

Most of the interior wood is presumed to have been stained in a dark-brown colour. I chose Tamiya Wooden Deck Tan as my base colour. To simulate the wood grain, the base colour was coated with a diluted Tamiya Nato Brown wash. Once the wash was completely dry, I used an old brush with hard, splayed bristles to dry-brush the surface with a lighter shade. The brush strokes of the wash and dry-brushing were both performed in the direction of the grain that I was trying to simulate.

On many parts I then used a brown wash to highlight the edges of any panels and details before finally brush-painting details such as panels, fittings and wiring.

The interior was gradually built up from the flooring. The parts were so well detailed and researched that I found very little opportunity for

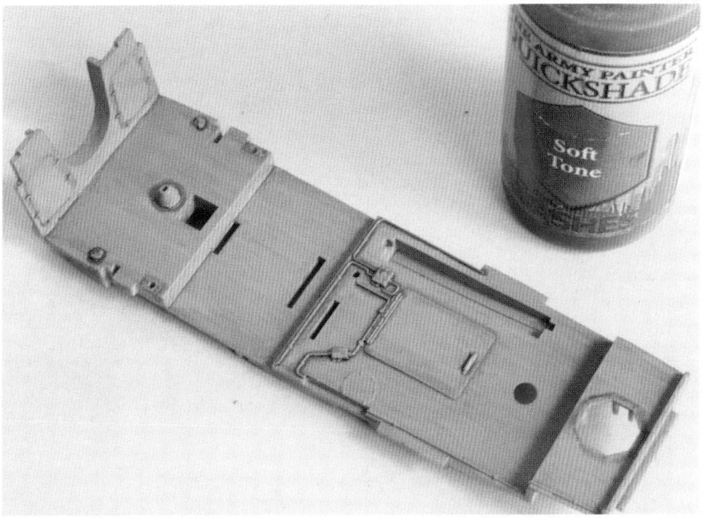

The cockpit floor has been given a dark wood treatment after which a brown wash is used to highlight details.

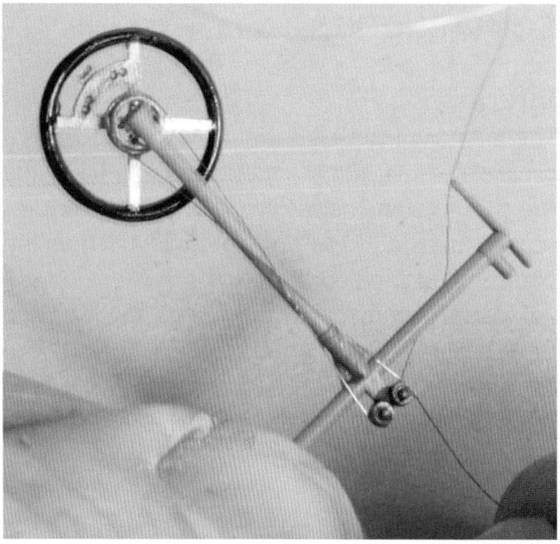

Control wires are fitted to the control-column assembly.

genuine improvement. As with the Albatros build, fuel-selector switches were made from brass rod, which were then fitted into holes drilled in the centre of each fuel-selector position on the instrument panel. Monofilament control lines were attached to the steering column before the assembly was fitted into the interior.

Once assembled and painted, the fuel tank, seating, control column, internal bomb rack and observer instruments were all fitted directly to the cockpit flooring part. The kit's photo-etch seatbelts were shaped and glued in position, once the seat and its surroundings had been fitted. Control wire made from monofilament was extended from the rear of the rudder bar to pulleys moulded on to each side of the fuselage flooring, leaving two loose lines.

Following the order suggested by the instructions, I began working on the framework. These parts were pre-painted before gluing to the main interior assembly. The only slight modifications I made were to wrap copper wire around the wireless aerial winder and to drill holes ready to accept the control wires. Most of the control-wire positions on the framework needed to be drilled, although some locations, especially on the starboard side, have useful nicks moulded into the plastic that can be used without any modification.

Once both framework parts were in position, I began the arduous task of fitting control lines along the length of each frame, beginning with the loose lines that had been fitted between the rudder bar and pulleys earlier in the build. Further lines were glued to the control horns on each side of the control-column bar. The loose ends of each of these lines were then subjected to the same process as the rudder-control wires, until there were three control lines running along the entire length of each frame.

One of the final acts in the construction of the interior was to add the observer's seat. This is

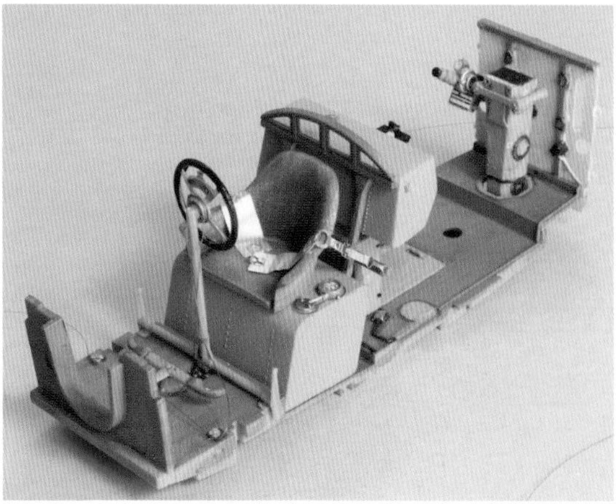

Initial assembly of the pilot's cockpit and observer's station.

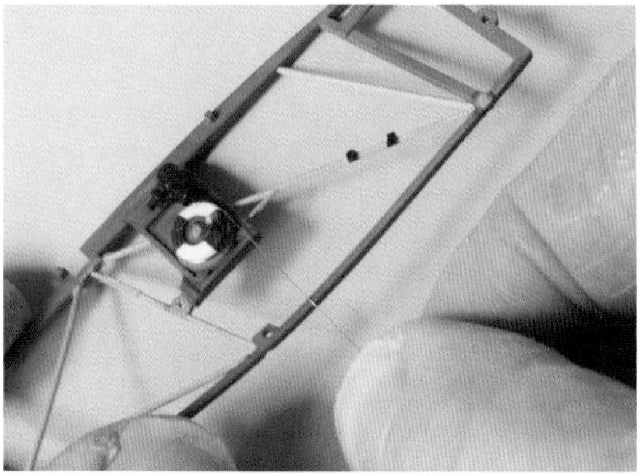

Copper wire is wrapped around the wireless aerial winder.

Control wires made from monofilament are fitted along each side of the interior framework.

The completed cockpit assembly.

a photo-etch part on which a plastic cushion is added, which is designed to simulate a seat that hangs from the framework a little like a hammock. The two pieces were glued together while the photo-etch part was still attached to the fret. Most of the paintwork was also carried out at this stage.

Engine

The Damlier-Mercedes' D.VIa engine included within the kit is similar in style to the Mercedes' engine assembled in the Albatros build and was built in a similar manner. Like the Albatros engine, I wound copper wire around each rocker spring and added spark plugs and wiring.

Many photographs of this engine in service appear to show strips of canvas wrapped around the intake manifold to help to insulate it. To simulate this, I wrapped strips of Aviattic clear, doped linen decal sheet around the part. Once completed, a brown wash was applied to highlight the wrapping effect and simulate staining.

I also used brass rod to simulate pipework present at the front of the engine. The shape of each rod was pre-formed before gluing the parts in position. The completed engine was then permanently fitted on to the engine-bearers.

To complete the forward interior position, an oil-tank generator and Spandau machine-gun were assembled and painted before fitting to the engine-bearer. I used the photo-etch cooling jacket for the Spandau, which needed to be annealed before shaping. Wingnut Wings helpfully supplies

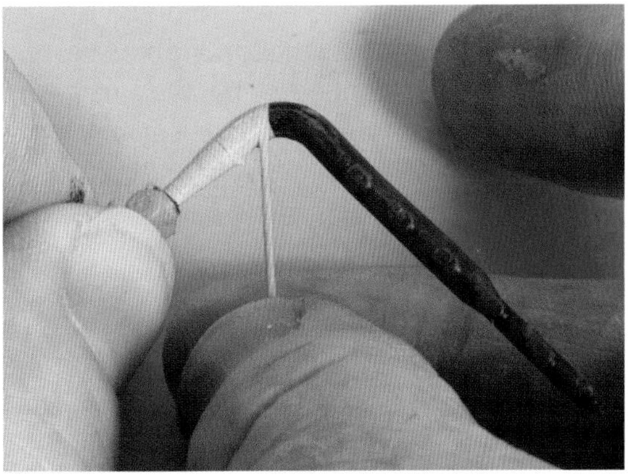

Manifold insulation is simulated by wrapping strips of Aviattic linen decal around the part.

The completed engine is fitted on to the engine-bearer section of the cockpit and interior assembly.

a small rod-shaped tool around which to shape the cooling jacket.

Fuselage Assembly

Before fitting the two fuselage halves around the internal assembly, the fuselage sidewalls required preparation on both the outside and inside surfaces. The kit developer has designed the fuselage halves to cover different variances depicting unreinforced and reinforced tail areas, which is differentiated by the stitching positioning toward the rear of the fuselage. Using the instruction manual as a guide, some of the stitching detail needed to be removed, which was done by sanding the unwanted detail away.

On the inside, the sidewall required painting. The main section around the pilot and observer stations is canvas, while areas fore and aft are wood. The instruction for the cowling area is a little unusual in that it is suggested that the area below the engine is painted in a grey-green primer, while the area above the engine-bearer is wood. As all of this area is one large metal panel, I can only assume that the wooden area above the engine-bearers is intended to simulate wooden blocks on which the metal panel is supported.

The inside of the fuselage was painted in stages, beginning with the fabric, which was sprayed pale-linen in colour and weathered with a brown wash lightly sprayed along the stitching lines. The stitching lines were then further accentuated by a brown pin-wash before lightly over-spraying the weathered areas with the original base colour.

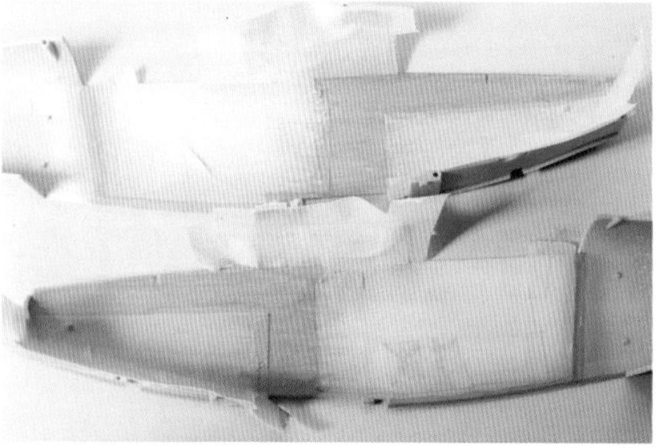

The fuselage interior colour was built up via a number of stages of masking and painting.

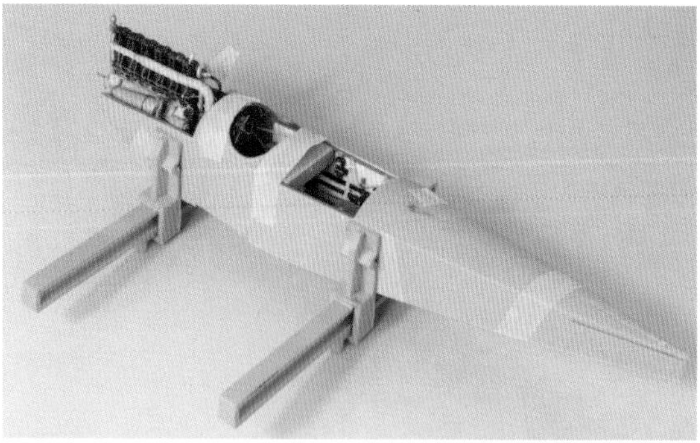

The two fuselage halves were glued around the interior assembly.

The fabric area was then masked and a grey-green primer colour was applied to the cowling area. Finally, wood areas were painted using the same brushing technique as I used earlier on the interior components.

The interior assembly was then glued into the starboard fuselage half, and both fuselage halves were glued together.

Painting

At this stage, all of the flying surfaces were removed from their sprues, cleaned up and, where necessary, assembled so that they could be painted at the same time as the fuselage.

Once all of the parts and assemblies were masked and primed, I began working on the underside, which was initially sprayed in a pale-blue colour. On a large-scale model, large, single bodies of colour, especially in areas that are intended to simulate fabric, can look a bit flat and so a little artistic licence can be used to add life to these areas. Wing surfaces, in particular, can benefit from some variation in the use of colour.

While it is sometimes assumed that the fabric on the underside of wings will have a translucent appearance, showing the wing structure through the material, this is only true if the entire wing is unfinished and in a natural doped state. A dark finish on the upper and/or lower surface of the wing will be enough to stop light penetrating through the fabric. Often the opposite effect can occur where the rib tape can have the appearance of being very slightly paler than the fabric surface because of the double thickness of material.

General wear and tear will also affect the appearance of the fabric coating. All aircraft were maintained in as clean a state as possible; however, there will inevitably be some residual soiling.

When trying to break up the flat colour of the wing, I tried to use this knowledge to my advantage. In the case of the Rumpler, I began by covering the rib-tape positions with strips of masking tape. This is a laborious job, but well worth the effort. I then sprayed very light patches and strips of brown wash, chord-wise. You can, of course, use more than one colour, but you don't want the patched areas to look too prominent.

I then removed the rib-tape masks. At this stage, the darker patches appear too stark in contrast to the masked rib-tape areas, so I then over-sprayed the entire wing area with a light coat of the original base colour, until I had a level of colour contrast that suited my taste.

Wingnut Wings has interpreted C.8037/17 as having a sprayed, three-colour, upper surface camouflage scheme. These colours are defined as dark-green, pale-green and mauve, which are applied in large patches. This scheme is fairly straightforward, with the exception of the fuselage, where the rear decking surface has a different pattern to the sides.

On schemes with a combination of colours, I find it helpful to do some basic testing before committing to colour selection. Mauve is the hardest colour to simulate and is often the lynch-pin to getting a colour scheme containing this colour looking right. Mauve is a difficult colour to mix, especially if a red is used as part of the mix. Some red paints contain yellow, which, when mixed with blue, results in a brownish burgundy colour, rather than a purple or mauve. Luckily, AK Interactive produces a reasonable World War I German mauve within their range of paints, which appears to be suitable for the Rumpler. For the pale-green, I settled on Wingnut Wings' recommendation of Tamiya Cockpit Green, although in hindsight I think that a slightly paler colour would have been more suitable, especially as I was spraying on to a grey base colour. For the dark-green, I chose a Tamiya Dark Green. This was not as dark as the colour that Wingnut Wings recommend, but I wanted a greener shade that was closer to Ronny Bar's artwork used in the instructions to illustrate the colour options.

After masking the under surfaces of the fuselage, I began the process of building up the upper surface camouflage scheme by spraying pale-green. The sides of the fuselage do not use this

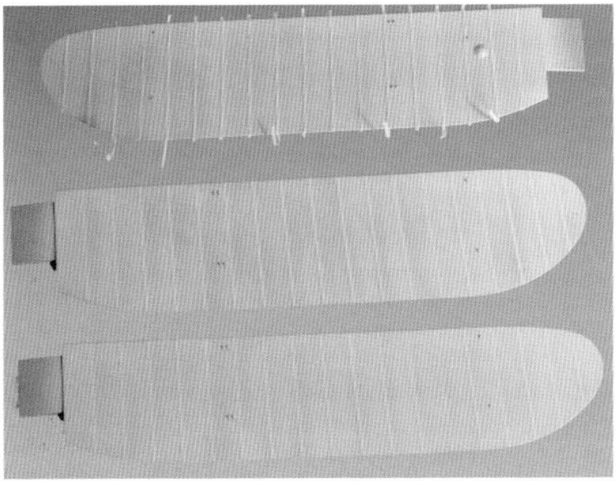

Three stages of adding weathering to the underside of the wing, illustrated from top to bottom, consisting of masking, spraying a brown wash and then over-spraying with a light coat of the base colour.

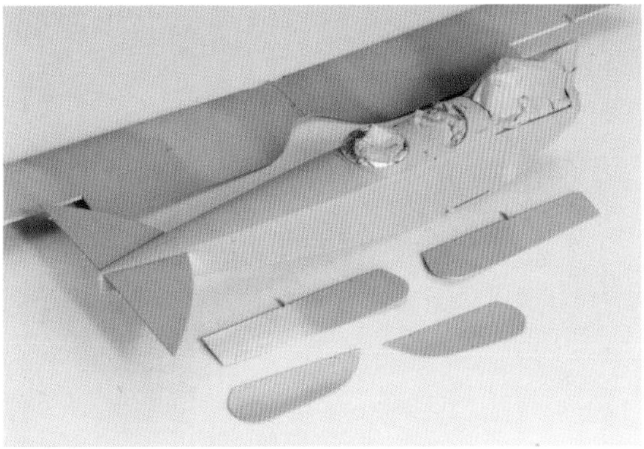

The first upper camouflage colour to be applied was the pale-green.

colour and so no additional masking was required at this stage. On the upper wing, the colour was sprayed freehand, as patches approximate to positions detailed in the kit's colour guide. However, on the upper surface of the fuselage, this colour was sprayed across the whole surface.

The rear decking of the fuselage was then masked so that I could spray the fuselage sides with the dark-green. The masking was stopped short toward the front edge of the decking, as at this point the dark-green pattern on the decking merges with the sidewall pattern.

Next, I applied the mauve. The patches were sprayed freehand. To do this you need to be able to trust your airbrush equipment and paints, and so I always strip and soak my airbrush in cleaner prior to fine, freehand work. I also test the paints out before committing to the actual job.

To produce a camouflage block without masking, I turn the air pressure down on the compressor. I then draw the outline of the patch by holding the tip of my air brush close the model surface and applying minimum pressure to the airbrush trigger. Once I have the basic outline, I begin to work away from the edges, gradually pulling the airbrush tip further away from the surface of the model and applying more pressure to the trigger at the same time, so that a greater area of model surface is covered without affecting the original soft edge of the patch. In this way, a reasonable block of colour with a slight mottled edge can be produced without the aid of masking. The procedure takes practice, but produces excellent results.

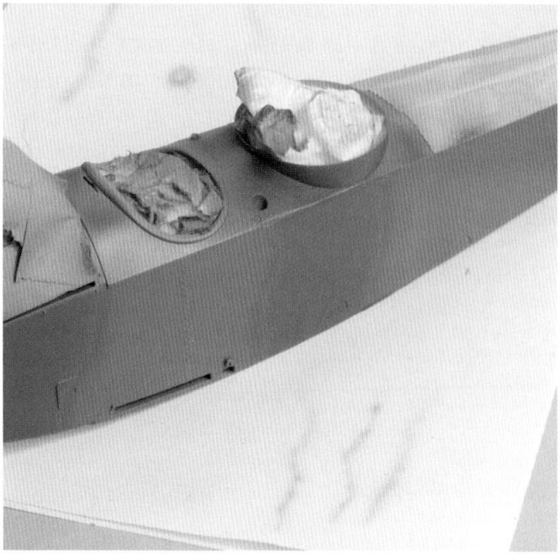

Mauve patches were applied freehand using an airbrush. Note the sprayed lines on the paper used as a test.

Thin washes are lightly sprayed in random strips to the upper camouflaged surface.

Next, the masking was removed from the rear upper decking and the fuselage sides were masked along the edge of the decking. Dark-green was then applied using the freehand method that was used with the mauve patches.

Once all the masking was removed, small details such as the cockpit collar were hand-painted. On the lower wings, the edges around the footplates were masked and the footplates sprayed aluminium.

Finally, I added a little weathering and depth to the camouflaged surface of the wings by masking-off the rib tapes and lightly spraying soil and shading washes in random strips chord-wise.

Wing Assembly and Rigging

Assembling the wings on larger biplanes with two or more bays can be more complex than on a single-bay aircraft. On the Rumpler, the first step was to glue the cabane struts into position. These are provided in the form of two V-shaped parts that are designed to butt up against each other along the top edge, which in turn is designed to

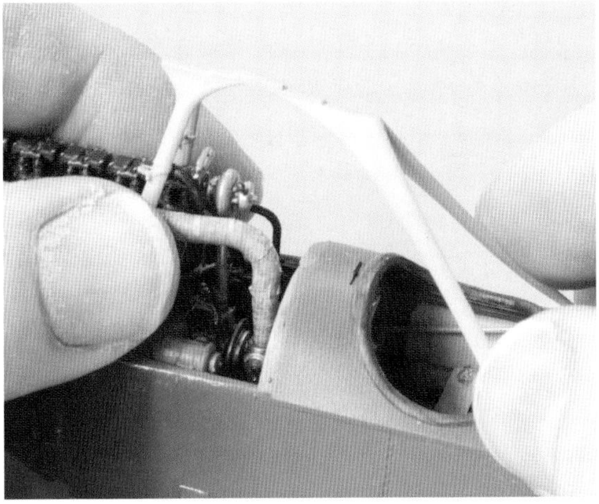

The two V-shaped cabane strut sections are fitted at the same time, so that they can be aligned correctly.

slot into the upper wing. It is, therefore, important that both struts are fitted at the same time, allowing their position to be adjusted while the cement is still wet. I used the top edge of the cabane assembly as a guide, trusting Wingnut Wings' engineering enough to work on the theory that if the top edge of the slot is exactly straight, then the struts are in their correct position. Once the glue was completely dry, I tested out this theory by dry-fitting the lower and upper wings and inspecting their alignment in relation to each other.

Next, I began to drill all of the rigging positions. These holes were all partially drilled into the wings. I also carefully drilled completely through the tips of the aileron-control fittings ready to accept control wires.

Turnbuckles were manufactured from wire and aluminium tubing, using the method described in Chapter 5. Once I had manufactured more than enough turnbuckles to complete the model, each turnbuckle was individually test-fitted and glued into position on to the lower wings and fuselage.

Looped pins were also manufactured using a method of twisting wire around a small drill-bit

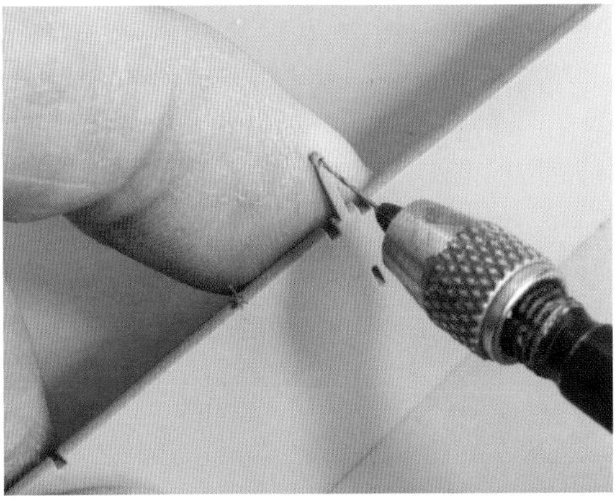

Holes were drilled through the tips of aileron control fittings ready for the control wires.

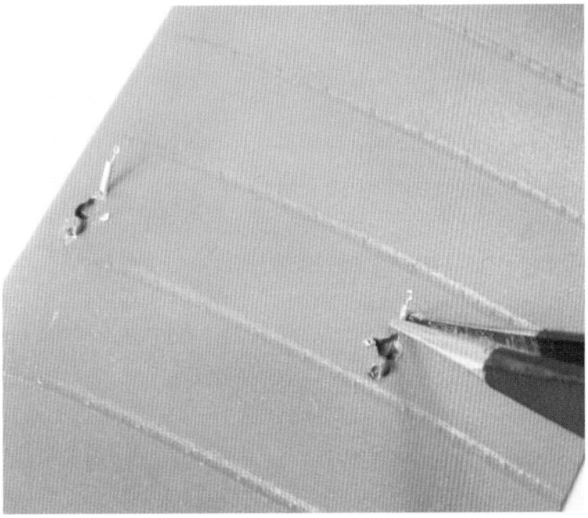

Homemade turnbuckles are fitted into the lower wings.

Looped pins made from wire are fitted into rigging locations on the upper wing.

and these were individually fitted into positions on the underside of the upper wing.

Each strut was dry-fitted into its position on both wings to make sure that the fit was not too tight. The struts were then sprayed in the pale-blue underside colour. On C.8037/17, the anemometer fits to the front edge of the inside, front starboard, interplane strut. There is no provision within the kit to position the anemometer in this way and so I set about fitting pins into the front edge of the strut by carefully drilling small holes into which brass rod was fitted and trimmed. Corresponding holes were drilled into the anemometer before gluing it to the strut.

Once the lower wings were permanently glued in place, I was ready to fit the upper wing. It is possible initially to glue the upper wing on to the cabane strut with only the front, inside bay, interplane struts fitted to support it. This is a lot easier than trying to fit all of the struts in one go and then struggling to slot all of the upper-wing attachments in place at the same time. I, therefore, began by gluing the front, inner bay, interplane struts into position.

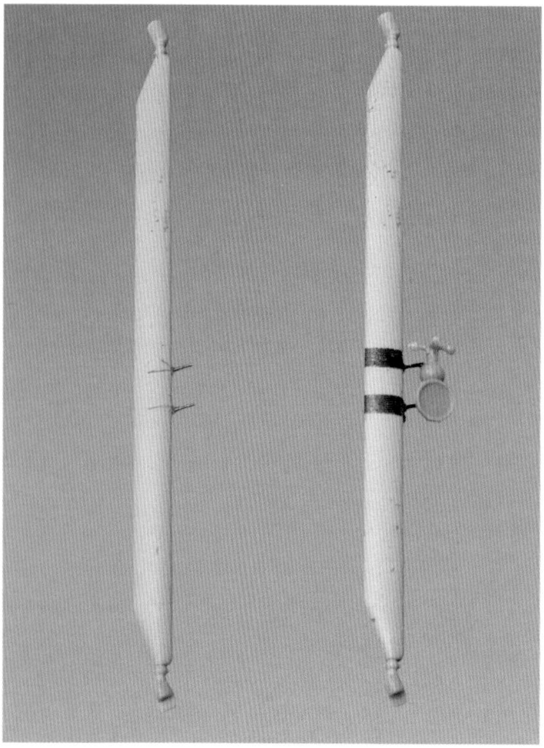

This photograph illustrates how the anemometer was fitted to the inside starboard front interplane strut.

Only the cabane and front inside-bay interplane struts were fitted before commencing upper-wing assembly.

I decided to fit the rigging wires that attach to the upper-wing cabane-strut position before the upper wing went on, as I felt that this would be a fiddly exercise to achieve otherwise. I don't really like pre-fitting rigging in this way, as loose thread has a tendency to get in the way and attract glue. For this reason, I used masking tape to hold the thread ends out of the way of my working area. The upper wing was then glued into position, checking that the upper wing aligned correctly from all angles.

The upper wing has been glued in position.

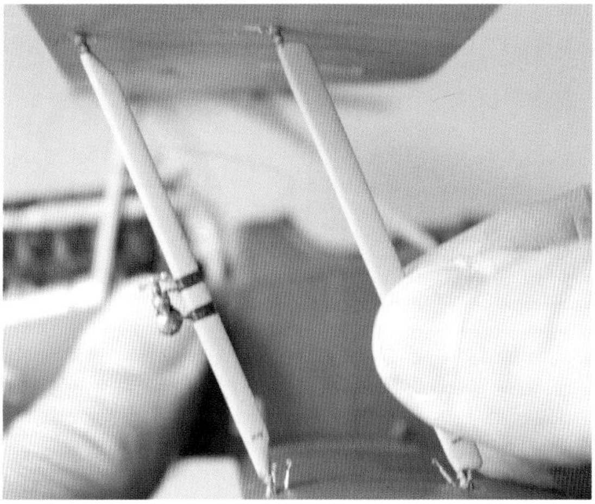

Rear inner-bay interplane struts are spring-fitted into position.

The rear, inner bay, interplane struts were then spring-fitted into place. During this process, a small amount of glue was applied to the recesses in which the strut was to be fitted, in order to avoid contaminating the wing surface with glue from the tips of the strut while fitting them in place. Too much glue should be avoided, as this will overspill the edges of the recess as the strut is fitted.

The loose end of the monofilament that had been fitted to the upper-cabane position was then threaded through the turnbuckle eyelet in the opposing lower-wing interplane position and locked in place. I then proceeded to rig the rest of the inner bay, including the incidence wires. The same process was applied to the outer-bay interplane struts until the wing assembly and rigging was completed.

Radiator and Undercarriage

The radiator is provided in two halves. One part is very slightly larger than the other, which required quite a lot of sanding, once assembled, to achieve a seamless edge.

To paint the radiator, I sprayed the grating black and then dry-brushed the grating detail with aluminium. Masking tape was then applied to this area and the remaining frame of the radiator was then sprayed underside blue. Shutters were painted before gluing them to the radiator. The completed radiator was then slotted into the front edge of the upper wing.

When I tried to fit the water pipe, I found it to be too long. In order to avoid losing any detail, the pipe was trimmed along the edge of the U-bend connector. Brass rod was used to reinforce the joint that I had made.

The undercarriage was assembled as recommended in the instruction booklet with the exception that I did not fit the wheels at this

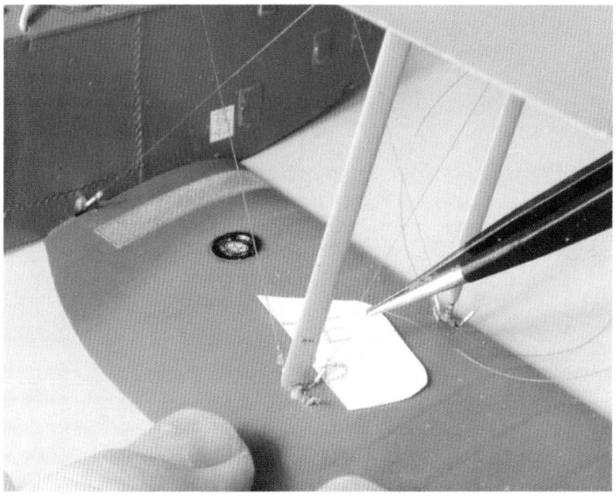

The inside bays are rigged using a similar process as was used in the Albatros build.

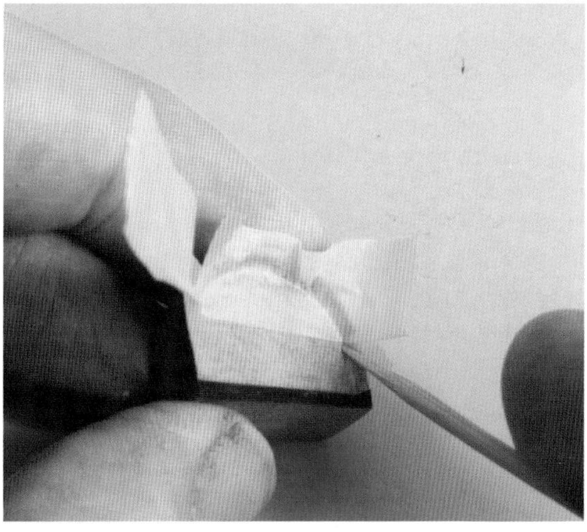

Masking tape is applied to the grated area of the radiator prior to spraying the edges.

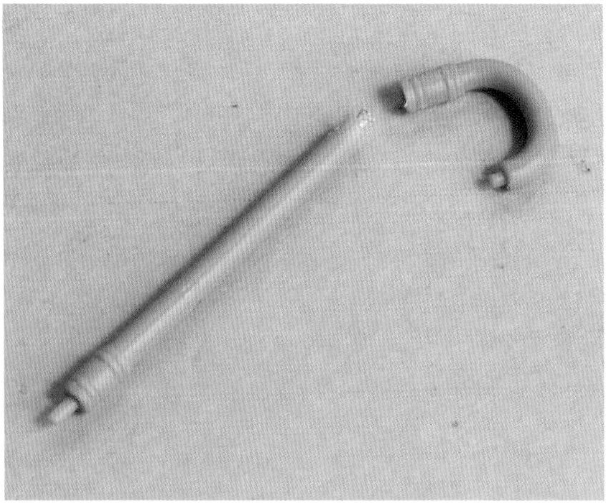

The water pipe required trimming to fit.

Bracing wires were fitted through holes drilled into the undercarriage assembly.

stage. I did, however, attach the generator, minus its propeller. Once assembled, the undercarriage was easy to fit to the underside of the fuselage. Bracing wires were then added through holes that I had drilled before the undercarriage was assembled.

Finishing Touches

The nose panel is the source of two bracing-wire points, one each side, which, in reality, are fitted to the framework on the inside of the aircraft.

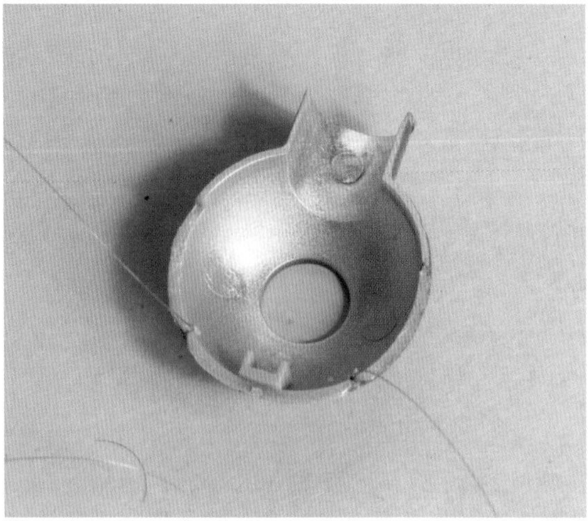

Bracing wires were fitted to the inside of the nose panel.

The flare rack and a scratch-built holster for the gun were fitted to the side of the fuselage.

To simulate this, two location holes were drilled on the inside of the nose panel and a strand of mending thread fitted into each hole. When the panel was glued on to the airframe, the thread was encouraged to exit through a pair of notches on the edge of the panel.

The kit includes a flare rack and *Eisfield* flare pistol. While the only photograph I have seen of

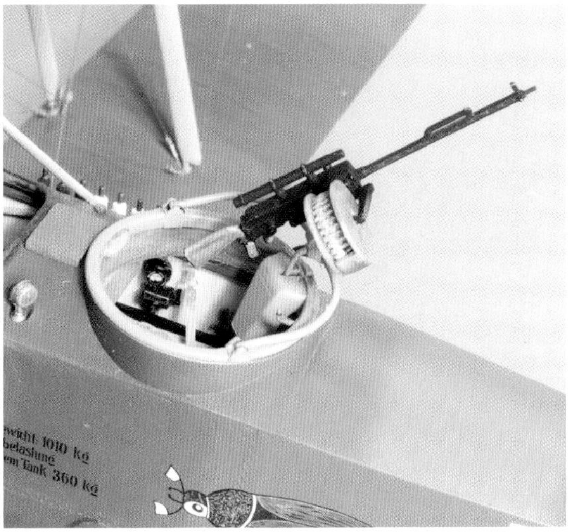

The Parabellum machine-gun and gun ring fitted to the opening in the observer's station.

C.8037/17 is taken from the opposite side of the fuselage, I liked the idea of including a flare rack, as it adds a nice touch of colour to the finished model. German flares were typically green, white and red in colours that could have a number of meanings when fired as a single flare or as a combination. The *Eisfield* flare gun included within the kit is moulded with a flare fitted into its nozzle. As the flare rack I was using was full, I decided to remove the flare from the gun.

I made a small pocket from plasticard to holster the flare gun. This was fitted externally next to the observer's station.

Aileron control wires were fitted to positions on the lower wing before threading them through the tip of the aileron-control fitting that I had drilled out earlier. Rudder and aileron control wires were fitted between exit holes in the fuselage and control horns.

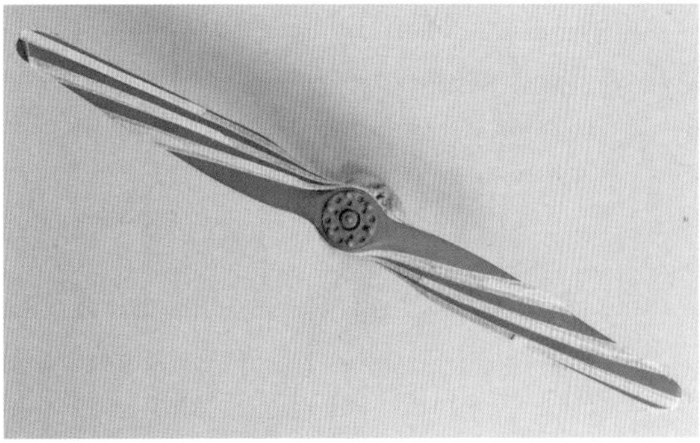

Strips of masking tape were used as an aid to painting the propeller laminations.

The wheels were painted and glued to the axle ends. The observer's Parabellum LMG machine gun and ring was also assembled and fitted in position over the observer's station opening.

Finally, the kit propeller was painted, using masking tape, to create the contrast in laminations that is typical of Axial propellers.

FINALLY

While larger aircraft with multiple bays may appear to be more challenging, in reality, the same techniques are used as single-bay aircraft. You will probably have noticed by now, as you work though these builds, that the routine for building aircraft of any size or shape is generally the same. When building well-engineered kits, such as those made by Wingnut Wings, it is generally not too difficult to work through the assembly. Where the process becomes more challenging is when manufacturers pay less attention to details, such as strut length, which we will see in the next build covered in Chapter 8.

Chapter Seven

Colours and Markings

INTRODUCTION

For many, colour is one of the primary factors that drives interest in German subjects from the World War I period. Arguably this period was the most diverse in the history of military aviation, as colours were experimented with and sometimes applied in what now appears to be an almost ad hoc fashion. In addition, the German Air Service was one of the most prolific users of colour as a method of identification.

While the British, and particularly the RFC (and later the RAF), actively discouraged the use of personal markings on aircraft, the Germans took the opposite view, which helped to create the mythology of World War I pilots being twentieth-century knights of the sky.

This chapter will aim to give a brief overview of German colours and provide tips on re-creating some of these schemes and markings in model form.

German World War I aircraft are well known for their colourful schemes, as illustrated by this Halberstadt CL.II.

Disclaimer

It is important to point out that the determination and interpretation of colours used during the World War I is not an exact science. Colour treatments were either sourced from an external supplier or mixed from pigments at the production site or even in the field. While it is reasonable to assume that suppliers had a good understanding and control of the colour of their products, whether aircraft manufacturers applied a similar level of control is debatable.

Very little first-hand detailed information on German colours still exists. The information that is available is typically vague and usually nothing more than a colour name. Most detailed information we have on German colours has been derived from the examination of surviving samples of fabric, which are likely to have altered with age.

Historians and enthusiasts have often used the Methuen colour system as a method of describing the colour of surviving samples. This is essentially a collection of colour blocks printed in a handbook, which at the time of publication was a fairly inexpensive solution to the problem of describing colour. For many of us, the Methuen colour system in itself is a problem in that the book has been out of publication for over forty years and now changes hands for large sums of money. As a result, the codes are of little help to the casual modeller in seeking guidance on colour. In addition, various editions and re-prints of the book are known to have had slight colour variations, which make it almost impossible for the serious scholar, with no access to the original fabrics, to obtain a perfect colour match.

To add to the confusion, a significant number of samples examined and colour-matched in publications during the eighties and early nineties were found to be counterfeits.

For these reasons, this chapter will not provide exact colour information.

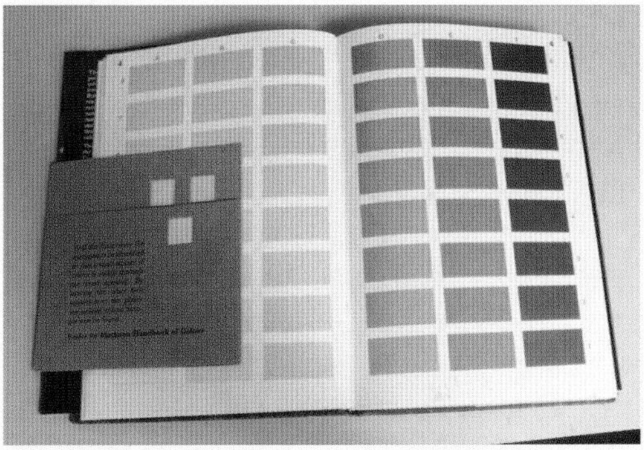

The Methuen Handbook *can, in theory, be used to compare paint chip samples to researched colours of surviving fabric. However, there are many pitfalls, including variations between different editions of the handbook.*

A Brief History of German Aircraft Colour during World War I

When war broke out, colour was not a consideration. Most aircraft from this period had a natural finish.

Linen produced in Germany used a process of applying steam and pressure to the fabric known as calendering, which essentially tightened the weave and reduced the spacing between yarns. The practical advantage of this process meant that the Germans were able to apply less dope to seal linen than the allies.

German fabric was used in both bleached and unbleached states. Bleached linen would tend to be an off-white colour, while unbleached linen was typically closer to a shade of beige.

Wood and plywood sections of aircraft would normally be stained or varnished, a process that would vary greatly between manufacturers.

The Germans began to use colour pigments on some of their aircraft from late-1915 onwards. At first, single colours were applied, either all over or to the upper surface of the aircraft. Common examples of this practice include the pale sky-blues

Some early Gothas are thought to have been finished in a colour, which is described as feldgrau.

applied by manufacturers such as Roland and Gotha, and what is thought to be a dark grey-green closely matching the *feldgrau* colour of infantry uniforms.

By the summer of 1916, some German manufacturers began using camouflage patterns on the upper surface of their aircraft. To begin with, these patterns were probably inspired by the French aircraft camouflage patterns, with early examples typically being made up of red-brown and green. Later, more colours were added to these patterns,

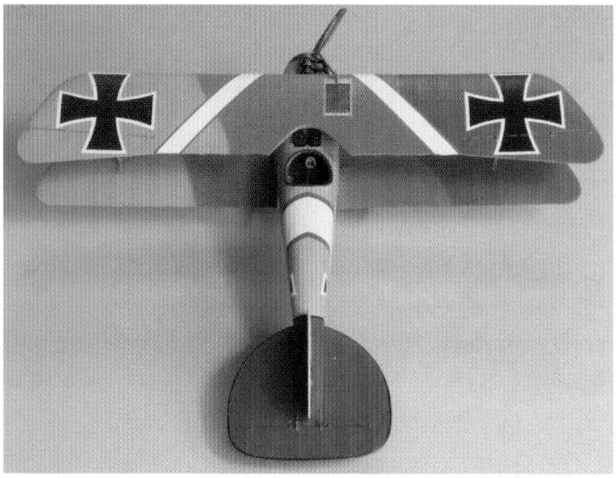

The camouflage scheme of this Albatros D.III features three common colours: pale-green, dark-green and brown. After April 1917, brown was replaced with lilac or mauve.

such as a dark-green and lilac. Lilac directly replaced red-brown as a result of a directive from the Idfleig in April 1917 because the combination of the brown and green had resulted in German aircraft being mistaken for enemy aircraft.

The biggest problem with applying pigments to the fabric surface was that they increased the weight of the aircraft, thereby affecting its performance. To counter this, the Germans developed a unique printed fabric designed to negate the need for any surface treatment other than doping and varnishing.

In October 1916, all aircraft linen was recalled from aircraft manufacturers to be printed with what we now know as a five-colour lozenge pattern. This was effectively an irregular polygon pattern consisting of five bright colours printed on to rolls of fabric.

The lozenge began to appear on aircraft toward the summer of 1917 and would continue to be used until the end of the war, by which time a second four-colour version had also been introduced, perhaps to address a shortage of certain pigments. Darker night versions are also known to have been printed.

Lozenge patterns were not just used on printed fabrics. Some aircraft had patterns hand-painted on their aircraft. This was often done to match wooden or metal parts of an aircraft with the

This Hannover provides an example of complex patterned schemes being painted on non-fabric areas of an aircraft to match the lozenge fabric.

lozenge covered flying surfaces, but there are also many examples of entire aircraft, including flying surfaces, being painted in this way.

Fokker used a method by which thinned pigments were applied to natural doped linen, which resulted in a streaked appearance. Whether this was originally done to address shortages or to differentiate Fokker aircraft from its competitors is not known, but the method was applied to many Fokker-produced aircraft from late-1916 onwards and the practice continued, even after the introduction of lozenge fabric.

Pfalz aircraft, such as the D.III, were finished in a form of aluminium dope known as *silbergrau*. This was essentially a pale-grey finish (mixed from carbon black and zinc oxide) with finely ground aluminium powder added to it.

Undersides of some aircraft were covered in a sky-blue colour; however, the shades varied greatly in intensity between manufacturers. The practice became less common after lozenges were introduced, although some manufacturers continued to use the colour until the end of the war.

Hexagonal-printed fabric, such as on this Hansa Brandenburg W.29, was used by the German Navy from early 1917 until the end of the war.

The history of colour in naval aircraft followed a broadly similar line as their land-locked cousins, although, understandably, two- and three-block camouflage patterns were never used. Typically, a medium-grey was used as a single colour covering of plywood, metal and, occasionally, fabric. The Navy did introduce a series of regular lozenge-patterned fabrics, which were usually applied to the upper flying surfaces of the aircraft.

It is not known when and where the idea of unit and personal markings began; however, it is reasonable to assume that the idea became a practical necessity as the number of aircraft in the combat area increased.

In the early years of the war, some aircraft were given names, which were adorned on the side of the fuselage. Unit markings began to appear in 1915 and were typically simple shapes or arrangements of stripes. As the number of aircraft involved in operations increased, there was a greater need for individual recognition and personal markings began to be used more frequently. Initially, these were fairly simple patterns or shapes, but as the practice became more common, these markings became an art-form.

In January 1917, a young cavalryman, who had begun to make a name for himself as a fighter ace in Jagdstaffel 2 was appointed commander of Jagdstaffel 11. Manfred von Richthofen wasted no time in overpainting his brand-new Albatros D.III in red. This single act sparked the fashion of painting aircraft in bright colours and schemes in the field. Many Jagdstaffeln also used overpainting as a method of unit identification.

Interpretation of Black and White Photographs

It is almost impossible to interpret an exact colour scheme simply by the examination of a photograph. However, educated guesses can be made by working through a simple checklist. The first thing you may want to confirm is whether part or all of the aircraft retains original factory colours. To confirm this it is helpful, but not essential, to know the serial number. You will need a good reference that describes various batch colour schemes and it is also helpful to examine photographs of other aircraft from the same batch as a comparison. At the end of this stage of your research, you will hopefully have some idea of the colours of at least part of your aircraft.

Another important question is: do you know what unit the aircraft was attached to and, if so, do you know the approximate time period? If the answer to these questions is yes, then does the photograph relate to any known unit markings

The chequered pattern on this Albatros appears to be painted on a varnished plywood base. The colour of the squares could potentially be black, red or yellow, but has often been interpreted as black. JACK HERRIS

from the period in question? An example might be that you have a photograph of a Pfalz D.III, which you know is a Jasta 10 machine from late-1917, which appears to have a black nose, wheel coverings and, possibly, even undercarriage and struts. Because we know that Jasta 10 aircraft of the period typically had a yellow nose and wheel coverings, then it's almost certainly the case that the black areas that you are seeing on the photograph are actually yellow.

To make sense of this, it is important to understand that many contemporary photographs of the World War I period were taken on orthochromatic film, which has little or no response to orange or red light and so yellows and reds were often depicted as black. A good example of this can be seen on many period photographs of Belgian aircraft, where the cockades of black, red and yellow simply appear as black disks.

If we do not know the unit, then much of the rest of the process is likely to be guesswork. If large areas of black are present in the photograph, try comparing this shade of black to the black of the national markings. If there is a slight difference in shade, then perhaps what you are actually looking at contains red or yellow pigments. The same principle can be applied to other situations where you have areas of a known colour and other areas of an unknown colour.

While the examples provided above can provide a starting point to interpretation, unless there is clear first-hand documented evidence of colour, then there will always be an element of guesswork involved.

PAINTING WORLD WAR I AIRCRAFT

Unlike World War II or any other modelling genre where subjects are primarily monoplanes, World War I aircraft require painting at an earlier stage of completion. Usually this will be once the fuselage is assembled, although the lower wings and tail-plane can also be in place. I always recommend that the model is primed before painting,

Three different colours sprayed on card provide examples of how a background colour alters the shade of the finish. The top row is sprayed on white card; the bottom row is sprayed on top of grey primer.

especially if airbrushing is to be the main method of paint application. This is because it reduces the risk of wear and tear caused by the amount of handling that the model receives, especially during the rigging process. For this reason, a protective finish such as varnish is also applied to the painted components. It should be noted that use of a grey primer will influence the shade of the covering colour and so colour selection may need to be adjusted to compensate.

Using an Airbrush

Airbrushes are not essential to World War I modelling, but will produce a notable improvement to your finished model. There are some finishes that were present during the World War I that are easier to achieve with an airbrush, such as the soft edges on sprayed camouflage schemes. The airbrush is also a useful tool when trying to produce subtle weathering or lighting effects.

I am not going to cover detailed use of the airbrush in this book as there are plenty of very good publications that specialize in this subject. However, the key to achieving a good finish is a combination of factors, including the general state of the airbrush, experience of paints being used and experience in using the airbrush itself.

It's vitally important to keep your airbrush clean and in good order. I always completely flush out paint between colours, a process that includes removing and cleaning the needle. After each spraying session, the brush is stripped down and given a thorough clean. Even following these good practices, you are likely gradually to suffer a reduction in performance due to a build-up of small particles inside the brush, and so regular stripping and soaking of the airbrush components in a good-quality cleaning solution, and subsequent lubrication of the brush, is important in maintaining your equipment.

Individual paints and paint manufacturers' products perform differently and, as such, require different levels of thinning and perhaps different thinning products. Some paints are best avoided altogether. This knowledge is only gained by experience and, as such, it is important not to expect too much too soon. The same logic applies to use of the brush itself. The more it gets used, the better and more refined the end result will be. In my case it took me a number of years before I was entirely comfortable in the use of an airbrush.

Masking

One of the most important parts of producing a good paint job is masking. Even if you are a brush-painter, there are many occasions when masking is essential.

Masking can be a slow process, but the more time and effort applied to the job, the better the end result will be. Often the process of masking can take a lot longer to complete than the actual application of paint.

When masking a World War I aircraft, you will almost always have to cover open cockpits and exposed engines. Any material that stops paint from reaching areas that you do not want to paint can make a suitable masking material. I habitually use small, scrunched-up pieces of kitchen roll to fill open cockpits and other large open areas.

Exposed engines are often particularly difficult to mask as you are not only trying to find a way to adequately cover the area, but are also trying to avoid damaging anything on the engine itself. For this reason, if it is at all possible to do so, I avoid fitting the engine until after painting is complete. This works well for rotary-powered subjects, but not so well for in-line engines. Engines can be masked with a variety of materials, including paper and masking tape. I try to avoid using Blu Tack as the material is difficult to remove completely from your model once painting is complete.

If masking includes sharp demarcation lines, then I always use a good-quality modelling masking tape, such as Tamiya tape, to reduce the risk of colour bleed. A thin strip of tape is usually used to create the actual demarcation line and then larger pieces of tape are built up behind the initial line. This allows the shape of the line to be finely

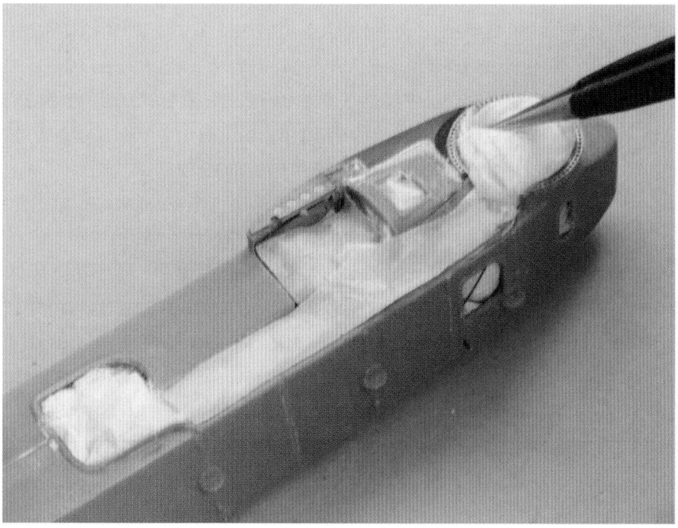

The open interior sections of the Gotha require careful masking before applying paint with an airbrush.

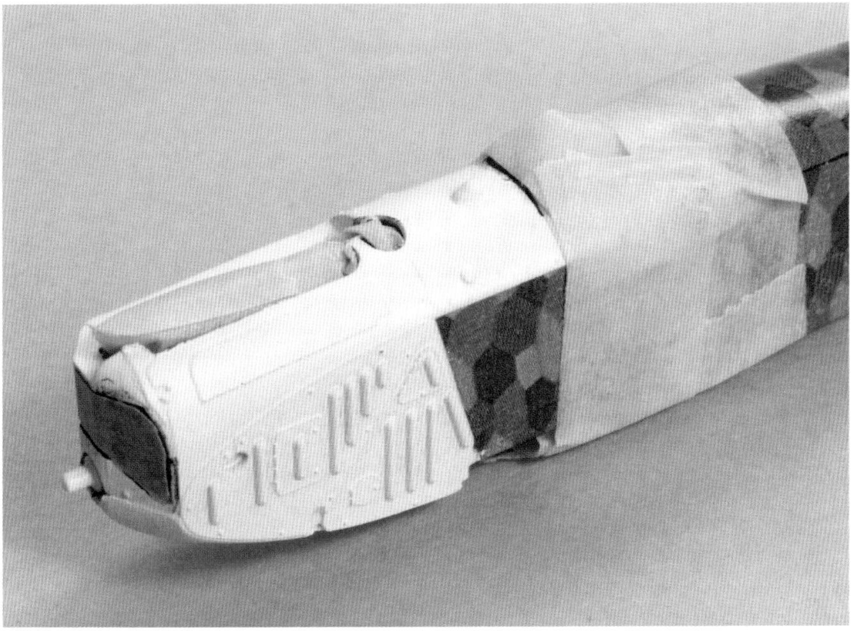

Masking tape has been successfully used over lozenge decals on this Eduard Fokker D.VII.

tuned and reduces the risk of creasing that would ultimately result in colour bleed. Colour bleed can also occur if the masked area is flooded with too much paint.

Decaled areas can sometimes be masked but I would suggest carrying out a test with unwanted decals before committing. The decaled areas should be sealed with a few coats of varnish before attempting to mask. It is also important to remove some of the tackiness of the tape's adhesive before applying masking tape to these areas. This can be done by simply applying the tape to your hand a few times before it is used.

Using Traditional Brushes

Whether you use an airbrush or not, the traditional brush still has a very special place in the modeller's armoury of tools. The secret to achieving good results with a brush is very similar to what I have described for the airbrush: keep your brushes clean; know your paints and how to get the most out of them. In addition, keep a good selection of brushes to suit different requirements. For example, a large, soft brush is perfect for laying down colour on large areas, while detail can be picked out with a small brush of medium stiffness and a fine tip.

Paints should often be thinned down before application, especially when applying a base colour to a large area. More coats of a thinner paint ultimately provide a better finish than a few coats of thick paint.

Brush-Painting Techniques

The brush-painter has a number of simple techniques that can be used to improve the appearance of painted components.

Washes are watered down mixes of paint that, when applied to parts of your model, can provide a level of depth, as well as accentuating detail, as the pigment congregates in recesses and around raised edges. Most paint manufacturers produce ranges of ready-made washes that are designed to provide an even flow. Artist's inks can also be used in some areas where you require a strong contrast of detail. However, a mix of water and acrylic will produce a good enough wash for most applications. If applied all over a large component, washes can cause unwanted tide marks and stains, and, as such, washes are best used on

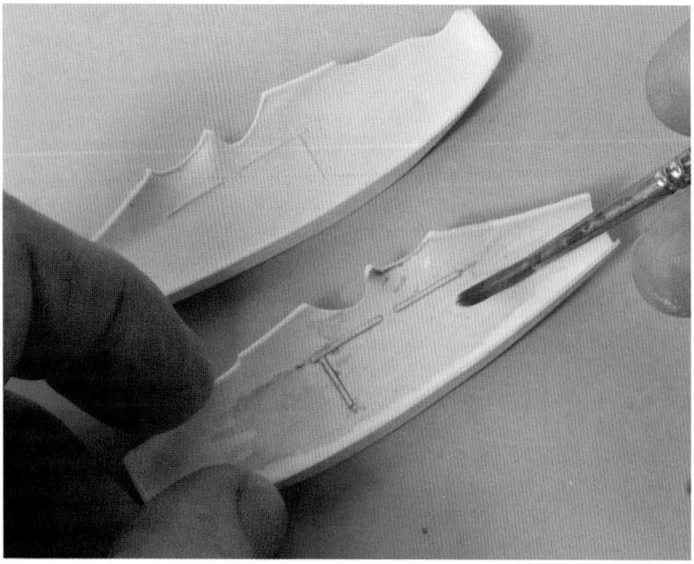

A brown wash has been applied to simulate wood staining. Note that the wash congregates around the edges of raised detail.

parts like engines and wood, in conjunction with other techniques.

Pin-washes are applied with a very small brush with a thin tip to specific areas of a component. Usually these will be recesses, such as panel lines or around the edges of raised detail. Unless you have a very steady hand, some overspill of pin-wash can occur, which can be wiped away while still wet. This can leave a small, light smudge around the pin-washed area, which can sometimes be beneficial, as it softens the overall effect of the wash.

Watercolours are a useful media for producing very clean, panel lines. Apply the watercolour on top of a varnished base. Use a damp cloth to wipe the excess paint away once it has dried. Once completed, the water-coloured areas will require sealing with varnish.

Dry-brushing is a process whereby a very small amount of pigment is applied to a part in order to highlight raised detail. This process destroys brushes, so it is best to use an old brush that is no longer adequate for other needs. Select a colour that is significantly paler than the base colour and apply a very small amount to your brush. Then use a scrap of paper to wipe and scrub the majority of the paint away from your brush until you can

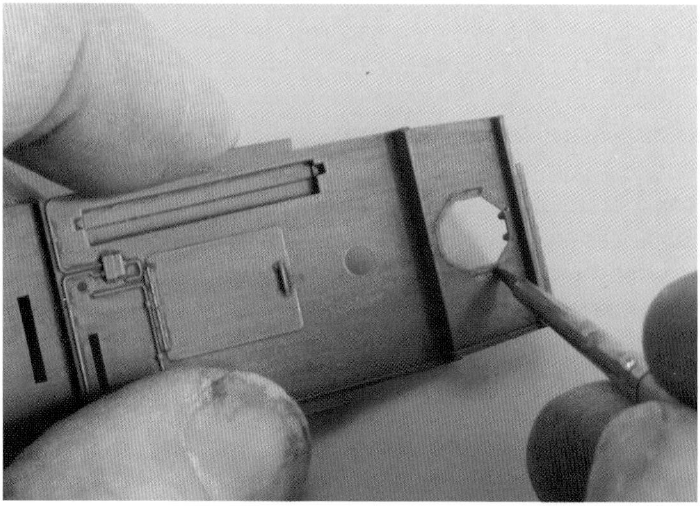

A pin-wash is being applied around the edge of fittings on this interior part for the Rumpler.

The black base colour of this exhaust is being dry-brushed with a metallic colour.

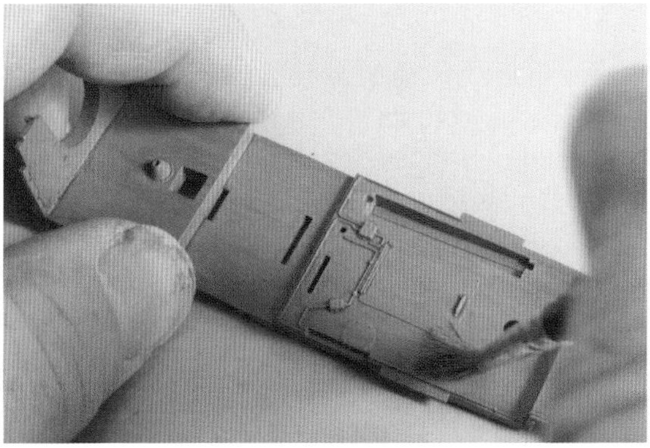

Dry-brushing can sometimes be used in conjunction with other techniques to produce a wood-grain finish.

only see a hint of paint on the paper. Apply what is left to the part that you are painting, using a scrubbing motion, which should have the effect of highlighting fine detail. Care needs to be taken not to scrub the base colour so hard that you begin to remove the original paint. If the effect is not visually apparent almost instantly, then use a paler shade or apply more dry-brushing coats of the same colour.

Dry-brushing can also be used to simulate wood grain. In this case, a stiff-bristle brush is used and less paint is removed on scrap paper. The grain then needs to be dry-brushed in one direction. This method can give variable results, depending on the brush you use and the amount of paint left on the brush, but with practice, a useful effect can be achieved.

SIMULATING GERMAN COLOURS AND SCHEMES

Fabric

It is very likely that the colour of fabric varied greatly as a result of treatments, ageing and base material colour and, as such, it is recommended that each project is treated slightly differently, so that when your models are viewed together as a collection, the models do not have a uniform appearance with the same fabric base colour.

From top to bottom, this simulation provides an example of how the colour of bleached and unbleached linen may change as varnish yellows with age.

All raw fabric, whether bleached or unbleached, was doped and varnished, and this is where most variations in colour will occur. Varnish, in particular, not only affected the colour of fabric but also the way in which light reflects from the material, which in itself changes the perception of colour.

Raw materials used within British varnishes caused the colour to yellow very quickly, which is why British aircraft are often depicted with a yellowish, clear, doped linen colour. While German varnishes would have certainly discoloured and yellowed to some degree with age, the general perception is that this was less pronounced, resulting in a clear difference between the appearance of German and British linens.

Ultimately, fabric base colour selection is likely to be a matter of personal taste; however, it is worth considering the age of the subject that you are building. If the aircraft is depicted as being fresh out of the factory, choose a colour that reasonably represents the base raw material. If the subject has been in service for a while, adjust your colour selection accordingly.

Alternatively, for those producing larger scale models, Aviattic produce an excellent solution to paint with a range of textile decal sheets that can be used to create very realistic fabric effects.

Simulating Fabric Effects

On its own, a single, flat, fabric base colour will look stark and unnatural, especially on larger scale models. A number of simple effects can be employed to break up the starkness of the base colour and give fabric covering a more organic appearance.

The build chapters of this book (Chapters 2, 4, 6 and 8) provide examples of how spraying or wiping a thin layer of brown in random streaks over the surfaces of the fabric areas can help break up colour. A popular way of doing this is to overspray or pre-shade the line of the rib tape with a darker colour. This technique can work, but it is important that this process does not become too uniform and mechanical. Once shaded or streaked, a light overspray of the base colour or a lighter shade of the base colour can help to blend in the darker colours.

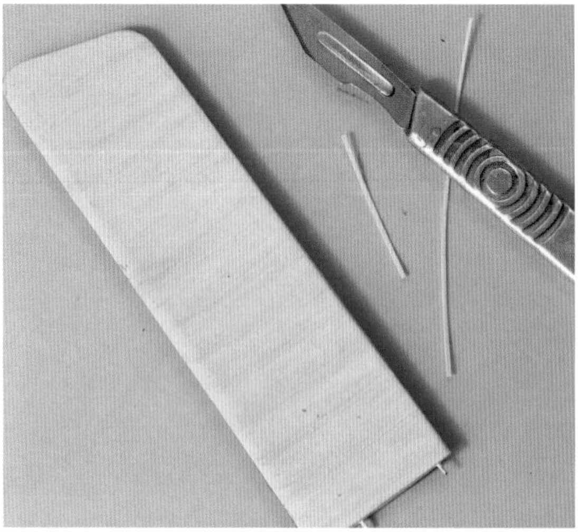

Strips of Aviattic textile decals are being applied to the wing surface. The slight difference in colour helps to give the wings a more natural appearance.

Masking rib-tapes or adding strips of decal rib-tapes can also help to give the illusion of organic fabric surfaces, especially when combined with random streaking.

Another useful technique is to simulate the effect of translucency when sunlight shines through a wing with a natural linen covering. In this case, you are attempting to replicate the effect of rib detail being visible through the fabric. The rib detail is accentuated either by masking and painting the ribs in a dark colour or by applying strips of a decal stock overpainted with a darker colour. Once the rib detail has been applied, it is advisable to overspray lightly with the base colour. This can be used in conjunction with other effects and treatments. Markings, such as crosses, can also show though the wings in some cases and this can be simulated in exactly the same way as the rib tapes.

It is, however, important to note that this effect is only applicable to the underside of aircraft with flying surfaces that are completely covered in natural linen. Any pigment applied to the upper side of the wing will impede light and the effect will not be present.

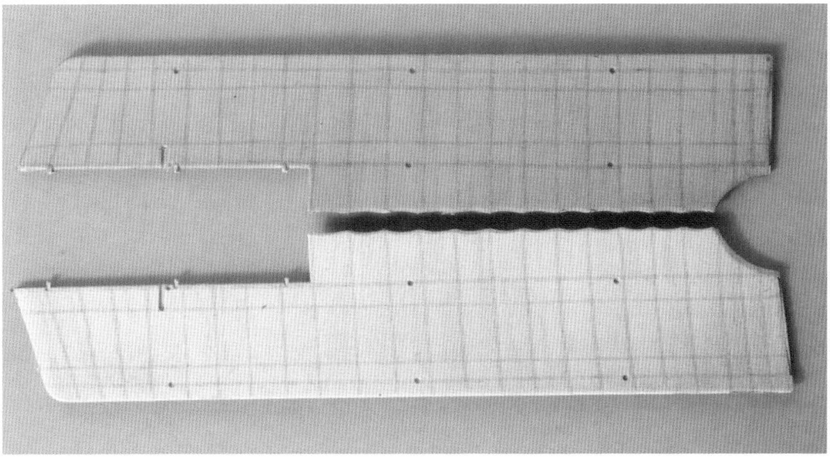

The undersides of the FF.33e wings have had strips of a base linen effect decal applied, which is then covered with Aviattic textile decal.

Plywood Finishes

Many German aircraft had fuselages that were partially or completely covered in plywood. Examples range from the box-shaped LVGs and early Albatros C-types, through to the semi-monocoque-style fuselages that became the trademark of manufacturers such as Pfalz, Roland and Albatros.

Plywood was typically nailed to the fuselage framework in panelled sections; however, the manufacturers of monocoque-style fuselages used various methods to shape the plywood. For example, Albatros moulded the plywood to the required shape before cutting and nailing panels to the fuselage, while Pfalz employed a system whereby layers of thin ply and fabric were built up on a master mould, creating a complete fuselage shell that would then be fitted directly to the framework of the airframe.

Natural plywood made from birch or alder was typically varnished or stained and, as such, colouring would vary from manufacturer to manufacturer.

Simulating a Wood Finish

There are many methods that can be employed to simulate a realistic-looking wood finish without too much effort. The first and most important part of creating any wood finish is the selection of the flat base colour. This should be lighter and paler than the finished colour that you are aiming for. Personally, I like to use base colours that try to simulate the original, unstained colour of the wood. In most cases this would be beige, sand or even a very pale-straw colour. If applying the base colour with a brush, it makes sense to apply the brush-strokes in the direction that you want the wood grain to run. Subtle variations in base colour can be applied to individual wood panels, but often it is easier and more effective to apply a uniform base coat and then use the top coat to individualize panels.

Once the base colour is fully dry, we can begin to apply layers of colour to simulate the grain and varnish. Essentially, what we are going to do is to apply a glaze of a darker colour to our base

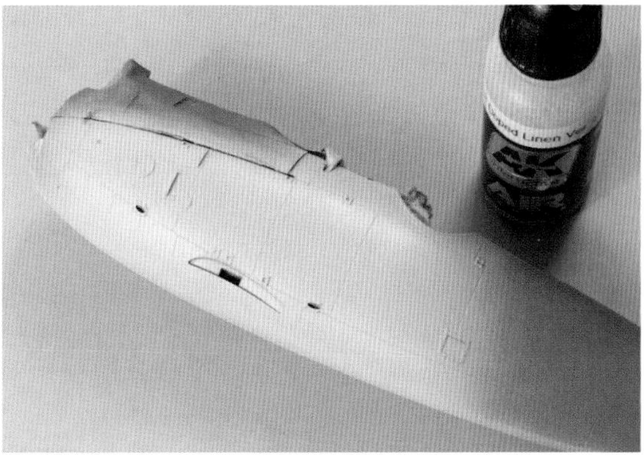

I used a base coat of clear doped linen on the plywood panels of this Wingnut Wings' Albatros.

coat. There are many variations on this theme and almost any artist media can be used, the most popular choices though are either oils or acrylics.

Creating a Wood-Grain and Staining Finish Using Artist Oils

As with the base coat, selection of colour is crucial to achieving the desired effect. For yellow varnishes, I typically use yellow ochre, directly from the tube, while for darker, browner wood finishes I am more likely to mix my own shade. Remember when selecting any colour for this purpose that you will be applying a thin layer to the base coat and so the colour that you select will lose some of its richness and vividness if applied correctly.

Apply a small amount of your selected colour on top of the base coat and use a piece of clean kitchen towel to wipe the oils in the desired direction of your wood grain. Using a clean piece of the paper towel, continue to wipe away the oils until only a very thin layer remains. At this stage, the original colour of the base coat should show through the thin layer of oils.

Now, while the oil paint is still wet, choose the oldest, worn-out brush that you own and brush in long strokes in the desired direction of the grain. This should create thin and faint lines giving the appearance of a wood grain. Try not to over-do this stage to the point where the contrast of the wood grain is too noticeable, as this will result in something that looks out of scale. This process can arguably be omitted on smaller scale models.

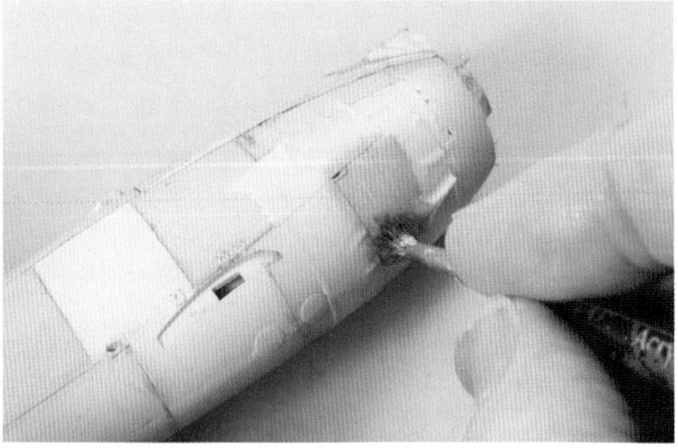

An old brush is being used to create wood-grain detail while the oil paint is still wet.

Oils take a long time to dry completely, especially if there are areas where thick paint has built up, such as panel lines. I would recommend leaving your completed wood finish at least overnight.

Creating Wood Grain Using a Wash Technique

A suitable wood-grain effect can also be achieved using standard hobby acrylics. This time we are going to create a wash that is brush-painted on top of the base coat. In order to create the wash,

Yellow ochre oil paint is wiped over the base colour in the direction of the grain to simulate varnish.

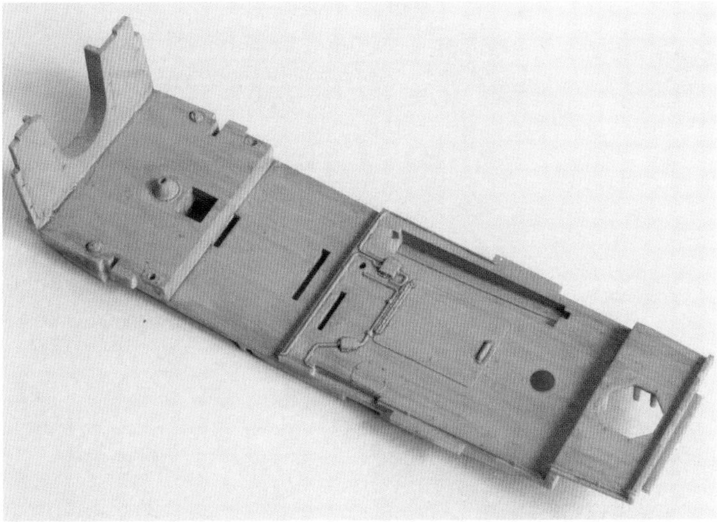

The wooden appearance of this part has been achieved by building up layers of acrylic wash on to a paler base surface.

a suitable colour of paint that is significantly darker than your base coat needs to be selected. Mix enough water with the paint so that when it is applied to the base coat, it results in a translucent effect. It's better to have too much water in your mix than too little, as weak washes can gradually be built up in layers to provide a pleasing effect. As with the oil technique it is best to experiment on spare parts or waste material before committing to your model.

Apply a generous coat of the wash to the surface of the base coat using a wide, soft brush in the required direction of the grain. As the wash begins to dry, use a small brush to create long, thin strokes in the direction of the grain. It can sometimes be effective to add more of the original wash mixture. This will have already begun to dry, making the consistency of colour a little stronger and so, by adding thin streaks to the drying wash, a grain effect can be achieved. Once happy with the wood effect, leave the area to dry completely. If necessary, repeat this process until the desired colour and effect has been achieved.

Dry-Brushing Wood Grains

Dry-brushing can also be used to create a suitable wood-grain appearance when used in conjunction with the wash technique. Dry-brushing can be used to tone down a washed grain that has too much contrast or a slightly wetter dry-brush can be used to create grains, although this technique can be problematic and requires practice.

Wood-Grain Decals

Another method of simulating wood grain is with the application of wood-grain decals, such as items produced by Uschi van der Rosten. Decals such as these can be used to simulate individual panels, although some products still require pre-painting of the model and also benefit from applying an oil paint-based stain on top of the decals.

Camouflage Patterns

One aspect of camouflage patterns that can be determined fairly easily from photographs is whether the demarcations between one colour and another are soft or hard. A soft demarcation line will usually indicate that the camouflage pattern was sprayed, while harder lines would most likely have been applied by brush.

For airbrush-users there are two ways that soft demarcation lines can be simulated:

- The first uses paper masks cut to the shape of the camouflage block. The masks are fitted to the model in such a way that the edge is raised up away from the surface of the model. The higher above the model the paper is raised, the

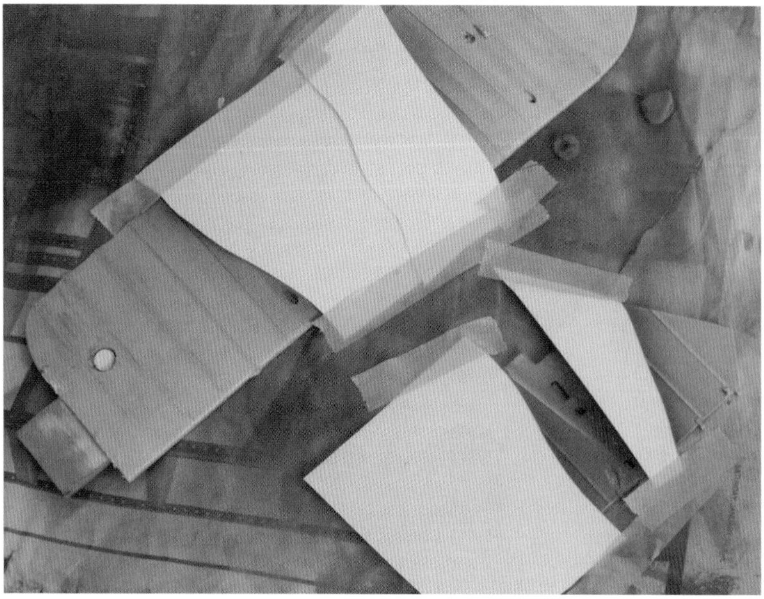

Paper masks raised above the surface of the wing can be used to create soft camouflage demarcation lines.

softer the demarcation line will ultimately be. When spraying a block of camouflage, begin with your airbrush nozzle at a 90-degree angle to the masked line and then gradually adjust the angle slowly so that some of the paint settles underneath the raised mask.

- The other method of achieving a soft demarcation line is by using a freehand technique, as described in Chapter 6 on the Rumpler build.

Soft demarcation lines are possible to achieve with a brush, but the results are generally not as effective. A small amount of paint is applied to a stiff-bristled brush and, in the same manner as a dry-brushing technique, almost all of the paint is removed by scrubbing the brush over a piece of scrap paper. Using a dabbing technique, begin to build up fine stipples along the edge of the demarcation line. Unlike airbrushing, where a soft demarcation line is produced by one colour on top of a solid block of another colour, using the brush technique you will probably need to apply the same process to both colours in order to achieve a satisfactory result.

The soft demarcation lines of this Ago C.IV have been achieved with a brush.

Lozenge Patterns

In October 1916, all aircraft linen was recalled from aviation factories to be printed with a new camouflage scheme. The resultant lozenge scheme was a pattern of irregular polygons printed on 54in rolls of fabric in two ranges of five colours, one

Restored LVG C.VI wings at Brussels Air Museum are covered in bolts of five-colour lozenge applied in a chord-wise direction. ALF SMALL

intended for the upper side and one for the lower side. The fabric began appearing on aircraft on the frontline in the summer of 1917, and in the spring of 1918, a second four-colour scheme was introduced. Lozenge fabric could be applied in three directions: chord-wise (across the width of the flying surface), span-wise (along the length of the flying surface) or diagonally to the flying surfaces.

Lozenge strips were also used as rib tapes by some manufacturers. Usually the tapes were cut to match the surface being applied to (for example, upper surface tapes to upper surface lozenge); however, there is evidence to suggest that upper-surface rib-tapes were sometimes applied to lower surfaces.

The Navy specified fabrics printed with regular hexagon patterns in three or four colours. Unlike the lozenge schemes of land-based aircraft, care appears to have been taken to match fabric during covering so that the flying surfaces appeared to be covered in one continuous piece of fabric. Rib tapes were not used on these lozenges.

Using Decal Lozenges

The most common method of reproducing a lozenge fabric is in decal form. Many decal manufacturers have attempted to produce lozenge-pattern decals over the years in virtually every popular scale. If you compare these products side by side you are unlikely to find any consistency in the colours used, although some products are more accurate to current understanding of lozenge colours than others. Of the decals currently available, I would recommend Aviattic products, which are accurate with regards to colouring and simple to use.

Kit lozenges are often a poor representation and, in the majority of cases, are best replaced. Even many Wingnut Wings' kits suffer from the use of colours that are bordering on unacceptable.

Aftermarket lozenge decals will either be supplied as individual strips replicating a role of fabric or as a continuous sheet. In both of these cases, the shape that is required needs to be cut by the modeller in the required direction.

Research is an important first step to the creation of any lozenge scheme. You will need to know what type of lozenge pattern was used, what direction the fabric was applied and, finally, what colour rib tapes were used.

Before application, the surface of the model requires painting and varnishing. The colour of paint may be partially determined by the decals that you are using. While traditional water-slide decals are printed on a white base, some may have a slight level of translucency that can be affected by the base colour and it is, therefore, worth experimenting with different base colours. Some modern aftermarket lozenge fabric decals are printed on clear decal paper, which requires a white or very pale-coloured surface underneath, otherwise the base colour of the surface will influence the intended colour of the decals too much. However, the advantage with these products is that weathering effects can be applied to the surface of the model before the decal goes on.

Gloss varnish is applied to the painted base surface in order to give the decal a smooth surface to settle on. Any roughness in the base surface increases the probability of air-trapping and the decal may not settle completely.

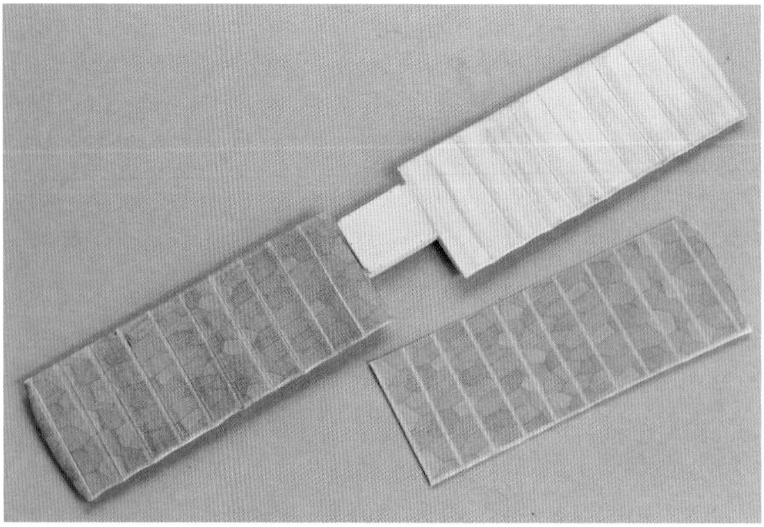

Simple weathering techniques have been applied to this wing section for the Eduard 1/72 Fokker D.VII before applying the lozenge.

Always begin by reading the manufacturer's application instructions when applying lozenge decals. I would also recommend performing a small trial, which should help iron out any potential problems before committing large amounts of lozenge decal to your model.

If the area being covered is a flying surface, such as a wing or tail section, I usually use the part as a template, adding a little extra to the chord to allow for wing-surface curvature. However, if I am covering a fuselage area, I normally create templates from masking tape. Masking tape is applied to the area that requires covering and the outline is traced on to the tape. Once the tape is removed from the model, it can be fixed to a piece of card or plasticard. The shape drawn on to the tape is then cut out to create a template.

I usually begin with application of the underside lozenge. I always try to position the decal along the most critical edge of the area that I am covering, so that if there is any excess decal, it can easily be trimmed from a less critical edge.

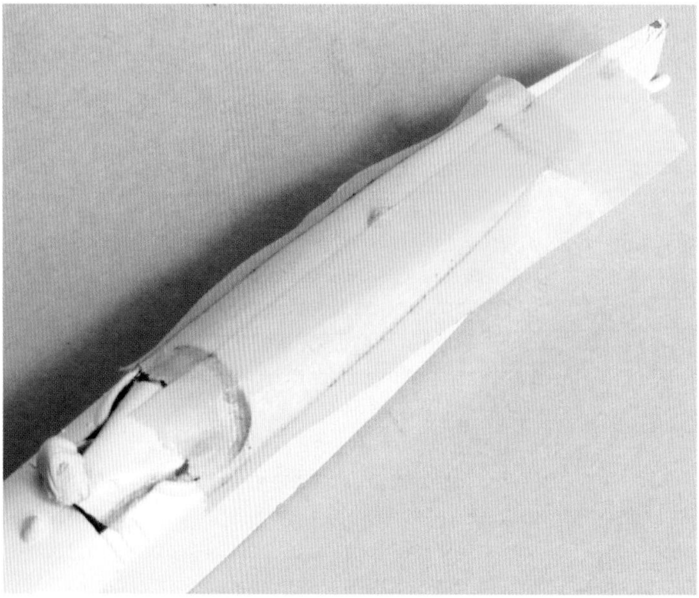

A template of the rear decking section of the Fokker D.VII is created from masking tape.

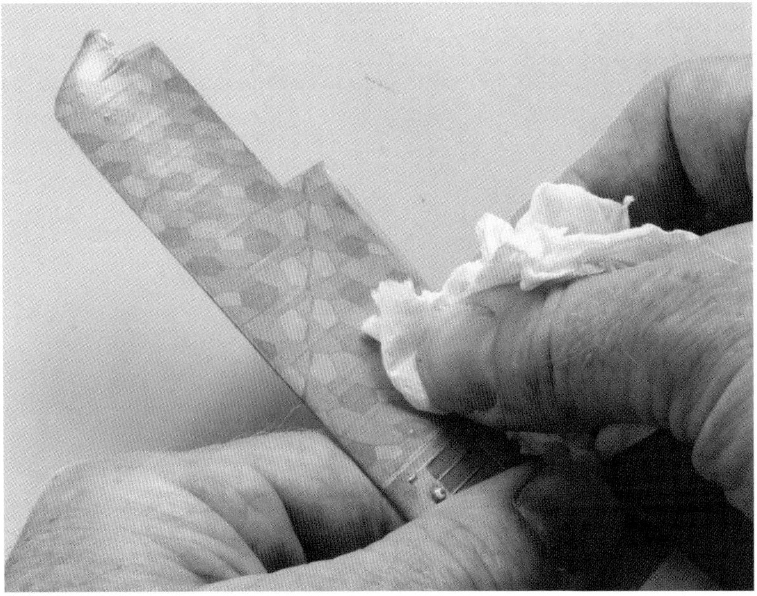

Air trapped under the lozenge decal is carefully being pushed out toward the trailing edge.

As an example, when applying lozenge to a flying surface, I usually recommend positioning the decal along the leading edge of the wing, so that any trimming is performed to the trailing edge. If applying individual bolts of lozenge, care should be taken to avoid any overlapping.

Once positioned, gently wipe the lozenge with a soft cloth or paper towel toward the trailing edge. The idea is to push any air out to the edge while maintaining the positioning along the leading edge. Depending on the decals being used, setting solutions can be used to help the decals settle. Always check decal instructions carefully before using such products, as stronger products such as Micro Sol can cause damage.

Allow the decals to settle overnight, once a surface has been completely covered. All lozenge areas should be sealed with a few coats of varnish in order to protect the decals during the construction of the model.

Rib Tapes

The application of rib tapes is a laborious job, but the inclusion of rib tapes, even in smaller scales, makes a huge visual impact on the finished model and is, therefore, well worth the extra effort. I almost always apply rib tapes to a wet varnish,

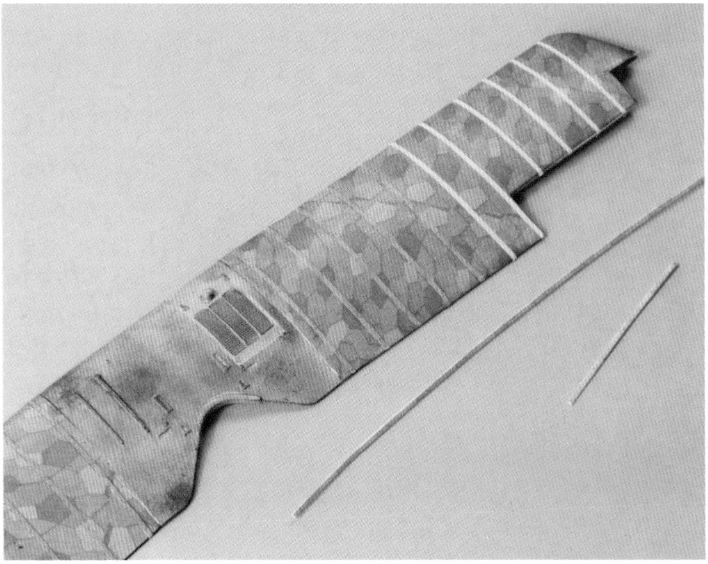

I would normally apply rib tapes from lozenge decal that has been printed on a white backing. However, in this example, clear-backed lozenge strips were applied on top of strips of white decal stock.

which helps the thin strips adhere to the surface of the wing. Once rib tapes have been applied and allowed to settle, they should be sealed with varnish. Coloured or linen rib-tapes can be cut from suitable decal stock that may either be printed or painted before cutting into strips.

Painting Lozenge Schemes

Lozenge patterns were not always printed on fabric. There are many examples of aircraft where the lozenge pattern has effectively been hand-painted. Simulating these patterns in model form can represent a challenge, not least because of the irregular and continuous way that the patterns were originally applied.

The first stage to creating a painted-lozenge effect is to map out your pattern on to the surface of the model using a pencil. This can be done freehand if the patterns are irregular. If the pattern is a regular one, then use of a template is helpful. When copying a pattern from a photograph or colour profile there is much that will not be visible and will require some artistic licence. However, the initial act of copying visible areas should help to provide a basic understanding of the rules of the pattern.

Once the basic shapes are marked out, each individual shape is colour-coded. This can be done either by applying a small sample of the colour

Using a colour profile as a reference, the position of each shape is roughly mapped out on the surface of the model.

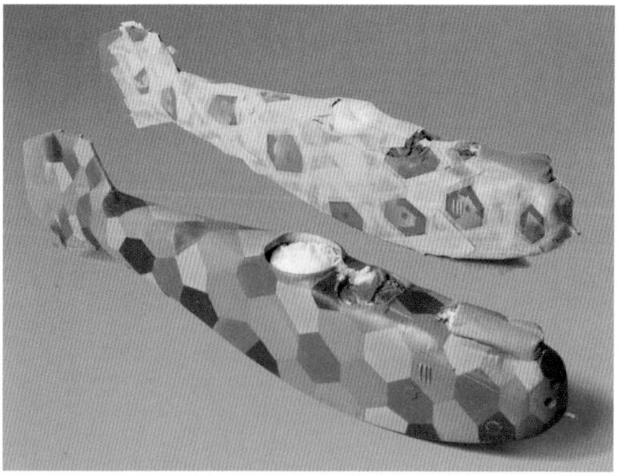

Each separate colour is masked and sprayed, resulting in a complete painted lozenge scheme.

itself or by writing a coded number representing a colour.

Masking tape is then positioned around all shapes containing the palest colour, so that only these areas are exposed. The entire area is sprayed in the first colour. The process is repeated for all other colours in the pattern until you end up with a completed pattern. Any break in the pattern can be touched-up with a brush.

Overpainting Lozenge

Often lozenge patterns were overpainted with a different colour. This may occur when an aircraft that leaves the factory in a lozenge fabric is overpainted with unit or personal markings in the field. The process was also occasionally used by manufacturers to tone down the bright colours of a painted lozenge.

Often the overpainting did not completely cover the lozenge pattern, resulting in an interesting effect that can easily be replicated by building up light coats of colour on top of the lozenge. This process works better with an airbrush, but to get the effect right, the airbrush needs to be in perfect condition. The paint needs to be fairly watered down, so that it can be sprayed at low pressure, but should not be so thin that it runs upon application.

The colour is then applied in light, even coats on top of the lozenge pattern, until the desired effect

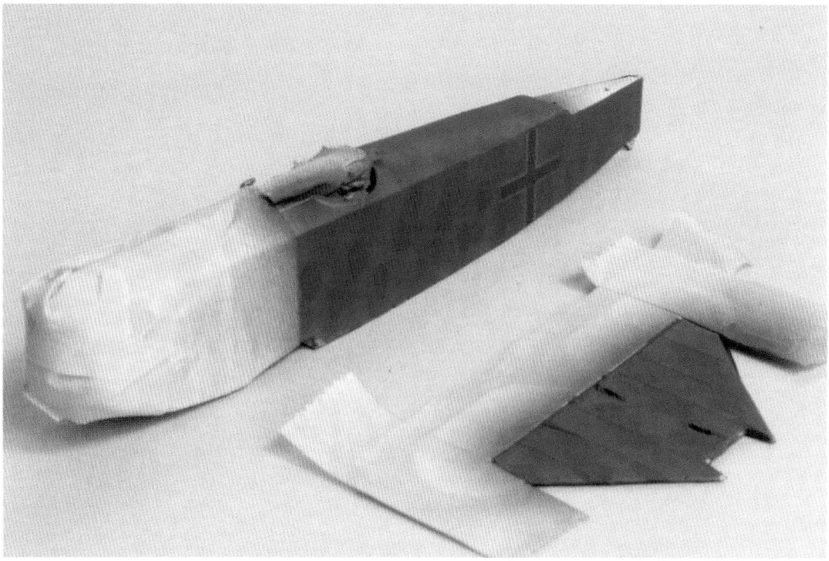

The lozenge decal and fuselage cross has been over-sprayed blue on this Fokker D.VII.

is achieved. Once this state has been reached, the paint should be sealed with varnish, as paint adhesion to a decaled surface is often very poor.

Streaking

Streaked finishes were specific to Fokker-manufactured aircraft and were produced by applying thinned colour in brushed streaks to a base surface, which was normally clear, doped linen. Coloured lacquers were applied to wooden-panelled wings using the same method on the Fokker E.V/D.VIII.

The most effective way of simulating streaking schemes with paint is to replicate the original method of application by applying a thinned paint to a base colour in a streaking pattern. Take care to research the direction of the streaking. Fuselage sides were typically streaked in a downward motion, while wings and decking were streaked diagonally. Using a slow-drying paint medium,

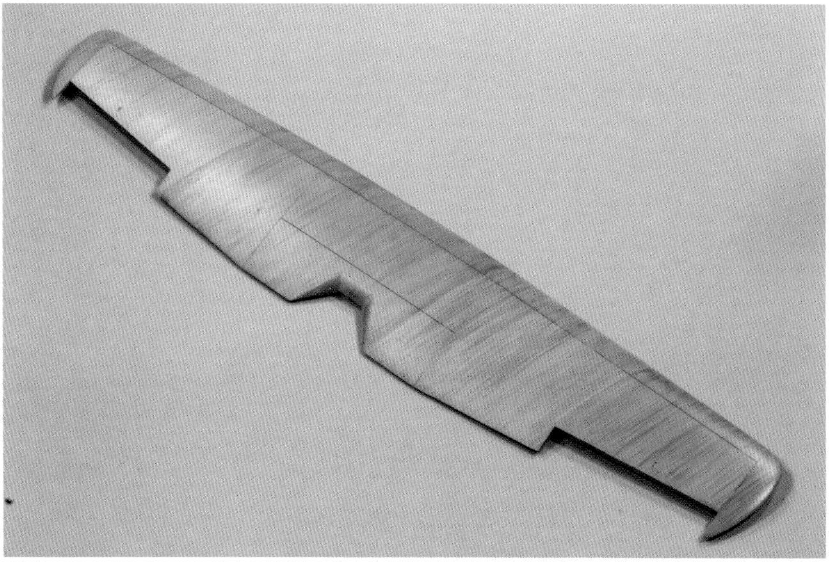

Thin streaks of Lifecolor Tensocrom washes were applied over a simulated plywood surface on this Fokker E.V wing.

Aviattic streaked decals have been applied to this Fokker F.I fuselage.

such as thinned oils, generally produces better results, but whatever medium is chosen, the key is to experiment and practise before committing to the model surface.

Alternatively, aftermarket decals can be used to produce a streaked finished. These products should be applied to the entire surface of the model using the same method as lozenge decals.

Stippling Effects

Some manufacturers applied stippling effects to aircraft surfaces. Perhaps the best-known exponent of this technique was Halberstadt, but manufacturers, including AEG, also experimented with stippling effects. In Halberstadt's case it is theorized that the colours of the stipples were intended to represent the lozenge pattern of the wing coverings.

To simulate stippling effects, I would normally use an old, round, hard-bristled brush with hairs that have become splayed outwards as a result of misuse. A small amount of paint is applied to the brush and the excess is scrubbed away on scrap paper in a similar manner to dry-brushing. Once most of the paint has been removed, dab the brush end a few times on the scrap paper at a 90-degree angle and examine the results. If the test has resulted in a reasonably consistent stipple effect, repeat the dabbing process on the model surface.

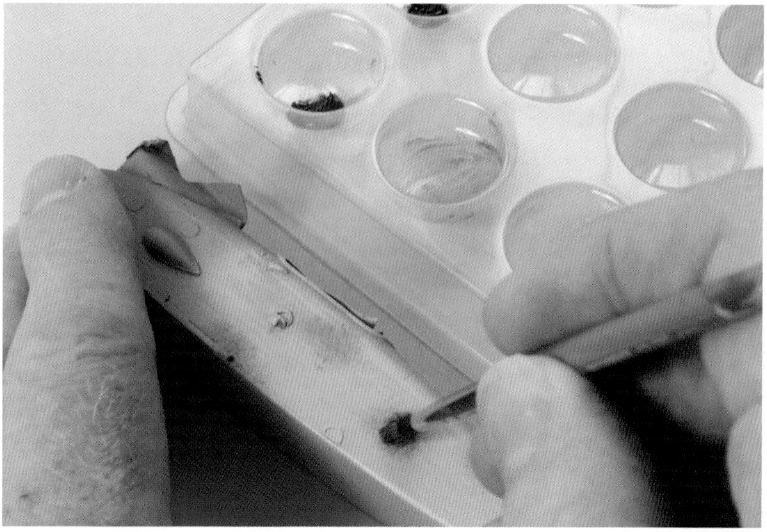

Oil-paint stipples are applied to the Halberstadt, using an old brush with splayed bristles.

I would recommend the use of a slow-drying medium, such as oils, as the finished stipple effect using a fast-drying medium, such as acrylics, will appear less consistent.

The base colour on which the effect is built up should either represent the natural covering material, which in the case of the Halberstadt would be plywood, or any initial finishing that the manufacturer would apply, such as a lozenge pattern.

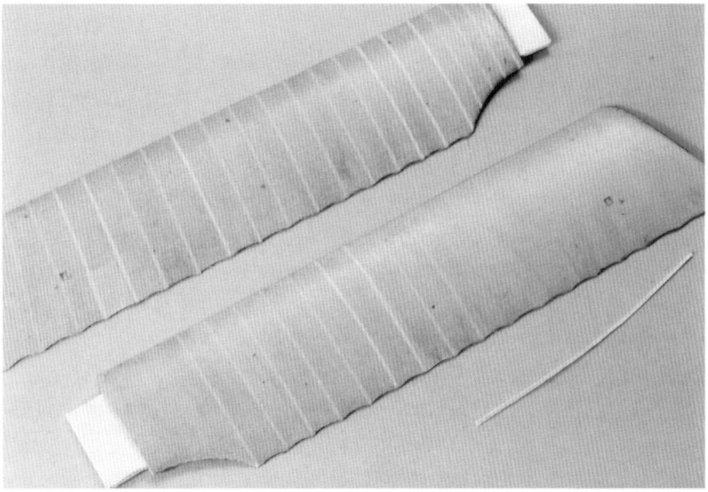

Variation in rib-tape colour and streaking effects help to give the illusion that this FF.33e has been in service for a very long time.

Weathering

Weathering is perhaps one of the most controversial aspects of World War I modelling. Weathering techniques in themselves could fill a whole book and, as such, cannot be covered adequately within this small section.

The majority of German aircraft on the frontline were kept clean during their lifespan. This is because a build-up of dirt would affect the performance of the aircraft and potentially the lifespan of the fabric covering. Even when the Germans were in retreat toward the end of the war, their aircraft were maintained after each flight. This does not mean that weathering effects are not applicable, but the modeller should avoid treating a World War I aircraft like an armoured vehicle.

Soiling effects should be applied subtly, so that they break up a flat colour, rather than become a feature. Heavier soiling effects could be used around stitching, which would also help to emphasize the detail. The one major exception is castor-oil staining on rotary-powered aircraft, which could significantly stain the entire length of a fabric-covered fuselage.

Parts and coverings were often replaced in the field, which can result in variations in colour between different sections. Even small components, such as rib tapes, can be varied in colour shade to suggest replacement.

Patches are a useful method of representing an aircraft that has been in heavy combat and can also be used to cover up any blemishes that may have occurred during the construction process. Simulating paint chipping around the edges of metal panels is also a useful method of suggesting wear and tear.

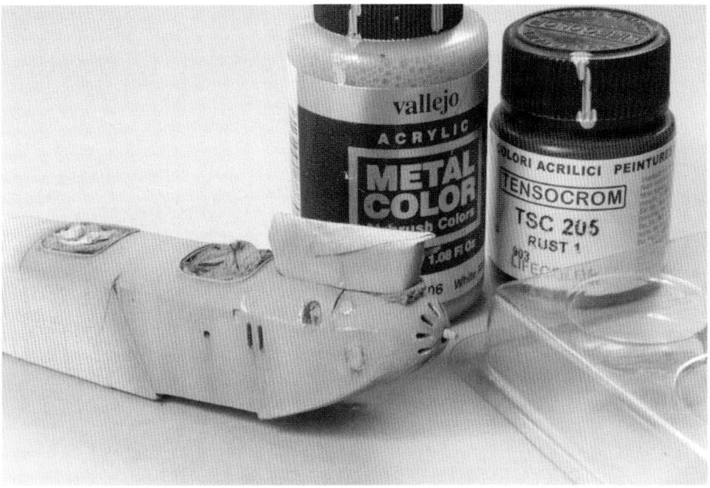

Chipped paint, colour fading and staining effects all combine to suggest a long service life in tough conditions.

DECALS

National Markings

Up until the end of March 1918, all German military aircraft bore the *Eisernes Kreuz* (Iron Cross) as a national marking. Styles of the *Eisernes Kreuz* varied, depending on the period that they were applied. Earlier *Eisernes Kreuz* had wider outside edges and a narrower central section than later versions. As aircraft began to be finished in colours and camouflage schemes, white outlines were added to help make the *Eisernes Kreuz* more visible. Almost overnight, the Iron Cross was replaced with the straight-edged *Balkenkreuz*. Idflieg orders were specific that all aircraft national markings should be altered by 15 April 1918. As a result of this order, many photographs of aircraft from this period will show evidence of the *Eisernes Kreuz* having been overpainted and the *Balkenkreuz* applied on top.

This effect can be relatively easy to simulate by applying an *Eisernes Kreuz*-style decal and then painting over the decal with a suitable colour before applying a *Balkenkreuz* decal over the top. Logic suggests that the Germans would have chosen a paint that was as close as possible to the original background colour when overpainting, but this may not always have been the case.

Choosing a Decal Scheme

Choice of a suitable decal scheme does not necessarily need to be limited to the options provided within a kit. Aftermarket companies, such as Pheon and Print Scale, produce a number of decal sets for World War I aircraft. Markings can also be sourced from spares, cut from coloured decal stock or even printed on your home printer.

When printing your own decals, it is important to understand that the printer is unable to print the colour white. This means that complicated white shapes, such as letters, are impossible to achieve. In addition, most colours, with the exception of black, require a white background in order to show up correctly. A complicated and colourful motif will either need to be printed on white decal paper and carefully cut around or printed on clear paper that is then applied to a white-painted background. These kinds of problems are not impossible to solve but it is important to be aware of them before embarking on a printing project.

Decal artwork can be produced in a number of ways, but each separate marking will need to end up as an image file. At this stage, the decal artwork should not be scaled and should be significantly larger than required.

On this AEG G.IV the Eisernes Kreuz *has been roughly overpainted with a grey paint. The* Balkenkreuz *has been applied to a different area of the fuselage.*

In the case of this Hannover, only the serial number was used from the kit decal sheet. The arrow was cut from white decal paper, while other decals were sourced from spares. The number '4' was originally from an FT-17 tank kit.

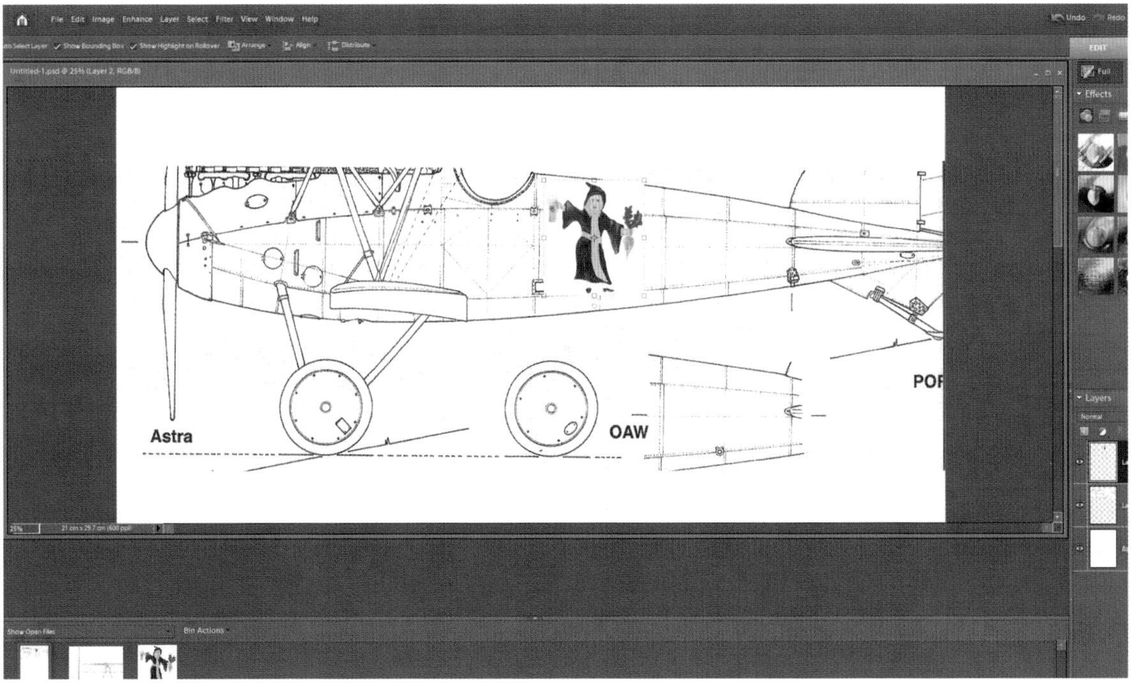

The Münchner kindl *motif from the Albatros build is scaled on top of scanned scale drawings.*

Scan suitable drawings of your subject in your chosen scale to a size of 300dpi and upload them into a suitable art program or word processor. The size of the plans should not be altered, so that if printed out, they will be the same size as the original. Upload your decal artwork on to the program and use the plans as an aid to scaling your decal artwork. Once happy with the scale, cut and paste your scaled artwork to a blank page and begin building your decal sheet.

I would suggest printing a test sheet on normal paper that can be used to check that the size of the decals correctly fits the model. Once everything is satisfactory, print the decal sheet on to white or clear decal paper and seal the surface with a few coats of varnish.

The decals can then be cut out and used as normal. I usually print twice as many decals as I require, just in case I experience problems.

The printed Münchner kindl *motif is applied to the model.*

Chapter Eight

Building a Gotha

INTRODUCTION

As an example of a larger twin-engine project, I have chosen the 1/72-scale Roden Gotha G.III. There are a number of reasons for this. First, the kit is easy to obtain and can be purchased for a reasonable price. Second, Roden kits tend to be a little rough around the edges and, as such, present a different set of challenges to previous builds in this book. Aspects of a kit that modellers of 'state of the art' products take for granted, such as exemplary fit and acceptable detail, do not always apply to Roden products. This does not mean that these kits are bad. On the contrary, they build into lovely little models, but they do require a little more work to get there.

The Gotha G.III was the forerunner to the Gotha bombers that crossed the channel and brought the war to the South-East of England from the summer of 1917. Unlike the G.IV and G.V, the G.III had a fuselage that was predominantly fabric-covered. Otherwise the G.III looked very similar in appearance to later variants.

The Roden Gotha G.III kit builds into an impressive model.

Roden Gotha G.III

The Roden G.III was initially released at the beginning of the millennium and was the first of a range of Gotha kits to hit the market. The kit itself consists of seven main sprues of which two are duplicates consisting of parts that are present in two or more positions on the model.

One of the biggest problems with Roden products is the decals – they generally don't age very well and often shatter as soon as they touch water. For this reason, whenever I build a Roden kit, I usually either use aftermarket decals or find creative ways of making my own markings.

To help detail this kit, I have also used an aftermarket photo-etch set produced by a company called PART. These sets are still available and generally very good value. Some photo-etch sets waste a lot of material trying to replace detail that is already present and to a satisfactory level of quality on the original kit. The Gotha PART set actually adds many extra details and, as such, is well worth investing in.

References

The main references I used during this build were the *Albatros Windsock special; 'Gotha'*, which covers the series of Gothas from the G.II to the G.Vb, and the Aeronaut book, *Gotha Aircraft of World War I.*

In addition, I downloaded the Wingnut Wings' instruction manual for the Gotha G.IV kit, as the G.III and G.IV have many similarities. With the absence of any internal photographs of the G.III, it appears that both PART and Roden have chosen to use photographs of the interior of later Gothas as a reference.

The *Windsock Special* includes a collection of 1/72- and 1/48-scale drawings of the G.III in the centre of the book that are particularly useful, especially when it comes to aligning the wings.

The initial source of inspiration for the markings that I would ultimately use also came from the *Windsock Special*, which includes a photograph of a G.III of Kaghol 2 with sets of three diamonds adorning the nose and fuselage sides. The Aeronaut book includes an artist's interpretation of this aircraft and it is on this profile that I based my model.

BUILDING THE GOTHA

Interior

No matter what scale I work in, I like to include a reasonable representation of the subject's interior. The Gotha's interior is very open and visible and, as such, any improvement that can be made will have a major effect on the finished model. Luckily, the PART set includes an excellent interior upgrade and most improvements that I made were based around this set.

The first thing I needed to do was to remove all the interior sidewall detail from the two fuselage halves, so that I could replace the moulded detail with photo-etch. I initially used a small,

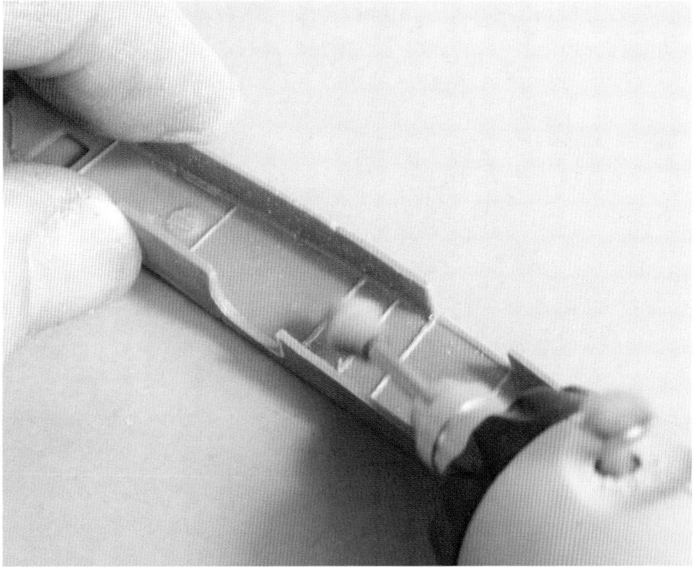

A powered rotary tool is used to remove internal detail from the sidewalls.

Photo-etch framework detail has been glued on to the internal sidewalls.

rotary-power tool to remove the bulk of the detail. These tools are useful aids but should be treated with care. I would highly recommend only using a rotary tool with adjustable speeds. Never use the tool at full speed, as it will almost certainly melt the plastic. A sanding stick was also used to clean up and smooth the surface of the plastic.

I decided to paint the interior before adding the photo-etch. Only the nose section, up to the rear of the cockpit, had a plywood covering, the rest of the airframe was fabric-covered. I began the process by spraying the interior with a very off-white colour to represent bleached linen, while the plywood areas were sprayed with a Tamiya Wooden Deck Tan base colour. Oil paint was used on the wooden areas to simulate staining and varnish. The photo-etch framework was then very carefully shaped and glued in position, gradually applying glue in stages to the underside of the framework, beginning at the nose and working toward the rear of the fuselage. The framework was then painted.

All of the internal bulkhead parts and photo-etch floor sections were then cleaned up and painted. Some of the crew seats that glue directly to the bulkheads were reshaped to round off the original square-shaped parts. Once painted, the bulkheads were all cemented into one side of the fuselage.

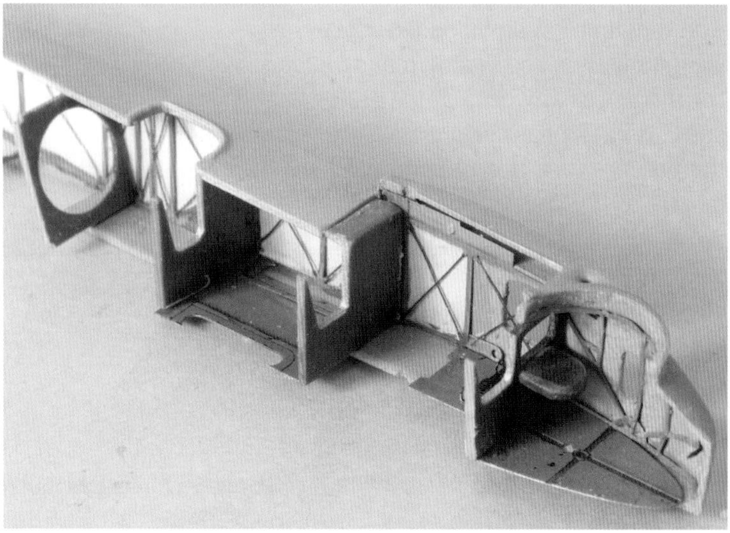

The kit bulkheads and photo-etch floors are fitted into the port-side fuselage half.

The control column and pilot's seat. The seat has been heavily modified from the original kit part.

The kit's pilot seat is depicted as having an arm on the left side. References for later Gothas suggest that there is a box-shaped control panel in this position and I can only theorize that this is what Roden were actually trying to depict. I removed this arm and also the block of plastic underneath the seat that made the part look like an armchair. Brass rod was shaped into a pair of leg supports, which were glued to the underside of the seat. A piece of plasticard was cut and shaped to depict the box-shaped control panel.

Most of the rest of the interior was assembled from the photo-etch sheet, although I did use the original kit interior bomb racks, as I felt that these parts were better than the replacements. The instrument panel was built up from layers of photo-etch and clear printed plastic sheet. The back of the clear printed sheet is intended to be painted white before assembly, but I chose to replace the rear photo-etch part of the assembly with white plasticard, negating a need for paint. A fuel pump was made from brass tubing with a T-shaped handle cut from spare photo-etch fret. Basic seatbelts were cut from masking tape and detailed with spare photo-etch to represent metal fittings, for most of the crew seats. Eduard pre-painted seatbelts were used for the pilot's seat.

The instrument panel, fuel pump and what I assume to be the fuel transfer pump were fitted into a separate cockpit canopy part, which is designed to glue into the port side of the fuselage. I found this particular assembly difficult to fit into the fuselage half to the correct angle and I ended up using a lot of filler to disguise the poor joint. The two fuselage halves were then glued together ensuring that the horizontal base rod

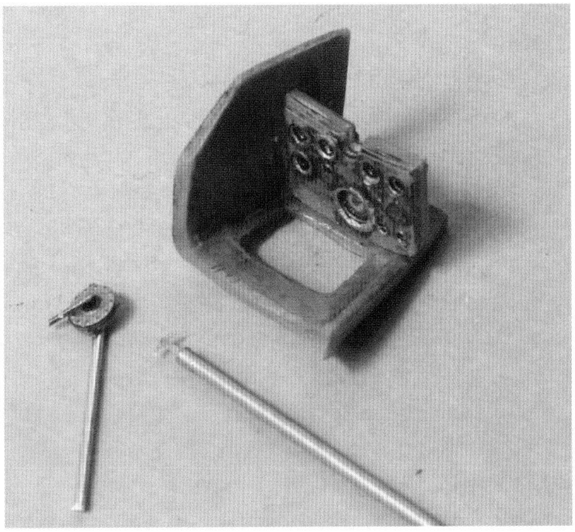

The photo-etch instrument panel fitted inside the cockpit canopy. The fuel pump is manufactured predominantly from brass tubing.

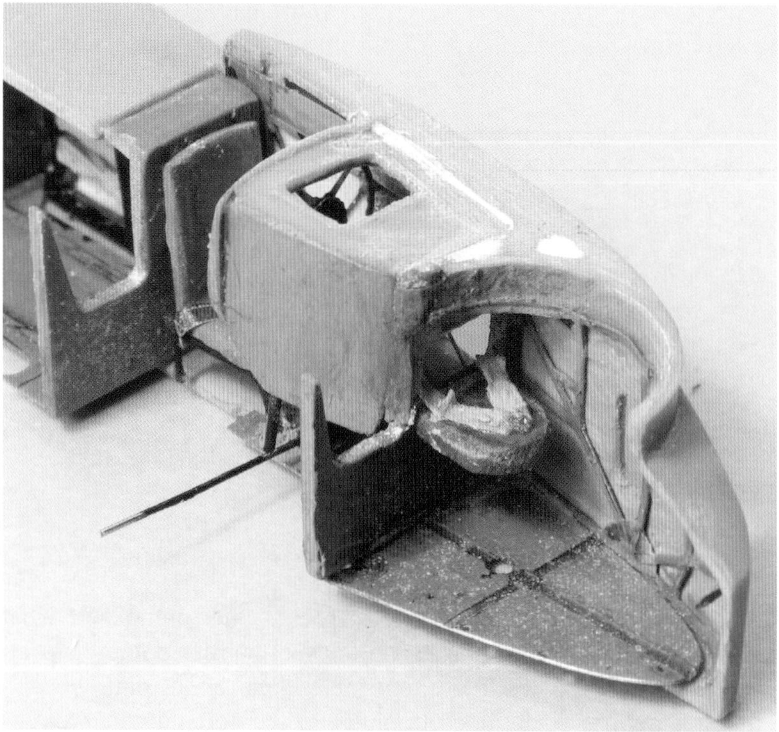

The cockpit canopy was difficult to align correctly with the fuselage.

of the control column fitted through holes that I had made in each sidewall. I also glued the central lower-wing section in position at this stage of the build.

Engines and Nacelles

The Roden nacelles require a fair amount of work before they are suitable for use. The opening in the top of each nacelle part is too narrow. This is not just an accuracy issue, but also makes it impossible to position the engines correctly within the nacelle. The width of the openings was extended using a razor saw to cut out the unwanted sections before cleaning up with sanding sticks and needle files.

A large number of louvres also need to be removed from each side of each nacelle. This is because Roden have produced generic nacelles that cover a number of different variants in order to reduce tooling costs. Early Gotha G.IIs and G.IIIs typically had four louvres on each side of each nacelle, although I would suggest checking references, as this was not always the case. I used a sharp scalpel to cut the unwanted louvres carefully away from each part. The nacelles were then cleaned up with fine sanding sticks.

The engines in this kit are fairly basic when compared to those that have been built in earlier chapters; however, almost nothing will be seen once they are fitted into the nacelle. I did, however, reshape the nose of each crankcase.

There is also no real benefit in using the kit's manifolds as they will not be seen and, ultimately, they make it more difficult to fit the engine inside the nacelle. Even with modifications to the nacelle, the engine was still difficult to fit, requiring alterations to the depth of the plastic lips that act as engine-bearers.

A razor saw was used to extend the nacelle openings.

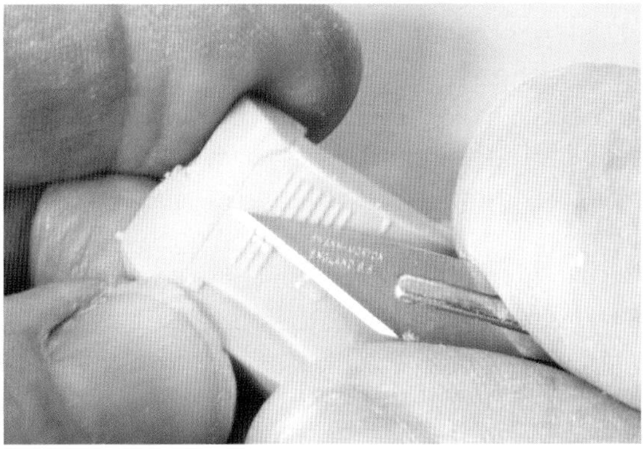

Unwanted louvres were carefully sliced away from each nacelle.

Replacement engine-covers were shaped from plasticard and glued into the nacelle opening.

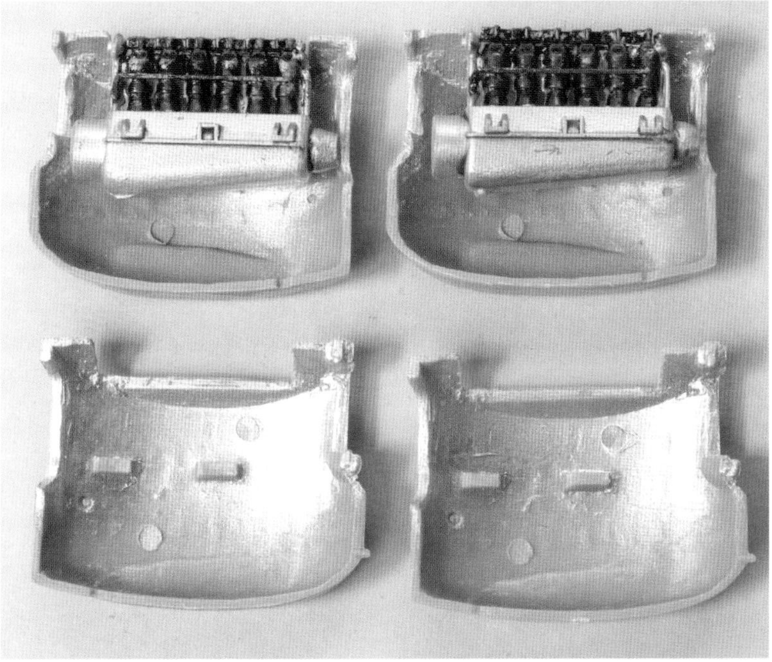

Engines are fitted inside the nacelles before the nacelle shells are closed.

This was achieved by trial and error – taking a little depth from each bearer at a time and dry-fitting.

Plasticard was bent to shape and used to replace the nacelle engine-covers, as my earlier adjustment of the opening had rendered the kit parts unusable. These were glued in place and then sanded to level the shape with the top of the nacelle.

Photo-etch radiators and access panels replaced the kit parts; however, I did not use the radiator filler cap/electrical thermometer. I chose to replace this part with a scratch-built item made by fitting a preformed piece of thin brass rod into the end of plastic strut stock via a predrilled hole. Both the wire and strut stock were then trimmed and shaped before fitting in place on to the top of each radiator.

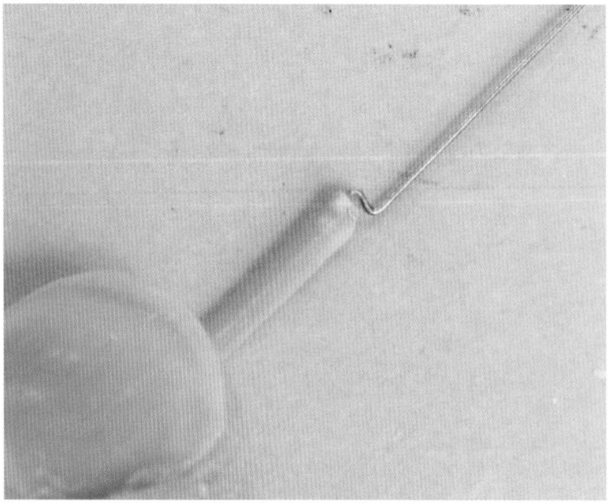

Radiator filler caps/electrical thermometers were made from brass rod and plastic strut stock.

Upper Wing and Rudder

The upper wing is provided in three sections. These parts required a lot of cleaning, especially along the trailing edge where an abundance of flash was present. Like most 1/72-scale models, the ailerons are moulded into the wing in a neutral position. I prefer to angle my ailerons. On most World War I aircraft, left and right ailerons should be angled in opposite positions, so that one faces up and the other faces down while the aircraft is resting. I used a razor saw to cut through the chord-wise edges of the ailerons and then carefully bent each aileron to the position I required. A coat of Liquid Poly was then brushed across the seam in an attempt to repair any weakness caused by bending the part. Once dry, I used small strips of plasticard to simulate aileron hinges.

The upper-wing attachments do not have any location lugs and so before fitting the parts together, reinforcement pins were made from brass rod. The three sections of the wing were then glued together, ensuring that the angle of dihedral dictated by the shape of the centre piece continued along each wing. Finally, the gravity tank was fitted to the central section of the upper wing.

The shape of the rudder does not conform to my drawings, as the bottom edge should have a more regular curve than depicted on the kit part. This was reshaped with a sanding stick. At this stage, I also fitted a pair of photo-etch control horns. The control horns were intended to be folded and fitted to each side of the rudder, but I chose to use each piece to represent one left and right pair of horns. To achieve this, the rudder was separated from the stabilizer and slots were cut into the inside edge of the rudder for the control horns. Each unfolded control horn piece was then slotted into position and glued.

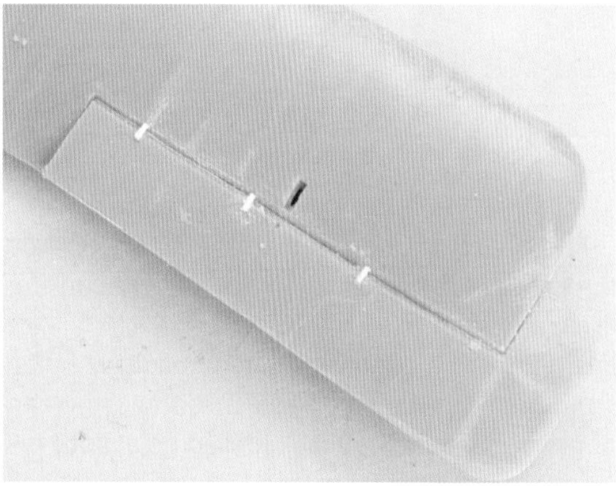

Once each aileron was bent into position, hinges cut from plastic strip were added.

Once the chord-wise edges of the aileron have been cut free, the aileron can be bent to shape.

The three sections of the upper wing were pinned together with brass rod.

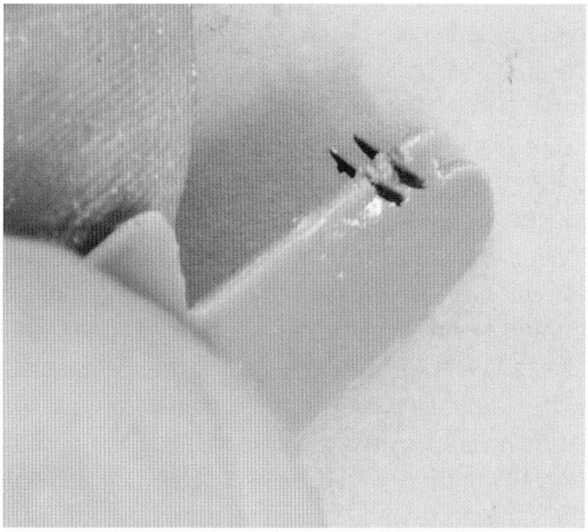

Photo-etch control horns are slotted into the inside edge of the rudder.

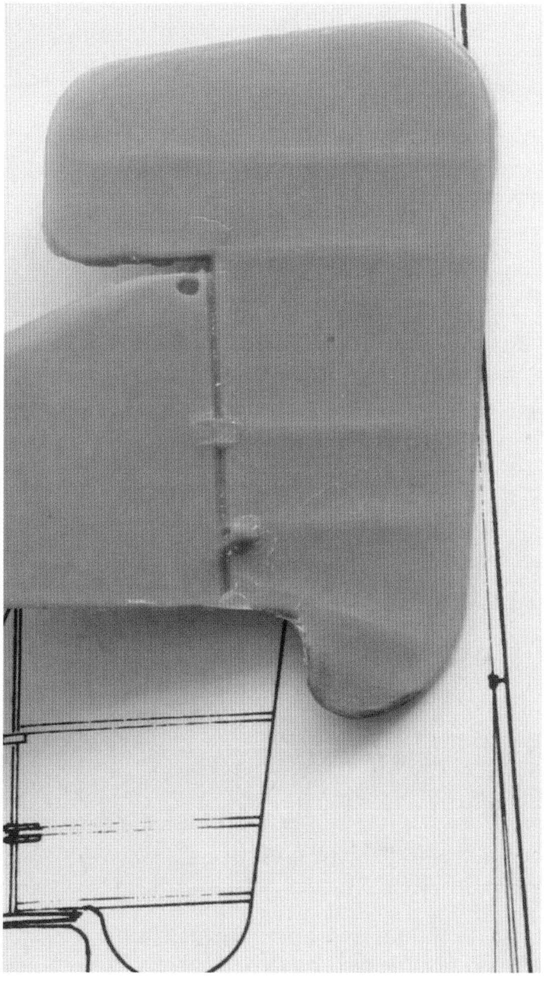

This photograph illustrates the difference between the shape of the kit part and Windsock drawings of the G.III. Note the difference in curvature at the base of the rudder.

Colours and Markings

As far as I'm aware, the exact colour of these early Gothas is unknown. The dark shade on photos has led to the belief that the upper sides of the aircraft were finished in an overall dark-green or perhaps *feldgrau.* The undersides of the fabric-covered areas appear to have been linen, while the wooden areas probably had a dark-stained finish.

I chose to use Tamiya RLM Grey as a representation of *feldgrau*, while the undersides were treated as bleached linen with yellowed varnish.

I began by spraying the base wood colour and then used a Burnt Sienna oil paint to represent the staining. Once this section was completely dry, it was masked and the base coat of the fabric colour applied, followed by the upper side *feldgrau.*

The undersides of the wings have very unrealistic looking sink lines to represent the rib positions. These sink lines are not particularly deep and I felt that they could probably be disguised by applying decal rib tapes. I randomly lightly sprayed lines of brown wash chord-wise and then over-sprayed the underside of the wing with a light coat of the base colour. I then applied strips of Aviattic linen decals to represent rib tapes.

The markings came from a number of sources. The series of diamonds on the nose and fuselage sides were cut from white decal paper. The Gothamaker's logos on both sides of the fin were sourced from a Gotha G.IV aftermarket set of decals. The *Eisernes Kreuz* national markings on the rudder and fuselage came from my spares' box.

Linen decal strips were used to disguise the sunken rib positions and simulate rib tapes.

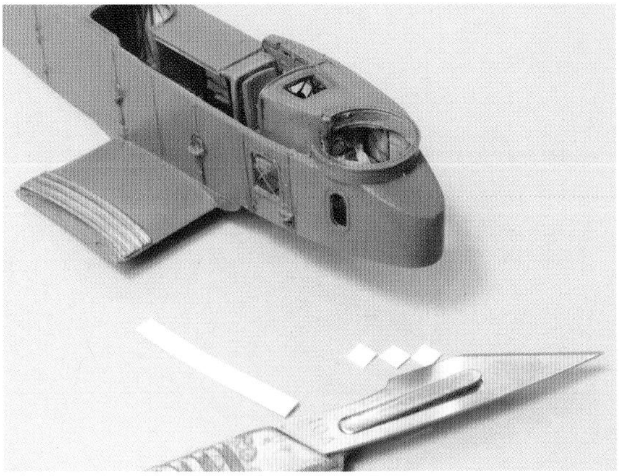

The distinctive diamond markings were cut from white decal paper.

Finishing the Fuselage

Even though the fuselage was now painted and decaled, there were still a number of finishing touches required before moving on to the wing assembly. To begin with, the horizontal stabilizers and elevators needed to be fitted. These were treated in the same way as the ailerons, in that the elevator was bent into position and the seam sealed with Liquid Poly. Hinges were made from plastic strip and control horns cut from spare photo-etch fret. To conform with drawings, the inside edge of the stabilizers needed to be reshaped, after which brass rod reinforcement pins were fitted.

The Gotha is fairly unusual, in that most of the control lines are fitted externally. For the modeller, this means that the wires need to be fitted before the wings are assembled, otherwise access to some areas will be difficult. I began by drilling a hole into each side of the forward section of the fuselage for the rudder control lines. Two pieces of mending thread were inserted into each of these positions and glued. Each thread was then located at various positions along the outside of the fuselage with a spot of cyanoacrylate and finally glued to each rudder control horn. Photo-etch elevator controllers were then fitted in place on to the

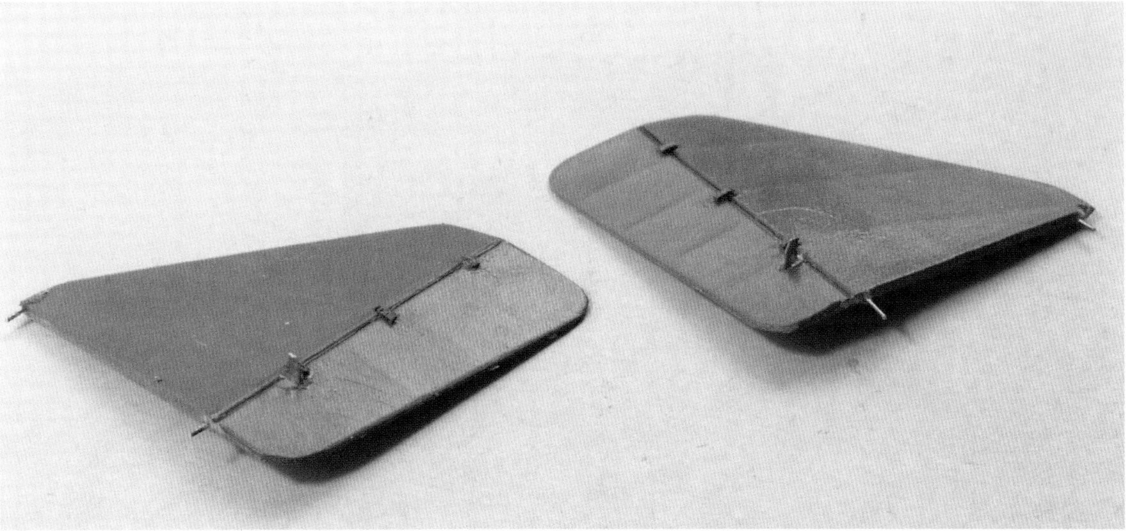

Horizontal stabilizers with adjusted elevator positions and photo-etch control horns.

exposed tips of the horizontal base of the control column. Before the controllers were fitted to the fuselage, two pieces of thread were glued to the opposing edges of each part. With each controller in position, these threads were then glued along the outside of the fuselage, following the same process as I had already done with

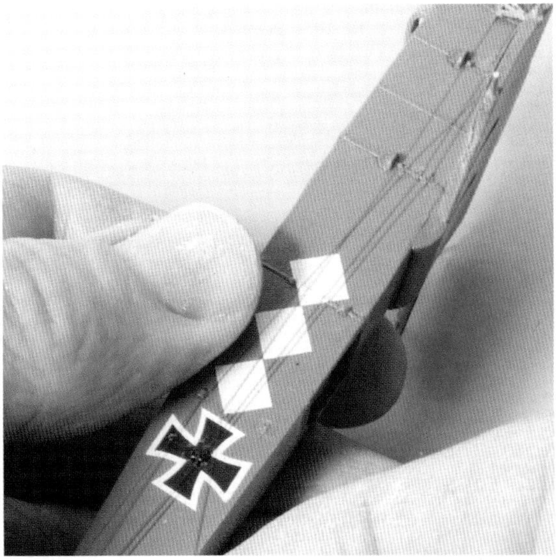

Control wires made from monofilament are fitted to the outside of the fuselage.

the rudder lines. At this stage, I did not trim the excess threads completely back just in case they needed repairing later in the construction process.

A small photo-etch throttle-control system was assembled and painted while still on its photo-etch fret. Once separated from the fret, the small assembly was fitted next to the pilot's position.

I used the windows that came with the photo-etch set, which are printed on to a small piece of acetate. Once they had been carefully cut out, each window was glued in position with white glue.

Wing Assembly and Rigging

Dry-fitting the engine nacelles to the central wing section exposed a potential problem with the angle of the nacelle when viewed from the side. As a result, the nacelle position was slightly adjusted to improve the alignment using brass reinforcement pins to hold the nacelles in place at the corrected angle.

In the case of the Gotha, it made more sense to assemble the upper wing to the central area first before fitting the lower wings in place. One problem with the kit seems to be that the strut lengths are variable. The cabane struts, however, did appear to be reasonably correct in comparison

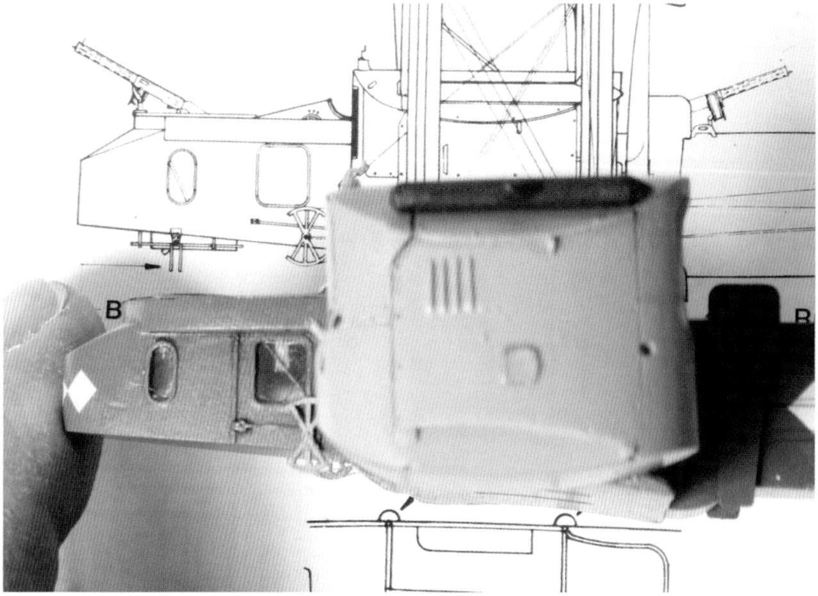

Note how the nacelle pitches slightly forward in its original position in comparison to drawings.

to drawings and so these were fitted first, ensuring that they were set at an angle, slightly leaning forward, as is apparent on the drawings. Once these were in place, the upper wing was very carefully test-fitted, mainly to check that the angle of incidence appeared reasonably correct.

The front nacelle struts appear to be too long, although this may be because they were originally intended to slot through the nacelle. Having adjusted the size of the engine covers, the nacelle strut location points needed re-drilling. The front nacelle struts were cut down to a size a little larger than the drawings suggested and temporarily spot-glued into place. I then followed a process of dry-fitting the wing and adjusting the strut lengths until everything fitted and aligned.

The original nacelle strut length is considerably longer than drawings suggest.

While these struts are not intended to meet at the upper tip, I decided it would be easier to glue the upper tips together and then make the location hole in the upper wing deeper and wider, giving the impression that they are separate. This created a much stronger base to which to fit the upper wing.

During this process, it soon became apparent that the nacelle strut location holes in the upper wing were incorrectly positioned and needed to be re-drilled. In order to determine the correct locations, the upper wing was laid upper side down on to a flat surface. The fuselage was then carefully placed on top so that the cabane struts aligned with the corresponding recesses in the upper wing. I then used a marking tool to pinpoint the new position of each nacelle strut recess. New holes were then drilled into the upper wing and the assembly was test-fitted.

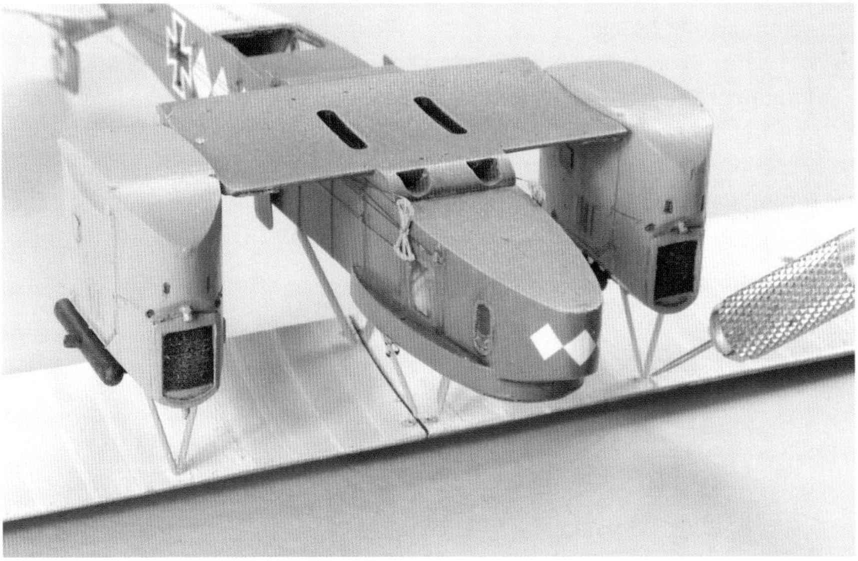

Revised strut positions were marked into the upper wing prior to drilling new locations.

The same process was followed for the remaining nacelle struts, ensuring that the upper-wing alignment looked correct from all angles.

Some G.IIIs, including the subject I was building, had a third support cabane strut resulting in an 'N'-shaped configuration. A brass strut was fitted between each front and rear cabane positions to simulate this.

The fuselage section, nacelles and wings were then prepared for rigging by drilling holes into all of the relevant positions. Because the wings are fairly thin, holes were drilled completely through the substance of the wing. The upper wing was then glued to the fuselage and nacelle assembly in an upside-down position, so that I could see that all the struts were located correctly and that alignment was correct.

The inner bay between the nacelles and fuselage was then rigged by gluing monofilament into location points on the fuselage, nacelle or through the lower wing and then feeding the opposite end of the thread through the corresponding hole in

Brass 'Strutz' was used to add a missing section to each set of cabane struts.

The upper wing is glued in position.

the upper wing. These ends were pulled tight and locked in position with cyanoacrylate.

One feature of the inner bay area of the Gotha is a 'Y'-shaped rigging section that runs from a single line in the nacelle to two lines that fit into the upper wing. To simulate this, it was necessary to knot two pieces of thread together, glue the knot and then cut one of the four ends away from as close to the knot as possible. One end of the thread was then glued into the nacelle, estimating the length required before the line branches into two. Once dry, the two remaining ends were threaded through their holes in the upper wing, pulled tight and locked.

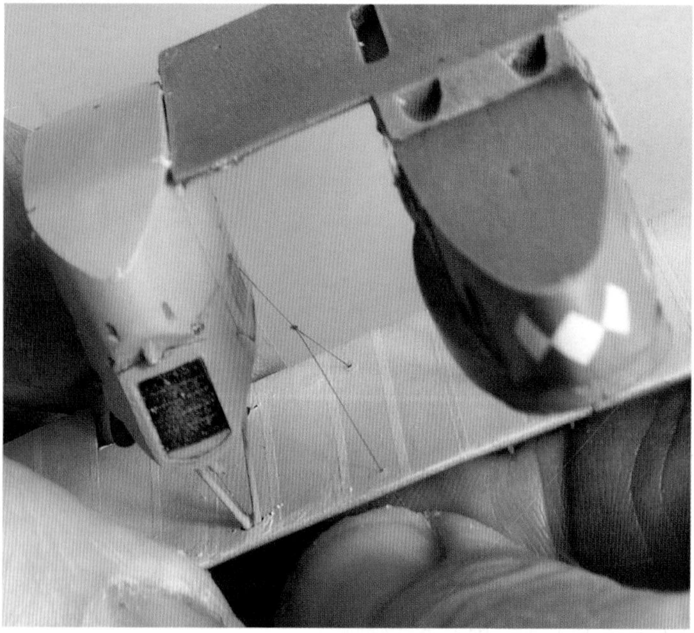

Two ends of a piece of Y-shaped rigging are simultaneously pulled through the upper wing and locked in place.

Each inner bay is completely rigged before fitting the lower wings.

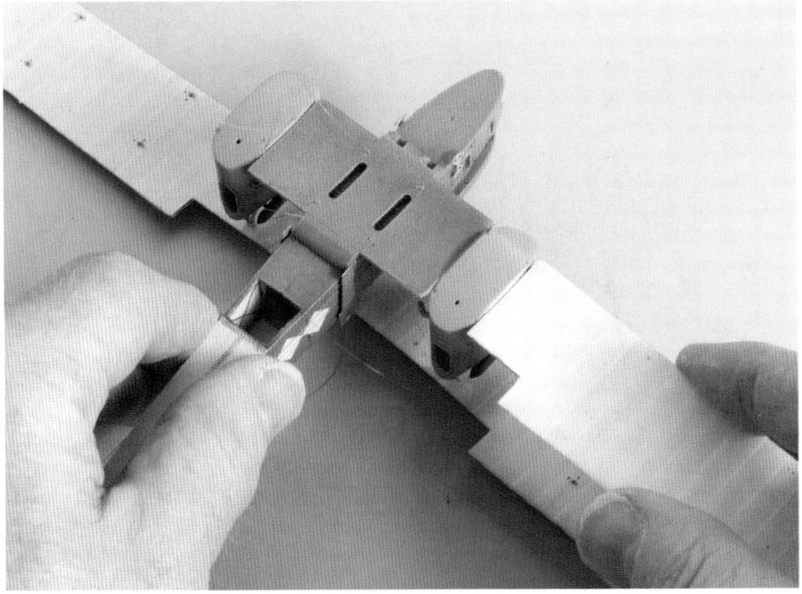

The first of the lower wings is slotted in position.

With the rigging of the inner bays completed, one of the lower wings was then glued into position, ensuring that it aligned with the upper wing from all directions.

I then began the process of spring-fitting interplane struts into position, beginning from the inside and working outwards. The kit struts were slightly too small and so I replaced them with items cut from brass 'Strutz'. Another problem I had was that some of the location holes didn't align very well with each other, which, if uncorrected, would result in incorrect strut angles. To rectify this, I made individual adjustments to the underside strut-attachment positions, using a marker and drill. For some reason, this problem was more acute on the inner bays.

One by one, interplane struts were spring-fitted into position. Some location recesses needed moving so that the struts would appear to stand at the correct angle.

Once all of the interplane struts on one side were fitted, the assembled area was rigged using the same process as in the central inner bay area, beginning with the incidence wires on each bay. The wing assembly and rigging process was then repeated for the wing on the opposite side.

At this stage, all the loose thread ends were still protruding from the outside of the wings. Each thread end was removed as flush to the surface of the model as possible. Any visible lumps of cyanoacrylate were also sliced away in an attempt to help reduce the amount of sanding required in the area. A small amount of filler was applied to each rigging position and, finally, the area around each rigging position was sanded with light grade paper until completely level. This is easier to achieve on the upper surface of the wing than the underside but, essentially, the same process was applied to both surfaces.

The completed wing and rigging assembly. Note, at this stage excess thread has not been removed.

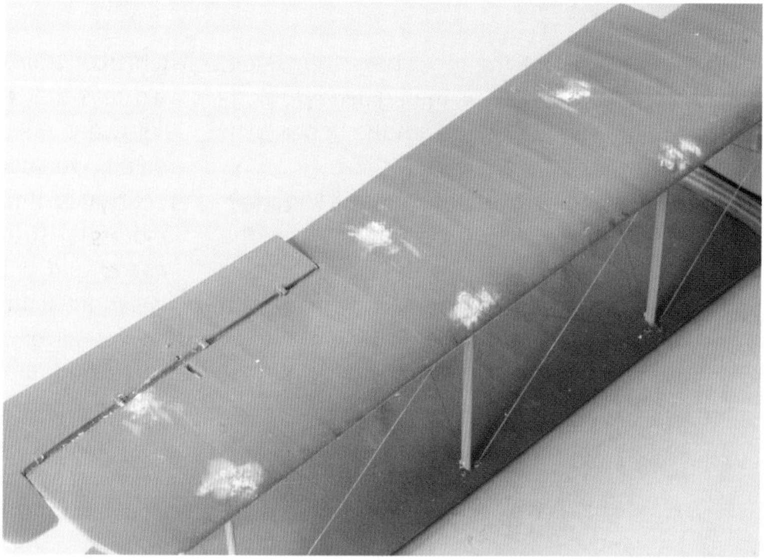

Cleaned up rigging locations prior to refinishing.

These areas were then resprayed by holding the tip of the airbrush very close to the model and applying very little pressure to the trigger. Using this method, only minimal masking was required.

I could not find any suitable replacements for the upper and lower wing *Eisernes Kreuz* and so attempted to repair the white outlined upper wing Roden decals using Liquid Decal Film. Liquid Decal Film is a solution that is painted on to the surface of the decal and dries into a film. It is useful when you have old decals that are cracked, as it can help to bond the cracked parts together. Once dry, the decal should be cut from its sheet as neatly and as close to the actual print as possible. I still experienced some shattering, but the decals were just about useable.

For the underside national markings, I cut the original decal from the sheet and used it as a template to cut identical shapes from larger spares.

The original decals are used as templates from which to cut replacements.

Undercarriage and Various Details

One issue that was very noticeable on my model was that you could see the inside seam where the fuselage halves were joined together from the large opening in the underside. To fix this problem, I used a piece of plasticard, cut to fit the width of the decking, to hide the seam.

Once the tail-skid was fitted, I used brass rod to replace its supports. Location holes for the undercarriage struts were drilled out and then the vertical V-shaped undercarriage strut parts were fitted in place. The axles were slotted in-between each set of struts.

Bomb racks were modified using the photo-etch updates. Once painted, the racks were glued to the underside of the model. The attachment positions needed to be drilled deeper before fitting the racks in place.

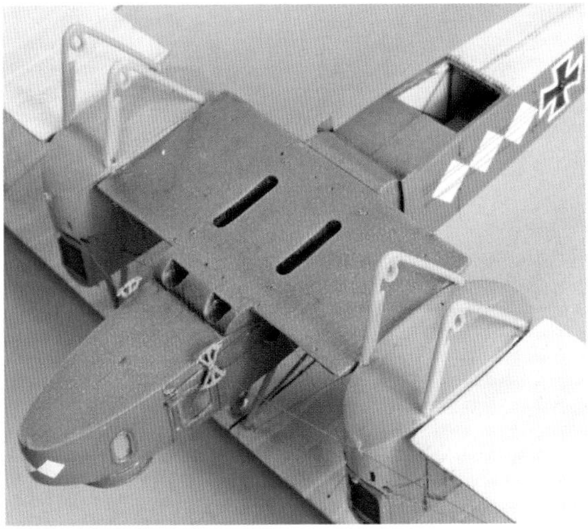

V-shaped undercarriage struts were fitted directly to each engine nacelle before adding the axles.

The bombload and wheels have been fitted to the almost complete model.

Wheels and bombs were painted and fitted. I used masking tape to create the black and white wheel covers, but the tyres were painted freehand.

A photo-etch replacement gun rail was folded and fitted to the rear upper-deck of the fuselage. Finally, two Parabellum machine-guns were assembled. The PART set provides complete photo-etch replacements, but I decided just to use the cooling jackets, as I felt that the original Roden parts were generally better. The guns were then fitted in position along with the propellers, marking the final process of the build.

FINALLY

The Gotha provides examples of a number of challenges that are typical of a more limited-run style of kit. Unlike the earlier builds in this book, which could, in theory, be built without the aid of any reference material or drawings, the Gotha would have been impossible to complete without such material. The Gotha also serves as an example of how a small scale, such as 1/72, can still include a reasonable level of detail, so that when viewed in a photograph it would be difficult to recognize that the model was constructed in a smaller scale.

Modellers who prefer 'state-of-the-art' projects have a number of twin engine subjects to choose from including this Wingnut Wings AEG G.IV.

Chapter Nine

Odds and Ends

INTRODUCTION

The purpose of this chapter is to detail modelling aspects that have not already been adequately covered. The sections in this chapter cover three distinct subjects. The first details some of those finishing touches that are added to the model in the final stages of the build. The second section provides a brief overview of techniques required to build kits manufactured from alternatives to injection moulded plastic. The final section will discuss aspects of the hobby that occur once the model is complete, such as photography and displaying at shows.

FINISHING TOUCHES

Machine-Guns and Ordnance

German machine-guns used in aircraft during the World War I can be split into two main types: those that were designed to be mounted in a fixed position and those that were designed to be mounted on a flexible platform.

Most German fixed machine-guns were produced by Spandau Arsenal. The original water-cooled MG08 was superseded by the lighter MG08/15, which, unlike its predecessor, was designed specifically for use on aircraft.

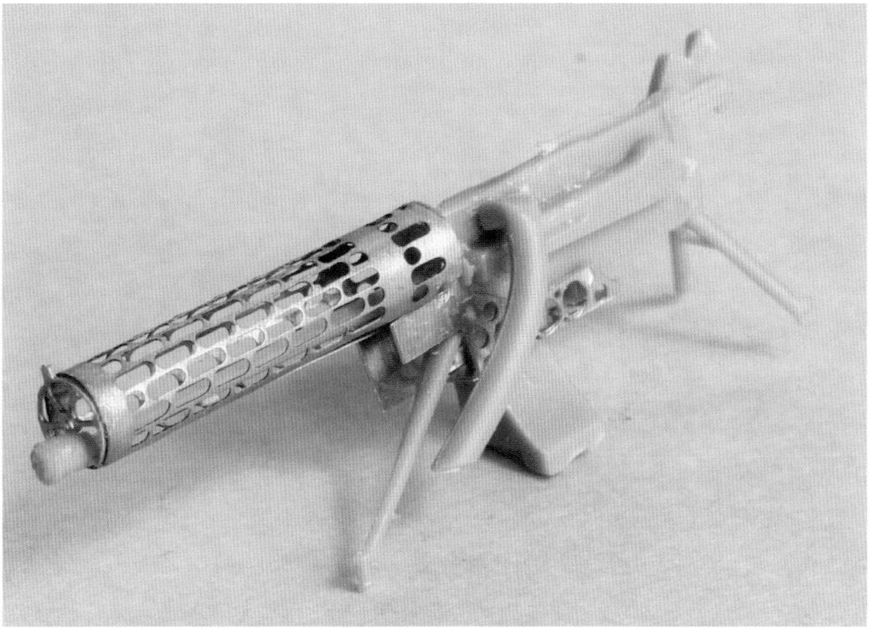

This Wingnut Wings' Spandau is a good example of a high-quality injection-moulded machine-gun with photo-etch details.

Machine-guns used on flexible mountings, such as gun rings, were known as Parabellum guns and were manufactured by Deutsche Waffen und Munitionsfabriken. Unlike the fixed Spandau guns, Parabellums had ammunition drums that could be easily replaced in flight. The design of the Parabellum also evolved throughout the war, as methods were employed to save weight.

There are three common methods of simulating machine-guns. The first is by using a simple, one-piece, injection-moulded, resin or white metal piece that would typically come with the kit. Alternatively, a gun can be assembled from a combination of moulded parts and photo-etch details. An option for this method is often included within premium kits or, alternatively, photo-etch replacements can be obtained separately. Another method is to replace the kit guns with aftermarket items, such as the 3D-printed products produced by Gaspatch. For most experienced modellers, the use of photo-etch is the most common method of constructing a German machine-gun.

Assembling Photo-Etch Detailed Machine-Guns

Assembling a photo-etch detailed machine-gun can be fiddly but, like most processes, becomes easier with practice. Assuming that the kit does not come with optional moulded parts for use with photo-etch, the first step is to remove the cooling jacket from the butt of the original plastic machine-gun part. If the tip of the gun barrel is well detailed, you may also wish to remove this area for later use.

I prefer to fit a barrel made from rod or tubing to the butt, as this usually helps to align the cooling jacket parts, although this is not always necessary. I would, typically, drill a hole into the cut edge of the butt to insert the length of rod.

Photo-etch cooling jackets need to be rolled around a suitably sized template in order to create their shape. Drill bits are often ideal for this purpose. Prior to rolling, some photo-etch products require annealing, otherwise it will be impossible to create a perfectly smooth shape. Annealing is a process whereby the photo-etch is heated over a cool flame, such as from a candle, which softens the material.

Once the photo-etch cooling jacket has been rolled into shape, it is not necessary to glue the two edges together. When gluing the cooling jacket to the butt, cyanoacrylate can be applied to one end of the rolled cooling jacket before it is completely removed from its template, making handling easier. Photo-etch guns usually include the front face of the cooling jacket as a separate piece. This part is usually easier to align to the jacket if a barrel has already been pre-fitted to the

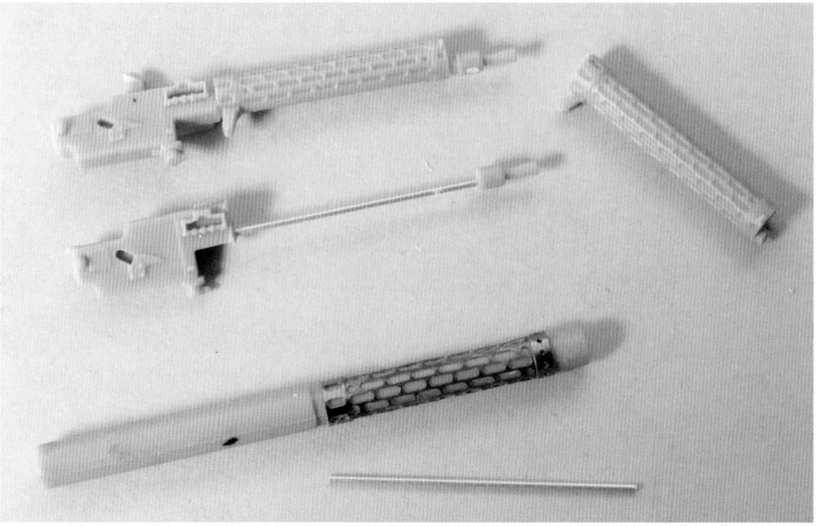

This photograph illustrates the most common process involved in upgrading a plastic machine-gun (top) *with photo-etch details.*

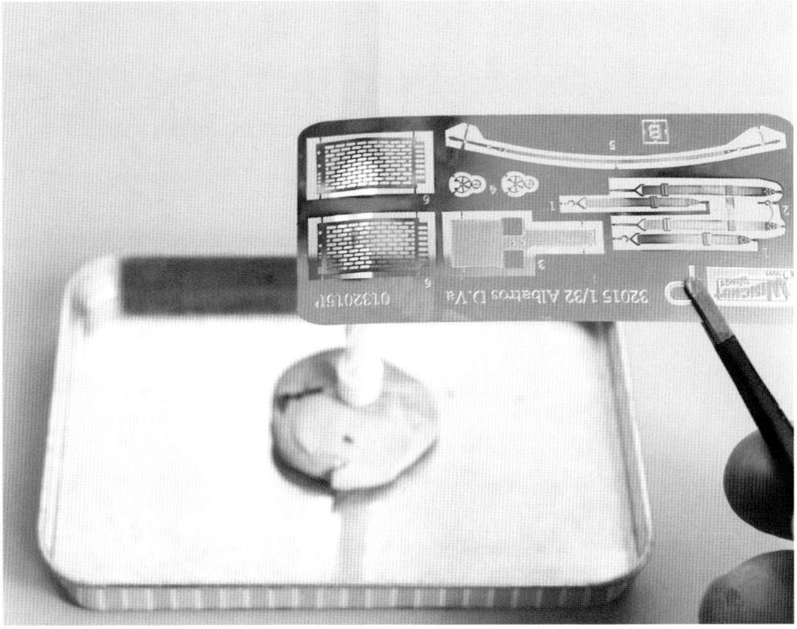

The photo-etch may require annealing over a cold flame if the material is inflexible.

butt. Further photo-etch details can be added as instructions for the product dictate.

Painting Machine-Guns

Machine-guns were typically gunmetal in colour. While there are some very good gunmetal paints on the market, the colour can also be simulated by painting the part with a flat black base colour and then dry-brushing metallic highlights. I find graphite from a shaved HB pencil a perfect material for this purpose.

Gun Mounts

The Germans used a variety of gun-mounting systems during World War I, most of which can be reasonably easy to simulate with basic modelling

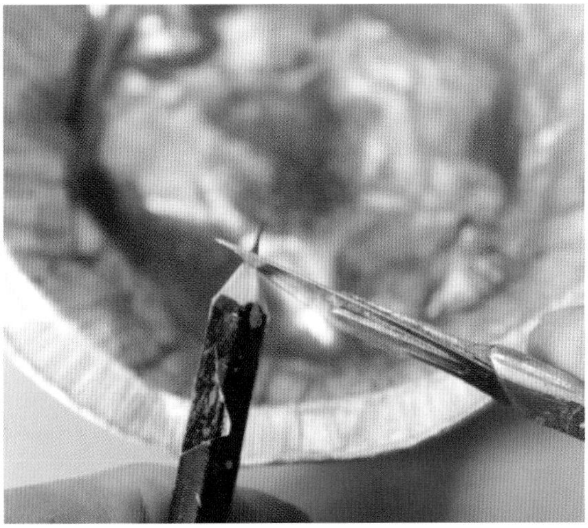

Graphite dust is scraped from the tip of an HB pencil into a container.

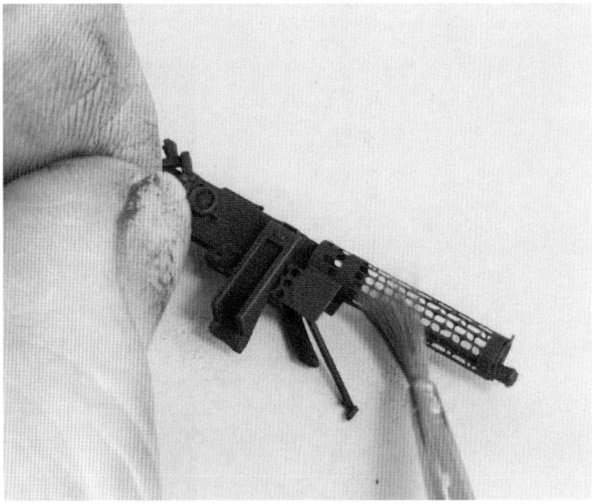

The graphite from the pencil is dry-brushed over a matt-black base to produce a convincing gunmetal effect.

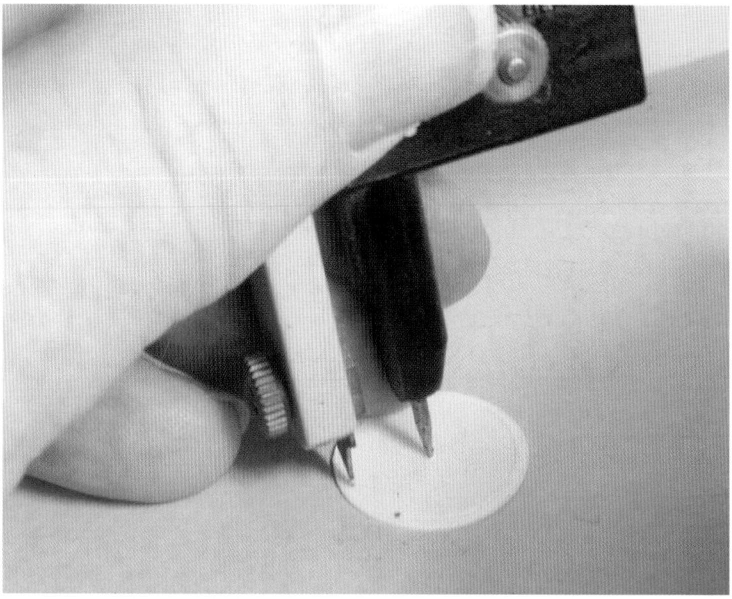

When cutting gun rings using a circular cutter, the outer edge needs to be cut first, so that the central pin locates in the same position when cutting out the inner circle.

materials, if the parts are either missing from the kit or of a poor quality. The most common type of flexible mounting was the gun ring, which can easily be cut from plasticard with the aid of a circular cutter.

Bombs

Most bomber kits come with a wide variety of bomb sizes, which usually results in a number of useful spares. Bombers could often be configured to carry varying sizes of ordnance up to a maximum payload. Examination of period photographs are the best method of determining size and positioning of suitable bombloads.

Bombs were typically painted either grey or pale blue.

Flares

Flares were used as a means of signalling to the ground or to other aircraft. German aircraft flares

A selection of bombs fitted to the underside of the AEG G.IV.

A close-up of flares and Eisfield *pistol supplied with the Wingnut Wings' Rumpler kit.*

were typically red, white and green, and the use of various combinations of colour had different meanings. Flares were often mounted to the side of the fuselage and can be simulated by grouping short lengths of plastic rod together, side by side, on top of a strip of thin plasticard. Once the required number of rods has been grouped, the top and bottom edges can be trimmed so that each flare is identical in size.

Undercarriage

A World War I aircraft undercarriage can either be pre-assembled as a separate part or assembled on to the main airframe. Which option is best will depend largely on the complexity and engineering of the assembly. A three-piece undercarriage for an aircraft, such as the Fokker Dr.1, will almost always be easier to pre-assemble, while a more complex design, limited-run style parts or scratch-built undercarriage will probably benefit by being built up in stages on to the airframe.

Brass rod is a useful replacement for axle parts, especially if a model is likely to be moved from

On this Albatros C.IX, the V-shaped undercarriage struts were fitted to the airframe before adding the axle.

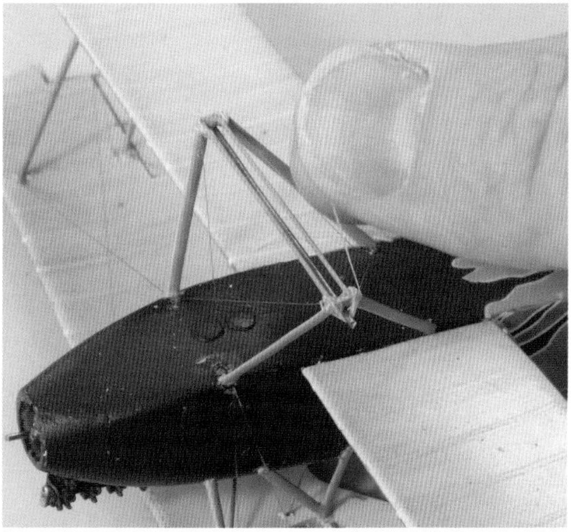

A bungee chord made from elastic is wrapped around the axle and tips of the undercarriage struts on this Halberstadt.

one place to another regularly once it has been built.

Bungee chords can be made from thread that has been soaked in diluted white glue or elastic chord. The end of the thread is glued to the inside edge on the tip of the undercarriage strut. The thread is then woven around the axle and undercarriage strut tips in a consistent pattern until the build-up of thread creates the desired effect.

Wheels

Wheels are particularly difficult items to manufacture, although there are methods of doing so. Where wheels do need replacing, perhaps because the original kit wheels are incorrectly sized, then the spares' box is usually my first port of call. Fortunately most modern kits provide a number of wheel options that result in a healthy collection of spares. When searching for replacements, the important aspect of the part will be the diameter. All surface details can be removed and replaced, if required. Tyres should be painted in a pale-grey colour. World War I tyres were never black, as the rubber did not contain carbon black, which is used as a filler in modern tyres.

Spoked wheels may occasionally be required. There are two methods of producing spoked wheels: the first requires the use of photo-etch spoked parts; the second is by completely manufacturing the spokes from wire or monofilament.

Photo-Etch Spoked Wheels

Photo-etch spoked parts of varying quality and accuracy are fairly common and easy to obtain. Sometimes the parts are designed to be shaped before fitting in place, while others are assembled as flat parts. Solid wheels will require the centre to be removed before fitting photo-etch parts, but often separate alternative tyre rings are supplied with kits where spoked wheels are an option.

Photo-etch spoked wheels are being assembled for the Wingnut Wings' Albatros B.II.

Once the photo-etch parts have been prepared, a small amount of glue is applied to the rim of the photo-etch part, which is carefully positioned centrally on to the tyre. Photo-etch spoked parts come in pairs that are designed to fit each side of the tyre. Often the act of off-setting the position of the front and rear spokes results in a more realistic appearance.

Scratch-Building Spoked Wheels

Spoked wheels can be scratch-built with the aid of a simple jig. The jig is essentially a solid base with a

The spokes on these beaching gear wheels have been made from monofilament.

An initial jig setup with half of the rim positioned centrally, on top of a tap washer. Monofilament has been tied to a nail positioned outside of the ring of nails.

number of nails representing the required number of spokes spaced evenly in a circle. A hole is drilled into the centre of the circle to fit the centre pin of the wheel. An additional nail positioned outside the circle is used as a starting position.

Exact methods vary; however, for each tyre section, you will require two parts representing two halves of a tyre or rim. These halves can be made from plasticard cut using a circular cutter and rounded on one side or, alternatively, they can be shaped from thick wire, such as can be found inside some heavy duty electrical cables. In this case, two complete rings are shaped for each required tyre. The cut ends are soldered together, cleaned up and then each part is sanded to half its original substance, so that you end up with two halves of a tyre.

One half of a tyre is mounted on top of a tap washer in the centre of the jig, so that its flat side is facing upwards. A length of brass rod is fitted into the hole in the centre of the jig.

Monofilament or wire is tied to the nail outside the circle and a suitable pattern is woven around the central rod and across the radius of the jig, so that every other nail is used. Patterns can vary and are likely to be the subject of experimentation, but should follow a consistent path around the jig.

Once the initial pattern to every other nail is complete, place a small piece of plastic or brass tubing over the central rod to act as a spacer and continue to follow the same pattern using the unused nails, but this time the wires fit around the central rod at the upper edge of the spacer.

With the required pattern complete, the second-half of the tyre is glued on top and pressure applied, so that the spokes are trapped and cemented between the two tyre halves. Once dry, the completed wheel is cut away from the jig and the outside of the tyre is cleaned up.

Initially, the monofilament is fitted around every other nail. Experimentation in different patterns can produce different spoked effects.

Once a spacer is fitted, the process continues using the remaining nails.

Once the spoked pattern has been completed, the second-half of the rim is glued on top of the assembly.

Floats

Floats on naval aircraft are typically more complicated to assemble than the undercarriage of land-based aircraft. However, the principle is essentially the same in that the structure is assembled in the simplest way possible to achieve the desired outcome. On a typical German floatplane, I would normally mount the floats to the airframe initially, so that alignment from all angles can be assessed and, if necessary, adjusted. Any structural strut arrangements would then be added using a similar spring-fitting technique to those employed with interplane struts, as detailed in Chapter 5.

On the Techmod FF.33e, the floats are initially fitted to the undersides of the wings. At this stage, care needs to be taken, as the attachment of the structure will be very weak.

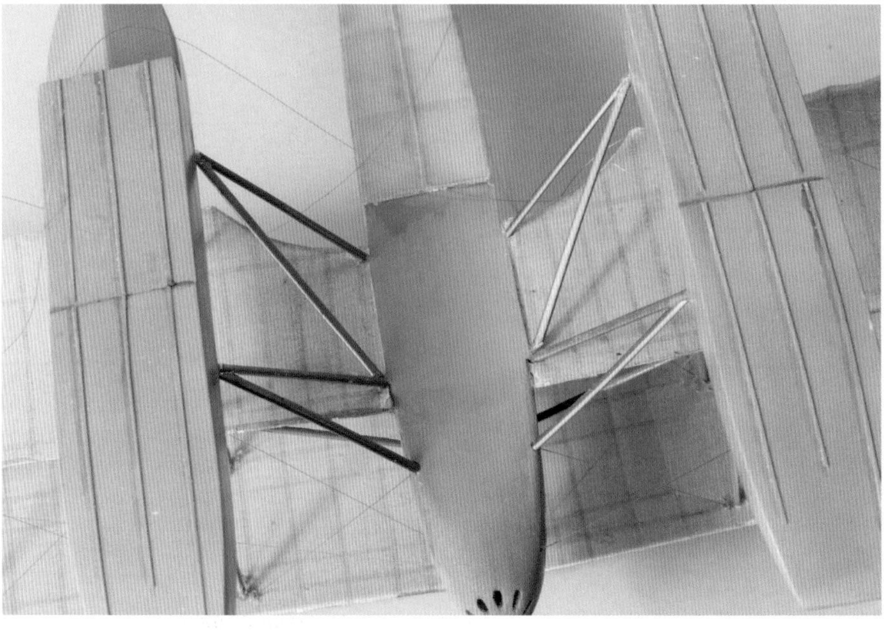

Supporting struts are added once the float attachment is in place.

Propellers

Most modern kits provide a selection of propellers, which make useful spares that can be used to replace poor-quality items. Alternatively, propellers can be shaped from plasticard or wood.

Painting German Propellers

All propellers from World War I were made from a number of laminations of wood glued together to provide a strong component. Many German propellers were made from two or three contrasting-coloured woods, which give them a distinctive appearance. This is difficult to reproduce using paints, especially when working in small scales where the only realistic option is to paint the laminations freehand. German propellers were typically made from seven or nine laminations and so smaller scales are more likely to be painted in a manner that provides an impression of laminations, rather than an accurate representation. On larger scales, seven laminations are fairly easy to achieve with the aid of masking tape. Once I have painted my laminations, I usually brush the entire propeller in a weak brown wash, which helps to represent any lacquers that have been applied. Propellers that have the appearance of a single colour can also benefit from this technique. Two distinct colour laminations are still applied, but a number of layers of wash are then applied on top until the laminations are barely visible.

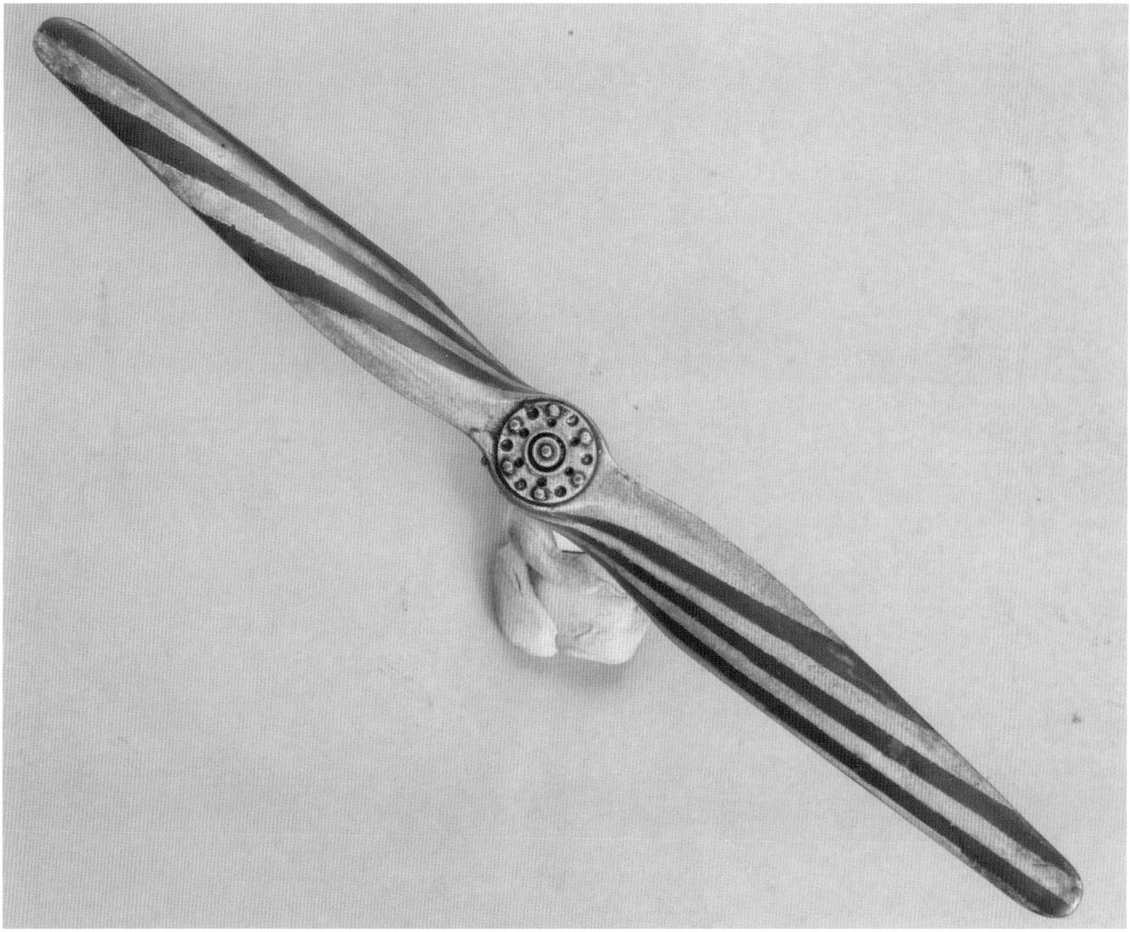

This propeller for the Wingnut Wings' Rumpler has been painted using strips of masking tape to create clean lines between laminations.

Making Wooden Propellers

Replacement propellers can be manufactured from wood veneers as an alternative to painting kit parts. The process is similar to the manufacture of real-life propellers, whereby the required numbers of light- and dark-coloured laminations of veneer are glued together with wood glue.

Once dry, the block of laminations is cut and shaped to match suitable drawings or the part that is being replaced. I usually cut the individual laminations to the rough shape of the propeller and then begin refining that shape to a size that is just slightly larger than I require, once the laminations have been glued together. Once the block resembles the flat shape of the propeller, I begin to adjust the angles of the blades. Wooden propellers can be carved with a knife; however, I prefer to use sanding sticks, which is a longer but safer process. The propeller boss can be shaved from the original plastic part and glued to your replacement propeller.

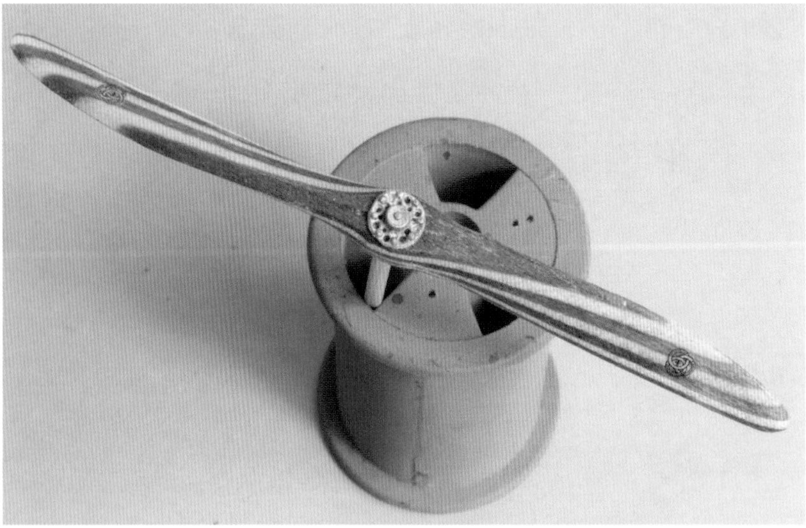

This propeller was created from laminations of veneer for the Albatros build in Chapter 4.

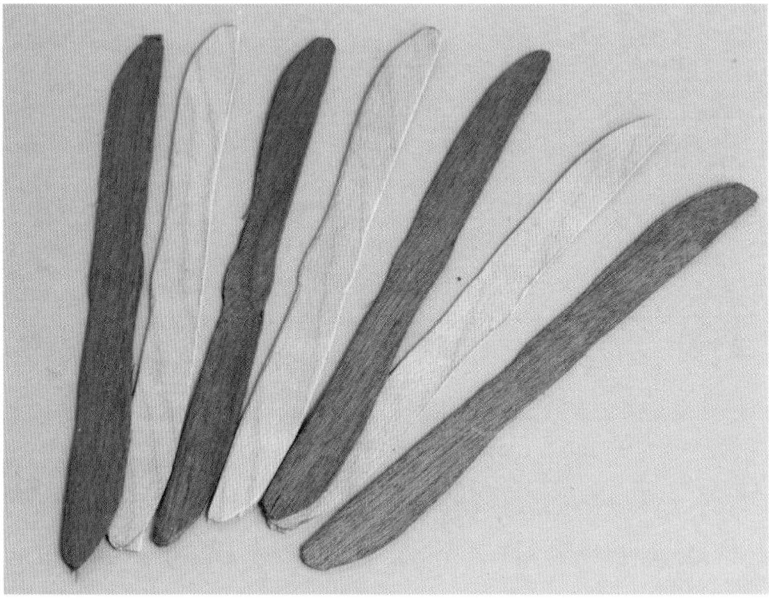

The Albatros propeller is made from seven laminations cut from two different wood veneers, which are glued together.

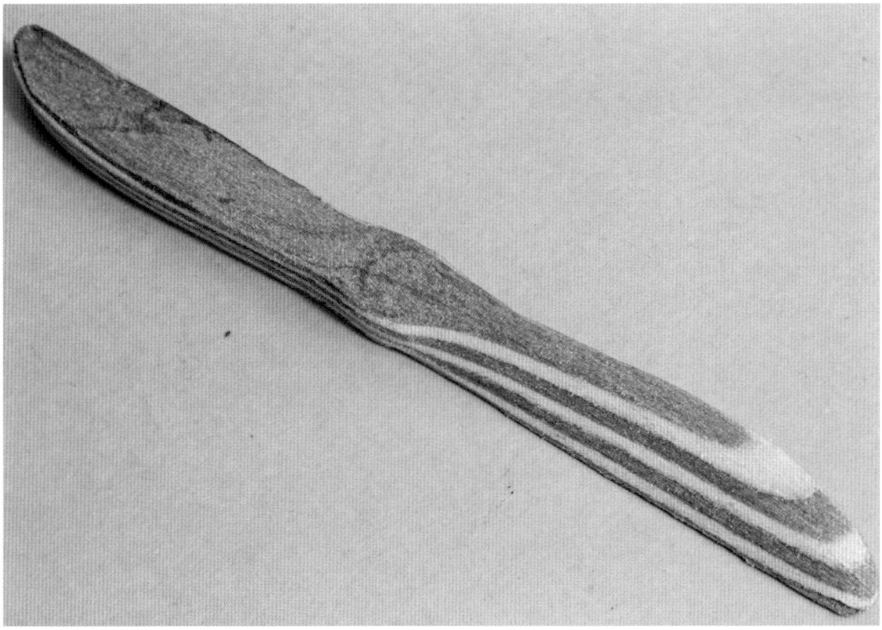

This photo shows the basic process followed when shaping propellers. The closest blade to the camera is in an advanced state, compared to the rear blade.

Displaying Your Model

Completion of the model may not be the end of a project, as there is always the option of mounting the completed model on to a base. Suitable bases can be manufactured from any solid material, although often they will be made from wood. Bases in a large range of sizes are easy to obtain commercially; however, they can also be made from off-cuts of wood or even everyday items, such as kitchen cutting boards.

Decoration of the base is entirely down to the skills and imagination of the modeller. Often this will be an airfield scene; however, an abstract design may be just as effective. The building of a scene is likely to use a number of elements that may include basic diorama building materials, figures or even accessories.

This scratch-built Dornier RS.III has been mounted on a base built to replicate the turntable on the shore of Lake Constance.

Figures and Accessories

The popularity of Wingnut Wings' kits has resulted in an explosion of figures and accessories to complement 1/32-scale model kits. The figures are usually manufactured from resin and are often supplied in three or four parts.

The scope of this book is not large enough to cover figure painting in detail, which as a subject could fill an entire publication. However, from the perspective of colour, German Air Service officers wore single- or double-breasted *feldgrau* uniforms. Flying gear varied, but was typically made from brown or black leather.

A German pilot climbs aboard his Fokker D.VII.

Companies such as Aviattic and Copper State Models have also produced a number of interesting accessories that range from bomb trolleys and fuel carts to trucks. These products are kits in their own right, but can also be used as part of a base scene or diorama.

ALTERNATIVES TO MAINSTREAM INJECTION-MOULDED KITS

Limited-Run Kits

The World War I aircraft modelling genre has not been as well supported by the large injection-moulded plastic companies as some other modelling genres. Cottage industry manufacturers have stepped in to fill the void and, as such, if the intention is to focus on building a large collection of World War I models, sooner or later your collection will include some limited-run kits.

Plastic short-run kits tend to be more basic with regards to detail than injection moulded kits. To compensate for this, manufacturers often use a number of different types of media, such as photo-etch, resin and white metal, to provide an acceptable level of detail. A few examples of these multimedia products have been used to illustrate this book, including the Eduard Hannover CL.IIIa and the Blue Max Halberstadt CL.II.

Limited-run plastic kits usually require more work to clean up the parts, but otherwise can be treated in a similar manner to mainstream kits.

Resin Kits

Resin kits are made from a two-part polyurethane compound, which has significantly different properties to plastic.

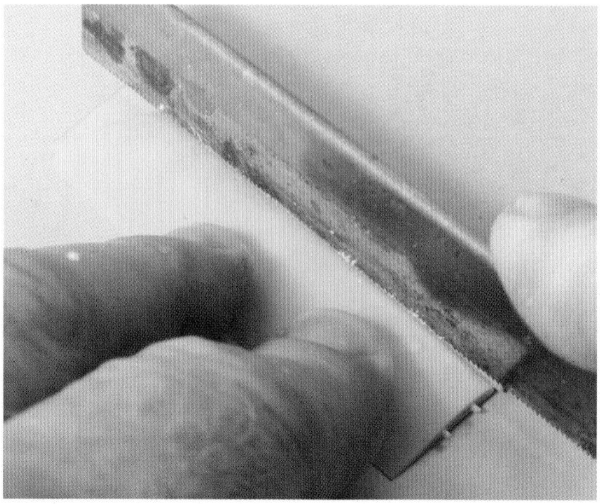

It is recommended that resin casting blocks are removed with a razor saw.

Resin compounds contain isocyanate, which is an irritant to the respiratory tract and it is, therefore, important to wear a dust mask when cleaning up parts. Parts are typically supplied on individual casting blocks that require removal. I would recommend using a sharp razor saw for this task, as the material is often too hard and brittle for knives to handle effectively.

Some resin kits have a tendency to warp, which is a feature that will most likely become apparent on wings and struts. I have been told that this is due to the castings being removed too early from the mouldings during manufacture, but it may well simply be a feature of some of the base compounds that are used. Warping can usually be corrected by soaking the affected part in very hot water, which should return the part to its original state without any need to force the shape. However, in my experience, the warping is likely to return in time and often it is safer to replace the affected part.

Unless resin struts have been reinforced by moulding a metal rod through the centre, I would recommend replacement, as the risk that unreinforced resin struts will warp after the model has been completed is very high.

Once cleaned up, a resin kit can be assembled in a similar manner to any plastic kit, the main difference being that the parts need to be glued together with cyanoacrylate. When gluing resin fuselage halves together, I usually apply the cement in stages, as it is easier to handle and manipulate by doing so.

Single-part plastic fillers such as Humbrol can be used to fill resin; however, I find the properties of two-part car body fillers much closer to the resin and provide better results.

Vacuum-Form Kits

Vacuum-formed kits are made by forming a plastic sheet that has been heated and softened around the master. A source of vacuum is used to ensure that the sheet forms tightly around the master.

While the sheets often look very basic compared to modern injection-moulded kits, the medium can be combined with scratch-building techniques to create a finished model that can look comparable to injection-moulded plastic products.

Parts are removed from the sheet by drawing around the edge of the part and then scoring the plastic along the line with a sharp knife. The part can then be snapped away from the sheet by bending along the score line.

The intended edge of the part is usually level with the top surface of the plastic and so the cut

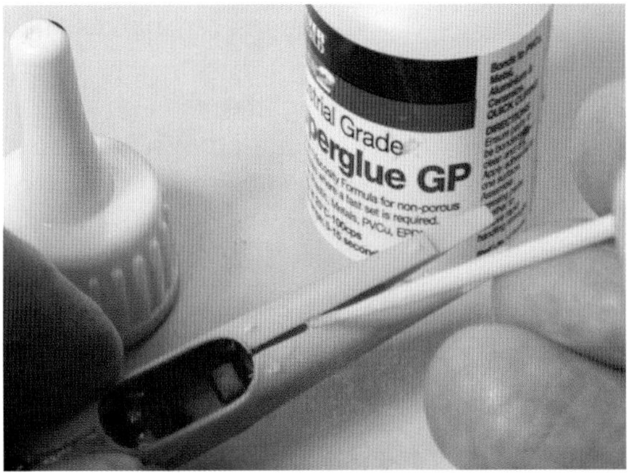

The quick-drying cyanoacrylate is applied to the resin fuselage in stages, which makes the process of aligning the two halves easier.

A pencil is used to define the outline of the vacuum-formed part.

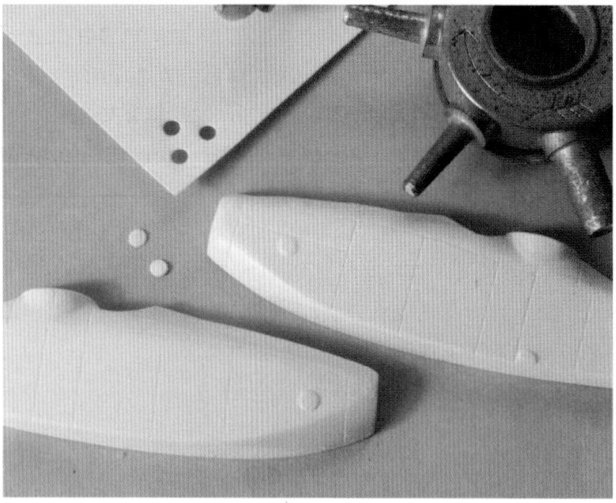

Inspection hatches cut from plasticard replace the hatches with rounded edges moulded into the fuselage.

edges will normally need to be sanded down to this level using a flat sanding surface, such as a sanding stick. It is often very apparent when this point has been reached, as small slithers of plastic will begin to peel away from the edge of the part.

Because of the way that vacuum-formed kits are manufactured, the parts do not have any sharp edges. Where such edges would be present, they can be introduced by gluing strips of plasticard along the rounded edge. Once dry, the strips can be sanded flush with the sides of the part, producing a sharp edge. However, sometimes it is easier to replace a box-shaped fuselage with sections scratch-built from plastic.

Raised detail, such as access panels and footplates, will also have rounded edges and are best replaced.

When gluing fuselage halves together, strips of plastic can be glued along the inside edges of the seam so that half of the width of the plastic strip is protruding from the edge. This will help to align the two fuselage halves and act as a useful reinforcement.

Vacuum-form flying surfaces typically only have detail on the upper side of the part. The underside will normally have concave details that will require filling. Once filled, the underside can be skinned with embossed plasticard or rib-tape detail can be added, as discussed in Chapter 5.

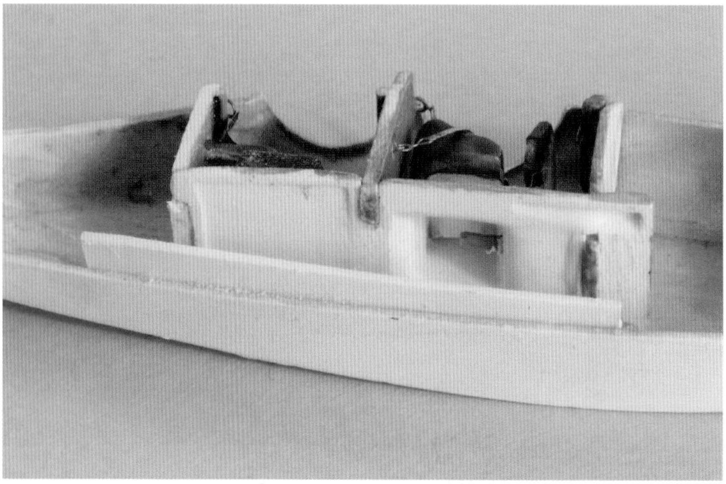

Strips of plastic are applied to the inside edge of the fuselage to reinforce the joints and aid alignment.

NON-PRACTICAL ASPECTS OF MODELLING

Photography

The use of photographic material has become an important part of modelling in the digital age, as many modellers use modelling forums and social media to document builds. While reasonable photographs can be obtained from almost any equipment, including the camera app on your phone, professional results do require a certain standard of equipment.

When choosing a camera suitable for taking good-quality photographs of models, it is recommended that a camera with the facility to change settings and focus manually is considered. Aperture size is also important, as this affects the amount of depth of field that

These two photographs illustrate the importance of using a camera capable of small aperture settings. The top photograph was taking on an aperture setting of F5.6, while the lower photograph was taken using F29. Both shots focused on the cowling.

can be achieved in a photograph. Depth of field defines how much of the model will be in focus. The larger the depth of field, the more of the model in the photograph will be sharp. Aperture size is defined as F-stops – the higher the F-number, then the smaller the aperture will be and the larger the depth of field. Most models require a minimum aperture setting of around F.13 to be completely in focus. I typically use F.26 or even F.30 for my photographs, unless I am deliberately trying to produce a photo that only focuses on a certain area. Often the only types of modern cameras that have the option for such a small aperture are SLRs.

In addition, the camera should have a macro lens, which will allow the camera to get closer to the model without going out of focus and should, ideally, have a focal length range that includes 50mm (for example, 35–70mm).

Tripods are normally essential because the use of a small aperture will require a shutter speed that is too slow for hand-held cameras.

Backgrounds can be as simple as a sheet of coloured card curved at a 90-degree angle in the centre. Avoid using white backgrounds unless you have a professional lighting setup, as the large area of white is likely to adversely affect the colour balance of your photograph. While reasonably good photographs can be obtained using natural light, they may not be easy to set up and usually require a number of reflective surfaces positioned around the model in order to control where the light hits. A simple indoor lighting setup consisting of one daylight bulb, a stand and reflective umbrella can be fairly inexpensive and worth investing in, although setups with a single light source will still require additional reflective surfaces.

A simple setup with a background made from blue card. In this example, the light source is behind and to the right of the camera. A white reflective surface is positioned on the left of the setup to reflect light on to the starboard side of the model.

Avoid taking photographs using wide-angle focal lengths, unless you are trying to achieve a particular effect. I usually take most of my photographs using a focal length somewhere between 50 and 70mm.

Clubs, SIGs, IPMS and Shows

While the general perception of modelling is of a solitary hobby, this is not necessarily the case. Membership of clubs and special interest groups, as well as frequent attendance and participation at events and shows, can make the hobby as sociable as you wish it to be.

The first step is likely to be membership of a local club. Many clubs are part of IPMS (International Plastic Modellers' Society). You can usually find details about local clubs in your local model shop or, alternatively, the IPMS website includes a full list of IPMS clubs and contact details.

Club membership will open up the door to participation in show displays, as most clubs will display at shows in their area. Shows are a good way of meeting like-minded individuals with similar interests to your own, and also provide the opportunity of showing off your latest models. When transporting models to shows they should be packed in a way that stops them from moving during transportation. In addition, the method of packing needs to be quick and easy, as breakdown time at the end of a show is limited. I tend to use a combination of packing foam and cocktail sticks to hold my models firmly in place during transportation. Small breakages can still occasionally occur and so I usually keep cyanoacrylate, a pair of tweezers and some spare cocktail sticks with me just in case a minor repair is required.

Membership of IPMS also provides access to special interest groups. These are groups that

Scale ModelWorld organized by IPMS is one of the biggest model shows in the world.

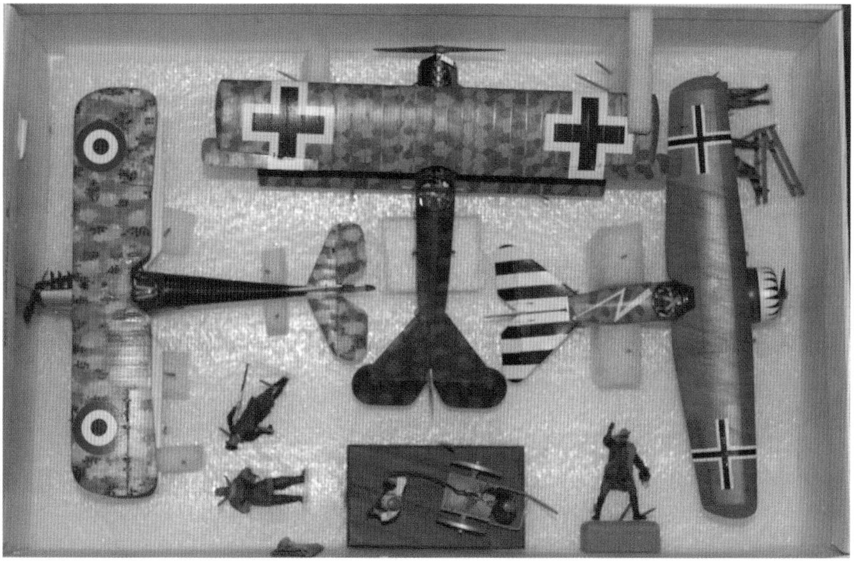

A photograph of the layout of transportation boxes is a useful reference for repacking your models at the end of a show.

specialize in a particular subject. Members of the SIGs usually stay in contact via digital media, but also meet in person at national shows. Currently IPMS lists one SIG that specializes in subjects from World War I period: The Great War SIG.

THE FUTURE OF WORLD WAR I MODELLING

As I finish writing the narrative of this book, the big news is that Wingnut Wings, one of the biggest names of World War I modelling, has ceased trading. This is significant as much of the current popularity of World War I modelling genre has been focused on Wingnut Wings and the regular stream of new 'state of the art' kits that they released each year.

Over the next few years it will be interesting to see whether mainstream manufacturers, who have up until now avoided competing with Wingnut Wings, will attempt to fill the void or whether there will be a decline in the number of new World War I kits being produced. It will also be interesting to see whether modellers that were tempted into the genre by the promise of Wingnut Wings will continue to support World War I modelling.

I can only hope that this is the case. As I hope that this book has proved, the World War I era provides a scope of subjects that is so numerous and diverse that Wingnut Wings could never hope to have done any more than scratch the surface. With or without Wingnut Wings, there are enough subjects and models out there to keep even the most prolific World War I modeller happy for a very long time.

Appendix

German World War I Aircraft in Kit Form

The following provides a list of the best kits that have been produced of some of the most popular subjects at the time of writing. Note that not all products listed below are currently available.

Subject	1/72	1/48	1/32
AEG C.IV	Ardpol	CSM	
AEG G.IV	Choroszy	Hi-Tech	WNW
Ago C.IV	CMR		
Albatros B.II	Choroszy		WNW
Albatros C.III	CMR	Special Hobby	
Albatros D.I/D.II	Roden	Eduard	Roden
Albatros D.III	Roden	Eduard	Roden
Albatros D.V	Eduard	Eduard	WNW
Albatros W.4	Roden	Eduard	
Aviatik C.I		CSM	
Brandenburg W.12	CMR	CSM	WNW
Brandenburg W.29	Toko	Flashback	WNW
DFW C.V	Ardpol	Karaya	WNW
Fokker E.III	Eduard/Airfix	Eduard	WNW
Fokker D.II		Special Hobby	Special Hobby
Fokker D.VI	Roden	Roden	Roden
Fokker D.VII	Eduard	Eduard	WNW
Fokker D.VIII	Roden	Eduard	MikroMir

Subject	1/72	1/48	1/32
Fokker Dr.1	Revell/Eduard	Eduard	Meng/Roden
Friedrichshafen G.III	Choroszy		
Friedrichshafen FF.33e	Choroszy	Techmod	
Gotha G.III/IV/V	Roden	Hippo	WNW
Halberstadt CL.II	Ardpol	Mirage	WNW
Halberstadt CL.IV	Ardpol	Mirage	
Halberstadt D.II	Pegasus	Blue Max	
Hannover CL.II/III	Airfix	Eduard	WNW
Junkers D.I	Roden	Roden	WNW
Junkers J.I	Eduard		WNW
LFG Roland C.II	Airfix	Eduard	WNW
LFG Roland D.IV	Mac	Fly	WNW
LVG C.VI	KP	Blue Max	WNW
Pfalz D.III	Roden	Eduard	WNW/Roden
Pfalz D.XII	Toko	Special Hobby	WNW
Rumpler C.IV	Pegasus	Planet	WNW
Siemens-Schuckert D.III	Toko	Eduard	Roden
Zeppelin Staaken R.VI	Roden		

WNW = Wingnut Wings
CSM = Copper State Models
Choroszy = Choroszy Modelbud

Index